Makeshift Migrants and Law

Makeshift Migrants and Law

Gender, Belonging, and Postcolonial Anxieties

Ratna Kapur

ROUTLEDGE Routledge
Taylor & Francis Group
LONDON NEW YORK NEW DELHI

First published 2010
by Routledge
912–915 Tolstoy House, 15–17 Tolstoy Marg, New Delhi 110 001

Simultaneously published in the UK
by Routledge
2 Park Square, Milton Park, Abingdon, Oxon, OX14 4RN

Routledge is an imprint of the Taylor & Francis Group, an informa business

Transferred to Digital Printing 2010

Typeset by
Star Compugraphics Private Limited
D–156, Second Floor
Sector 7, Noida 201 301

British Library Cataloguing-in-Publication Data
A catalogue record of this book is available from the British Library

ISBN: 978-0-415-59629-9

Contents

Acknowledgements vii

1. Introduction 1

2. The Making of the Migrant 27

3. Victims, Whores, and Wives: Migrant Women and the Law 58

4. Sexual Restraints: The Construction of Female Sexual Subjectivities in Anti-trafficking Discourse 96

5. The Citizen and the Migrant Subject: Postcolonial Anxieties, Law, and the Politics of Exclusion/Inclusion 138

6. The Fear Factor: Muslims, the Gujarat Riots, and the Purge from Within 167

7. Conclusion: Insurrectional Subjects 195

Bibliography 207
About the Author 231
Index 232

Acknowledgements

Every book is a journey that is travelled with many companions, and never walked alone. I am grateful to all those who have encouraged me to write this book and have also been integral to its development. I would like to thank all those associated with the Centre for Feminist Legal Research for their support and assistance. In particular, I am thankful to Eve Gallagher, whose positive and cheerful disposition, as well as thoughtful and meticulous research helped to make this project such a meaningful and fulfilling one. I would also like to thank Gayatri Sharma and Manusmriti for their research assistance and Shashi Bala for compiling and documenting the research materials. My thanks also to Jyoti Sanghera, senior research consultant, and all the members of the Global Alliance Against the Trafficking in Women who were able to put me in touch with network members in India, Nepal and Bangladesh. These contacts provided very helpful inputs and proved invaluable. Thanks also to all the staff at the Women's Rehabilitation Centre, Kathmandu, in particular, Renu Rajbhandari, Babu Ram, Safala and Sabitra, as well as all the staff and members of Ain-O-Salish. Special thanks to Sara Hossein and Meghna Guhathakurta. There were many women and organizations in India, Nepal and Bangladesh who shared their valuable time and comments and provided information that was essential to carrying out this research. My deep gratitude to all of them. I am grateful to all the participants of the Gender, Migration and Law consultation, held in January 2007, from Bangladesh, India and Nepal. I would especially like to thank Aneeqa Ahmad, Natasha Ahmad, Flavia Agnes, Shahnaz Begum, Xonzoi Barbora, Jagannath Adhikari, Bharati Dey, Jeanne Devos, Bernard D'Sami, Sonia Faliero, Ganesh Gurung, Padma Mathema, Mumtaz, Pratima, Hari Phuyal, Renu Rajbhandari, Anubha Rastogi, Deep Rai, Anupam Roy, Dunu Roy, Sharu Joshi Shrestha, Navsharan Singh, Eleanor Taylor-Nicholson, Amrita Thebe, Meenakshi Thapan, Lakshmi Tripathi and Kalpana Viswanath.

On the specific chapters, I would like to thank the participants of the Feminist Theory Workshop organised by Duke University in March, 2008 for their inputs into Chapter 1, especially on the theoretical framework of this book. My thanks to Dr Samarjit Jana and Care India, as well as to the secretariat of the Global Alliance Against the Trafficking of Women, Bangkok for their feedback and comments on an earlier version of Chapter 2. I am grateful to Vanessa Munro and Carl Stychin for their detailed comments on an earlier version of Chapter 4. I am also grateful to Yishai Blank for his comments on an early draft of Chapter 5. I would also like to thank all the participants of the Why Citizenship workshop, University of Toronto, May 2006, for their comments and inputs into an early draft of Chapter 5. Different versions of Chapter 3 have been presented at the Institute for Migration and Ethnic Studies, University of Amsterdam; the seminar on Dispersed Trajectories: Feminism, Postcolonialism and the Road Ahead, Oxford University; the Faculty of Philosophy, University of Zurich; the Consultation on Gender, Migration and Human Rights, organized by the Centre For Feminist Legal Research, New Delhi; and at the Pune Law Institute, Pune. I am grateful to all those who provided helpful comments and constructive criticism on the chapter at each of these gatherings. I would like to thank the editors of the Columbia Journal of Gender and Law for all their helpful comments on an earlier version of Chapter 6. I am particularly indebted to Natalie Levine for her patient and thorough editing.

My thanks to the International Development Research Centre (IDRC), Ottawa, for providing generous funding to undertake this research study. My thanks also to Mama Cash, HIVOS and IDRC for the generous support provided to enable the holding of a regional consultation on female migration and law in January 2007.

1

Introduction

> We are the people you never see.
>
> *Traffic Signal*, 2006

> [Y]ou begin to give up the very idea of belonging. Suddenly, this thing, this belonging, it seems like some long, dirty lie.
>
> Smith (2000: 337)

> Come on, mohajir! Immigrant . . . Pack-up double quick and be off to what gutter you choose.
>
> Rushdie (1983: 89)

> From the internal colonialisms of the sixteenth and seventeenth centuries to the overseas colonialism of the late eighteenth through the nineteenth centuries, this fully evolved [Western concept of law] . . . was the gift of civilization to be brought to others; as an incomparable vehicle for establishing peace and order, it was simultaneously the vehicle through which the forces of violence and disordering were legitimated.
>
> Rosemary J. Coombe, 'Contingent Articulations' (1998: 27)

Traffic Signal is a compelling Bollywood portrayal of migrant workers and the underclass, whose livelihoods and day-to-day living depend entirely on the functioning of a traffic light on the corner of a busy intersection in Bombay. As long as the light is red, they are able to ply their goods to a captive group of customers huddled in their luxury vans or ramshackle taxis. These lives are far from the ritz and glitz of Bombay city life, the grandeur of Victoria terminus, or the charms of the Gateway of India. *Traffic Signal* is the story of outsiders, about those who migrate to and reside in the underbelly of Bombay life, making a living in the murky shadows of India's financial capital.

The film delves into the complexities of the existence of subaltern life and the life of the 'Other' who has either migrated into the city, or simply lives on its margins. The spectator is visually exposed to the considerable risks that accompany the lives of migrants in such peripheral spaces. The film embraces a clutter of over 60 characters, a derelict lot, led by the main protagonist, Silsila. Silsila is a street-smart young man, born and bred as an orphan at the signal that he now manages. For him, the traffic signal is his workplace and a home where he lives. He collects a weekly percentage from the earnings of each of the signal's inhabitants. There is also a bigger boss, Bhaijaan, who runs the entire traffic signal industry in Bombay, which rakes in an annual profit of over 180 million rupees (4 million dollars). In turn, these sums line the pockets of corrupt and seedy politicians.

Silsila leads the traffic signal's band of have-nots, who service the city's high-heeled and well-to-do, keeping Bombay moving, shifting, and throbbing. They include a cluster of Bangladeshi migrants willing to beg for a living, a young ragpicker from the southern state of Andhra Pradesh, named Tsunami, having lost his entire family in the 2004 tsunami, the attractive Rani, who fancies Silsila, and her sister, Chutki, who have migrated from Gujarat, a western state in India, to make their fortunes selling their traditional garments. They live with the regular community of beggars, hookers, and other 'Others', many of whom have migrated from their villages into the bustling metropolis in search of livelihoods and in pursuit of their dreams. They are spectral subjects, who are barely legible humans — aliens — excluded into the realms of disenfranchisement, dispossession and displacement. They all experience marginalisation, abuse and hardship, yet nevertheless remain resilient and buoyant.

The climax of the film involves the construction of a flyover at the very traffic signal where the community resides and works. The fly-over symbolises India's surge towards progress as it is propelled into the global market economy. The country is barely able to keep up with the consumer demands of a hungry population, which include the latest car fashions of SUVs, Toyota Innovas, and BMWs, as well as a revamped infrastructure to accommodate these new luxuries. The inhabitants of the traffic signal become the central casualty in India's pursuit of progress. While Silsila goes to court to fight against their inevitable displacement, the writing is on the wall. The film's ending includes a shot of the traffic signal being yanked out of the ground and carried away on the shoulders of several workers, like a cadaver by pall bearers. Both the traffic intersection and the lives of all those who reside within its circumference are forever transformed. Progress produces more migrancy with little tangible protection or security for the displaced population. These are subjects who are excised from the domain of juridical entitlements and belonging. They become the 'interiorized outside' (Butler and Spivak 2007: 16). Yet they remain resilient and their continued presence in the heart of the 'city of dreams' renders unstable the boundaries of the nationstate and its inhabitants.

The space of the subaltern represented in *Traffic Signal* serves as the location for this book's central concern: to expose how the complexities and layering of the migrant's existence are rolled and flattened through the apparatus of law. This apparatus obscures the broader material and normative processes that produce migration and construct the migrant's subjectivity. I elaborate on how law can both advance and impede the rights of the migrant subject and how legal interventions are makeshift arrangement. They are constructed and dismantled against the boundaries of difference, protection of the sovereignty of the nation-state, and the myth of the all-embracing liberal subject. Such interventions produce the 'Other' and reinforce essentialised assumptions about difference. For example, the poor migrant woman is reproduced as passive, in need of protection, and incapable of decision-making, or the Muslim as an outsider and potential threat to the security of the nation-state, to be incarcerated, deported, or even eliminated.

Dominant, state-centric accounts of migration sit at odds with the accounts of migrants. In this book, I critically dismantle these state-centric accounts where migration is invariably defined in relation to territorial boundaries. I present a decidedly different perspective by foregrounding the migrant subject, and in the process draw attention to the peripheries of the nation and the ambiguous space occupied by this marginalised subject. Migration in these chapters is not simply confined to the physical act of movement and the legal regulation of such movement. Nor is the migrant subject constituted solely against the geographical boundaries of the nation-state. Each chapter seeks to explore the normative and material dimensions of migration and the migrant subject. These dimensions inform the legal regulation of the migrant subject and produce the line between belonging and non-belonging.

Throughout these chapters I use the term 'migrant' to refer not only to the subject who crosses borders, but also to the one who occupies a subaltern position. These are the workers who are not crossing borders as IT professionals or welcomed because of their class, educational, and professional backgrounds. These include the women who are either left behind by migrating male family members or who cross borders as migrants, sometimes at great risk to their lives, as a result of increasing border controls and the tightening of immigration, security, and anti-terror laws or whose internal migrations within the domestic context are barely recognised in law. They also refer to those who may be citizen subjects, but are rendered as lesser citizens, outsiders, or 'Others' through dominant sexual, cultural, and familial norms that inform the law as well as the postcolonial anxieties that determine who constitutes the legitimate subject in the postcolonial nation-state. These are the migrants whose lives are either addressed within a law and order or criminal justice framework or regarded as sexually exploited victims who must be rescued and rehabilitated.

Dominant sexual, cultural, and familial norms shape and determine the legal responses to the migrant subject. These normative boundaries are constructed against the idea that the 'Other' is a negative, threatening, corrupting, or contaminating force. It is where the fear factor is most explicitly made evident. She must be constrained, confined, incarcerated, and even eliminated lest she undermines the nation's identity. The definition of who constitutes the legitimate subject remains undefined and ambiguous, and is what remains after all remnants of the 'Other' have been eliminated or suppressed. The distinction between the two remains fluid and ambiguous, contingent in part upon the success of challenges by the 'Other' to refashion dominant cultural, familial, and sexual norms.

The partition of the subcontinent in 1947 into two national identities, constituted primarily through religious difference, and a subsequent partition of Pakistan along lingual divides has produced persistent migrations, rendering India's borders fluid and not fully determined. Thus, state sovereignty has always been an intensely contested terrain within the subcontinent. The postcolonial nation remains in a constant state of flux as it is unable to achieve a sense of completeness given that the nation's territorial, material, and normative borders have been constantly challenged by the migrant subject ever since its formation. These 'cartographic anxieties' are written into the nation's genetic code (Krishna 1996: 196). It seeks to address these uncertainties by drawing bright lines between the citizen and the Other, in particular the migrant, where even insiders, such as beggars, sex workers, and Muslims are rendered suspect, untrustworthy, and alien through dominant ideological and normative structures. These lines range from treating all women as upholders of the nation's integrity, whose appropriate place remains within the home, to regarding all Muslims as potential traitors and terrorists. Such extreme positions are stridently asserted by the Hindu Right, a movement that seeks to establish a Hindu state in India. It regards all Muslims as outsiders, and also seeks to restore women to a place that they once enjoyed in some long lost mythical golden era of Hindu supremacy — an era that firmly situated women in the home. Such assumptions were constitutive of the nation-state's identity at its inception and continue to inform the legal apparatus that governs the nation's 'Others'. These normative building blocks of the Hindu Right have come to dominate, with relative ease, the national common sense, in spite of the presence of countervailing forces.

The responses of the state are expressed partly in and through law, exposing the levels of anxiety on the part of the postcolonial nation over the survival of its very identity. While this book supports efforts to lobby for more legal avenues for migration, it seeks to do so by unpacking the fears, anxieties, and opposition to such efforts. I expose the deeper issues that are implicated in the debates over migration and the rights claims of migrants. And this analysis is conducted primarily in the context of women and religious minorities in India. This focus is illustrative and not intended to exclude or minimise the significance of other differences, such as caste and ethnicity, and how these mediate the legal regulation of migration and the constitution of the migrant subject in law.

Any discussion of the legal regulation of migration and the construction of the migrant subject also entails a brief analysis of citizenship. Inclusion and exclusion are partly determined against the boundaries of citizenship, which is not merely about rights and belonging. The technologies of citizenship include compliance with the normative assumptions that inform citizenship law and constitute part of the relations of ruling.

As discussed below, the technologies of citizenship are used to correct the deficiencies of the citizen subject. These technologies promote autonomy and self-sufficiency, and are simultaneously coercive as well as voluntary (Cruikshank 1999: 4).

FEMALE MIGRANTS, SUBJECTIVITY AND LAW

Global estimates suggest that nearly half of all international migrants are women, though the official figures do not necessarily account for the unknown number of undocumented migrants (GCIM 2005; UNESA 2006; UNFPA 2006). Yet the issue has remained at the periphery of an already peripheral issue, that is, international migration. Until recently, women have either been excluded from migration analyses or, when included, have been perceived as either non-migrants waiting for their spouses to return or as passive dependants of male migrants or coerced into moving (Brettell and Simon 1986; Lingam 1998). The gender dimensions of migration were only seriously addressed at the international level in the early 1990s (Chant 1992; Jolly et al. 2003; UNESA 2005). Increasingly, scholars and policy makers are beginning to acknowledge the importance of developing a broader and more complex gender perspective in the study of migration (Boyd and Grieco 2003), examining the roles of women in the labour market (Cheng 1999), documenting experiences of female migrants from particular ethnic communities or in particular countries (Brettell and Simon 1986), and analysing immigration policies and their effects on female migrants (Kelson and DeLaet 1999).

Despite some recognition of the importance of female migration and the need to address their human rights, the attention given to the female migrant at the legal and policy level, both globally as well as domestically, remains inadequate. Female migration has primarily been addressed through the discourse of trafficking or smuggling, rather than within the framework of the global economy and the search for better economic opportunities. As discussed in greater detail in Chapter 3, the focus on the coercive aspects of female migration has often been driven by sexually and morally conservative agendas (Agustin 2007). And these responses are based on and reproduce the specific idea that women, especially from the global south or poor women, are victims, infantile, lack agency, and the capacity to choose. The result is that legal discourse often reproduces and reinforces the migrant woman as a disempowered subject in a perpetual state of victimisation.

In the context of South Asia, the response to the issue of female migration is linear and myopic, invariably intrusive, protectionist, and morally judgmental. In legal discourse women are largely regarded as either economic dependants or victims of exploitation, especially sexual exploitation. Instead of protecting and empowering women while ensuring them greater autonomy, state-structured policies and laws thwart their chances and opportunities for advancement (Thapan 2005: 53). There is an assumption that female migration does not occur independently or with the informed consent of the woman, but rather, must entail a dependant or coercive element (Palriwala and Uberoi 2005).

Within India, the literature dealing with female migration has focused predominantly on the period of partition (Bagchi and Dasgupta 2003; Butalia 1998; Menon and Bhasin 1998) and distress migration due to religious persecution (National Commission for Women 2005a). More recently however, women's cross-border movements have been addressed within the context of human trafficking and advocacy in favour of anti-trafficking laws. The focus remains on coercive movement. And as discussed in Chapter 3, these interventions have resulted in restricting or curtailing women's migration or increasing the moral surveillance over their lives. Trafficking is frequently conflated with migration on the one hand and sex work on the other. These conflations and confusions lie at the core of the failure to distinguish and effectively address female migration.

Focusing on migrant women as wives who follow their husbands or as victims of religious persecution or trafficking discounts the importance of migration as a livelihood option for women and the empowerment it can lead to for the individual migrant woman. Female migrants are not merely responding to the changing market realities — they are making conscious choices to move. And they are also constantly negotiating both the normative and material apparatus that construct these choices. The female migrant's situation is never fully resolved, but remains ambiguous and riddled with tensions. Yet these tensions and ambiguities are not captured in frameworks, legal or others, that treat her almost exclusively as a victim, forced to move, primarily into a sexually exploitative situation (Gardner and Osella 2004: xlii). Even when migrations are not coerced, the official discourse continues to address women as 'vulnerable' to trafficking, constructing all kinds of female migrations as coerced — whether physically or materially. In one case involving a ban on bar dancing in Bombay bars, the migrant women dancers in these bars are not perceived by the court as working out of choice — rather, they are assumed to have been forced into the profession. The ban is struck down by the court not because it is regarded as violating the right to life and livelihood of the dancers, but because it is discriminatory. It is not applicable to all women who work in the bars, including non-dancers such as waitresses. This approach views the women as victims lacking in agency and in need of protection. And it is an approach that overwhelming informs judicial responses to female migrants, as discussed in Chapter 4. Female migrants remain invisible in law and when they do appear, it is as victims of oppression, sexual or otherwise.

The global economic agenda, which demands the surrender of sovereignty in the interest of free capital flows and also produces a demand for cheap exploitable labour, has given rise to fears over the erosion of national sovereignty. Part of the state's renewed efforts to reassert its sovereignty is being articulated in and through its women and women's bodies. The construction of women as wives and mothers, upholders of the nation's integrity and cultural values, has been partially constitutive of women's legal status as citizens in the contemporary period. And this construction continues to be delineated within the confines of a Hindu-nationalist identity as well as distinct from the 'loose' or 'fallen' woman. At the same time, the legal regulation of women in and through this register of norms sustains their marginalisation, subordination, or exclusion from full legal subjectivity and enjoyment of the rights to which all citizens are entitled. These norms sometimes operate to 'protect' women and feed into assumptions about cultural authenticity on which Indian national identity is based. When women have been good wives and mothers, when they have lived up to normative expectations, they are more likely to be the recipients of rights and benefits associated with citizenship. By the same token, a woman whose life has deviated from the roles demarcated by these norms may often be denied such rights and benefits. This exclusion from juridical entitlements is produced precisely through her failure to meet the tests for social intelligibility required for minimum recognition. She is disqualified from these entitlements because she is produced as a non-member or lesser member of the nation-state.

Symbols of the Nation

The reluctance to acknowledge consensual or voluntary female migration is partly historical. During the late nineteenth century, women became the embodiment of an incipient national identity. They were the symbols of the nation, of its purity, honour, and distinction from the imperial power or the 'West'. The legal regulation of female migration continues to be informed by this earlier construction. Acknowledging women's presence outside the home amounts to acknowledging the erosion of the constituting feature of Indian nationalism. This feature regards women as upholders of the purity of the nation, whose purity lies within the private domain, that is, the family and realm of spirituality (Chatterjee 1989).

The legal regulation of the female migrant focuses on the tensions produced as she moves outside of the private sphere. These include a challenge not simply to the delineation between the public and private, but also to the normative features of gender identity in which the identity of the nation is deeply implicated. This tension has remained central in the emergence of the postcolonial nation, where the concern has rarely been over the human rights of migrants, but rather on the very survival of the nation-state's identity. This concern has directly informed the legal regulation of female migrants who are impacted by the anti-immigrant measures taken up by various governments. Recent calls by local residents in Assam to 'oust Bangladeshis' in an effort to stem the ostensible inflow of Bangladeshi migrants into India and prevent a cultural tsunami, or restrictions on women below the age of 30 from leaving the country for jobs in the Middle East are overwhelmingly informed by concerns over the survival and stability of the nation-state's identity. The increased entry and exit restrictions are likely to lead female migrants to resort to clandestine migration, which may, in turn, put them in an increasingly vulnerable position. Since undocumented migrants are viewed by most countries as 'illegal', once identified, they may become subject to prolonged detentions and deportations. Fear of 'being discovered' by immigration authorities may even prevent women from reporting substandard working conditions or abuse.

There are also discriminatory overtones against women belonging to religious minority communities such as the Muslim. Increased detentions and expulsions of migrant workers curtail women's mobility, which, in turn, restricts their access to economic and social independence. The detention and deportation of male migrants may indirectly curtail the freedom and opportunities of a female migrant. For example, women who enter the country as dependents of their male spouses may become deprived of income and may themselves be forced to leave the country. Moreover, anti-immigration policies tend to propagate anti-immigrant rhetoric among the general population. This further leads to mistreatment, abuse, stigmatisation, and failure to recognise the rights of female migrants.

The legal regulation of female migration, which is overwhelmingly determined within an anti-trafficking framework, attests to the ways in which certain movements are privileged over others, and they operate to discipline and control one element of the population — its women. Foucault's power–knowledge paradigm is relevant here not only as an example of how legal discourse is a terrain of power, but also how universal assumptions about women are produced and sustained by law. The legal responses to female migration are entrenched in a protectionist approach, which accepts traditional and patriarchal discourses that construct women as weak, biologically inferior, and modest. These so-called feminine characteristics are perceived as natural and sacred, and thus as the appropriate starting place for legal regulation. While feminists have entered this terrain through concerns over women's equality and freedom from violence, they have inadvertently also fallen into the trap of re-entrenching women's victim status, especially of poor women, and hence their need to be rescued and protected by a paternalistic state. The campaigns against trafficking have frequently reinforced assumptions about women as weak and subordinate — and thereby in need of protection — and the need, therefore, to treat them differently in law. Women's ostensibly natural differences are deployed to justify any differential treatment in law and, in effect, to preclude the very equality feminists have sought to bring about. This approach explains why female migration is so often regarded as forced or coerced and taken up within an anti-trafficking paradigm, while male mobility is equated with voluntary or consensual migration.

Addressing the issue of female migration and subjectivity from a postcolonial lens is critical from the point of view of both law and policy. While anti-trafficking campaigns may genuinely be based on concerns about women's human rights, the reference that frames this issue needs to be addressed. This reference denies women any recognition of their agency as economic actors. It fails to understand that female migration is challenging dominant/universal assumptions about women, especially poor women, from the postcolonial world as invariably subordinated, oppressed, and victimised. Through the example of postcolonial India, this book evaluates the implications of viewing female migration in law almost exclusively through the lens of trafficking, victimisation rhetoric, criminal justice, and the moral purity of the nation.

THE MIGRANT AND THE HINDU NATION

Religion has always been part of the discourse around migration though it is not the only, nor the primary, concern. It has been an important factor in determining the constitution and identity of the Indian nation and hence also the constitution and legitimacy of the migrant subject. Cleavages along the lines of religion informed the anti-colonial agitations and the subsequent birth of national identity as well as the consolidation of sovereignty in the postcolonial period.

While the notion of borders has been an indispensable part of the process of modernity and in the making of the nation, this is only a part of the story of the birth of the postcolonial nation-state (Banerjee 2002; Chaturvedi 2001; Murayama 2006: 1351). In the subcontinent, the process of demarcating borders was carried forth by the British, delineating in the process the territorial boundaries of what would later become the independent state of India. However, this process was not without its complications, contradictions, and challenges. The present tensions between religious majorities and minorities emerged partly as a result of the particular form of decolonisation that took place — one that granted self-determination — in the form of political independence to nation-states which were yet to be consolidated while at the same time ceding to demands of Hindu nationalists who imagined the Indian nation-state partly along religious and cultural divides. There was subsequently an attempt to achieve the promise of the nation-state system, of being a collective of states in which a perfect symmetry existed between the geographical boundaries of each territorial unit and the normative boundaries of the social units that respectively occupied them. In 1947, a plan to partition the region into India and Pakistan along religious divides produced a widespread programme of ethnic cleansing that saw millions of people forced to migrate to a 'homeland' with which they had no particular affiliation. However, even after the implementation of one of the largest forced migration policies the world had ever known, primarily along religious divides, the battle was only half over as the myth of nation-statehood had to be maintained.

This process of the formation of the nation-state in India has not been fully resolved as illustrated through the history of the partition and the inability to draw clear lines between who belongs and who does not. The formation of the postcolonial nation-state remains elusive partly because of the persistent and perennial cross-border migrations that have continued to undermine the prospect of a nation that is territorially complete and socially and politically aligned with its inhabitants. It is this aspect that leads to issues and concerns over migration that are specific to postcolonial states.

In this context, the symbols of the nation take on a life of their own, as do perceived attempts to undermine them. The border is needed to convey the idea that the nation is 'a fixed unit of sovereign space' (Samaddar 1999: 21). Continued migration across territorial boundaries thus disrupts this spatial imagery by highlighting the 'complex interdependence of states' as well as the fluidity of political and religious communities across time and space (ibid.). More importantly, when it comes to nation building, the 'disruption' of the border is as important as the border itself. By crossing borders, migrants subvert the inviolable territorial lines drawn up by nation-states and ironically ensure that the concept of the nation-state is 'saved', 'strengthened' and 'valorised'. In other words, by 'subverting' the boundaries of the nation-state, migrants confirm that the nation-state exists (ibid.: 131).

This history of territorial demarcations has been entangled with religious cleavages in the subcontinent. In India, the treatment of the Muslim more generally and the Bangladeshi migrant in particular needs to be understood against this historical backdrop. In the contemporary moment, the rise of the Hindu Right in India has been coupled with the resurgence of the myth of the Hindu nation. The Hindu Right has its basis in revivalist and nationalist movements of the nineteenth century, which sought to revitalise Hindu culture as a strategy for resisting colonialism. The Hindu nationalist political and ideological processes have been in formation since the nineteenth century and continue to impact on contemporary politics (Bhatt 2001; Jaffrelot 2005; Ludden 1996). As these processes developed through the twentieth century, they took on a distinctively right-wing, anti-minority stance, particularly in the 1920s with the publication of V. D. Savarkar's *Hindutva: Who is A Hindu?* ([1923] 1989) and the founding of the Rashtriya Swayamsevak Sangh (RSS — Association of National Volunteers) (Pandey 1990: 210).[1]

The basic precepts of the ideology of the Hindu Right, based on *Hindutva*, are that Muslims and Christians are to be considered suspect because, unlike Hindus, their holy lands lie outside of India. Even though they share the same 'fatherland', India, their allegiances are often questioned on the grounds that they have their religious fealties in foreign lands. Sarvarkar developed the idea of *Hindutva* as a communal discourse, which seeks to constitute Hindu subjects to understand their fractured society in a particular way. *Hindutva* is based on the myth of a continuous 1,000-year — old struggle between Hindus and Muslims as a structuring tension in Indian history. Both communities are constructed as homogenous blocks, and Hindus presented as chivalrous patriots who have heroically resisted the tyrannical, 'foreign Muslim rulers' (Basu et al. 1993: 2). Thus, the Hindu Right and the political philosophy of *Hindutva* are antagonistic to difference. Madhav Sadashiv Golwalkar, who led the RSS from 1940–73, stated, for example:

> [A]ll those . . . can have no place in the national life, unless they abandon their differences, and completely merge themselves in the National Race. So long, however, as they maintain their racial, religious and cultural differences, they cannot but be only foreigners . . . [T] he strangers have to acknowledge the National religion as the State religion and in every other respect inseparably merge in the National community. (Golwalkar 1947: 53–54)

M. S. Golwalkar was very clear that there was no place for religious minorities who failed to assimilate. They were instructed to shed their notion of separateness and merge themselves in the national race. They had to adopt the Hindu culture and language, respect and hold in reverence Hindu religion, and glorify the Hindu race and culture. They had to cease to be foreigners or else remain in the country as subordinate to the Hindu Nation, making no claims, deserving no privileges or preferential treatment, and denied citizenship rights (Golwalkar 1947: 55–56). The Hindu nation was thus constituted in the writings of Golwalkar through an attack on the very legitimacy of religious minorities, and on a denial of any protection of minority rights within the Hindu nation.

If non-Hindus failed to conform then they could be regarded as disloyal and incarcerated or even be eliminated. In V. D. Savarkar's *Six Glorious Epochs of Indian History*, Muslims are cast as enemies and traitors intent on the destruction of the Hindu state and the establishment of Muslim domination throughout the country (Savarkar 1971: 143–44). And the Hindu male must rise against this threat and demonstrate his manhood and masculinity. This version of history also assumes that Hindus are Aryans, with an unbroken lineal descent for 5,000 years, and that the *Vedas* (the oldest layer of Sanskrit texts originating in ancient India) are the bedrock of Indian civilisation (Thapar 1975). It is a version of history that draws on the colonial interpretation of Indian history as based on religion. While the Muslims aspired to and acquired their own country, Pakistan, the Hindus are still aspiring to establishing their Hindu *rashtra* (land).

The Hindu Right has sought to promote and spread this communalised discourse to an increasingly large segment of Hindu society through legal, political, and religious discourse. It has continued to use *Hindutva* to attack the legitimacy of minority rights. *Hindutva* continues to mean the assimilation of all minorities into the majoritarian way of life. The concept of *Hindutva* retains its oppositional meaning: that is, it continues to be constituted largely in relation to that which it opposes — Muslims and Christians. For the ideologues of the Hindu Right, it is this effort to assimilate minorities back into the folds of Hinduism that has given *Hindutva* its political character. The current phase of popularising the agenda of the Hindu Right through the Vishwa Hindu Parishad (VHP — World Hindu Council), the promoter of the religious ideology of the party, has not fundamentally changed this political attack, but rather simply popularised it through the invocation of religious discourse. *Hindutva* is a call to unite against religious minorities; at best it is a call to assimilate these minorities into the ostensibly more 'tolerant' fabric of Hinduism, and in its more radical form, it is a call to simply destroy them. In either mode, *Hindutva* is an attack on the rights, and indeed, on the very legitimacy of religious minorities. As a call to assimilate or otherwise undermine the very identity and integrity of minority communities, it is based on a total disregard and lack of respect for other religious groups.

The aspirations to complete the nation remain present in the contemporary moment. This completion is determined by drawing clear lines between those who belong and those who do not. This delineation is manifest in the response of the state to the Bangladeshi migrants as well as the Hindu Right's portrayal of Muslims more generally, even those who are Indian citizens. The Muslim is recast as an outsider, a migrant man or woman, whose true loyalties lie elsewhere.

Religion was a marker of difference during the colonial encounter, an indicator of the primitive past from which the native subject needed to be recuperated and brought to a state of civilisational maturity. Within the colonial context, difference in treatment of the native subject was justified partly on the grounds that her ancient practices and traditions relegated her to the primitive end of the civilisational spectrum. The transition from the primitive into the modern, ahistorical, and evolved form required the shedding of religious attributes and the historical past (Brown 2001; Kapur 2005: 21). In postcolonial India, the Hindu Right has deployed a similar logic in terms of its response to the Muslim minority community, which is regarded as backward and uncivilised, and has urged that the Muslim community surrender its 'special treatment' and assimilate into the Indian (read Hindu) mainstream in order to receive full entitlements to citizenship. Otherwise, it risks being regarded as untrustworthy and subject to justifiable violence, incarceration, and exclusion.

CITIZENSHIP

Citizenship in postcolonial India cannot be captured within a territorial conception of citizenship, which is tied to geographical location. It has been and remains a highly contested concept. There has been a proliferation of citizenship scholarship over the past decade and there exist very diverse approaches to the concept. While an exhaustive analysis of the debates is beyond the scope of this book, I briefly identify at least three strands in the scholarship that are indicative of the many positions. The categorisation is deployed purely for the purpose of providing clarity as these positions frequently overlap and resist any rigid categorisation. My primary focus is to articulate how a postcolonial inquiry reveals the ways in which certain exclusions and hierarchies are constitutive of citizenship rather than examples of how the project is merely in need of mending or correction.

The classical position argues that citizenship amounts to formal legal status of membership in a nation-state. T. H. Marshall has set forth the classical notion of citizenship as based on three sets of rights: legal, social, and political. This position equates citizenship with the enjoyment of a range of formal rights and entitlements, including economic and social rights, and is understood as universal and inclusive of all those who inhabit a certain physical space provided they adhere to some specific prerequisites. It is an understanding of citizenship that is egalitarian and capacious, based on free and equal membership (Marshall 1950; Marshall and Bottomore 1992).

A liberal theory of citizenship tends to remain tied to a notion of citizenship premised on community that is bounded and exclusive, committed to removing subordination of members within that community. There have been many challenges to the classical position stated by Marshall, some which view citizenship as relational (Faulks 2000) or dialogical (Yuval-Davis and Werbner 1999) or based on hierarchies (Baxi 2002). Others have focused on the need for a more robust understanding of economic, social, and cultural rights (Vasan 2007; Salgaonkar 2007). With the opening up of the market and the omnipresence of neoliberalism, there has been increasing attention paid to consumer citizenship (Evans 1993; Sparke 2004; Hindess 2002; Ignatieff 1987) as well as the erosion of social citizenship (Fraser and Gordon 1994). While the critiques of citizenship are vast and varied, many remain focused on redefining the multiple, substantive understandings of citizenship and developing more expansive notions of citizenship (Bosniak 2000, 2006: 17–36).

A second strand of citizenship scholarship has focused attention on the political responsibilities and active engagement in political life as a means to enjoying citizenship, rather than mere enjoyment of rights. This approach emerges from a sense of increasing crisis in the area of citizenship, which is being eroded by the loss of family values, infiltration, bogus citizens, terrorism, and Islamic militancy. It is regarded as being under siege from globalisation, mass migration, and transnational flows of capital. While the notion of republican citizenship has not featured heavily in contemporary debates on citizenship within India, it is nevertheless significant. This approach critiques the citizen as a passive recipient of rights and regards this subject as one who should be required to perform political obligations as a citizen (Walzer 1970: 203–25). Its core features include a sense of belonging to a political community, loyalty toward one's homeland, and the predominance of civic duties over individual interests. This approach is an additive rather than critical of liberal conceptions of citizenship. It seeks to add responsibilities and obligations to rights for a fuller theory of citizenship, rather than critiquing the foundations of citizenship or its failures.

A third cluster of scholarship can be categorised as postcolonial and Foucauldian critiques, which bring to crisis the very normative content of citizenship by viewing it as serving a normalising function. Some scholars have demonstrated how citizenship has operated through exclusions and how women, racial, religious, and sexual minorities have been excluded from the full and equal enjoyment of rights (Cossman 2007; Guru 2005: 260; Gorringe 2008; Kannabiran 2006 on caste/Dalits; Lister 1997 on gender; Narain 2007; Richardson 2000; Roy 2005; Thapan 2005; Vasan 2007; Voet 1998; Weeks 1999 on sexual citizenship). The critique of the normalising role of citizenship brings to crisis the very notion of the emancipatory potential of citizenship. While this is a broader critique and not limited to the specifics of a postcolonial experience, a postcolonial perspective raises more critical questions about whether concepts of citizenship as developed in countries with histories, social and cultural contexts that are so different from postcolonial ones can have much purchase. Do they help illuminate the social and political postcolonial reality? Postcolonial societies have had a tense relationship with modernity and postcolonial scholarship has problematised the terms of modernity (Chakrabarty 2000; Said 1993). It has addressed the specific cultural underpinnings of modernity and the implications of the cultural encounter between the West and the 'Other' (Said 1993). These encounters enabled the former colonial power to establish its cultural and political foothold, but not without in turn being challenged, altered, and shape-shifted. What emerged cannot be understood through the interpretative grid of modernity of the West.

A postcolonial lens provides a method of inquiry that grounds the concept of citizenship within the historical and material reality of India. Simultaneously, it unpacks the discursive role of citizenship in constituting subjects along the axis of inclusion and exclusion as well as a tool of power of governance (Roy 2008). This approach, influenced by Foucault's work on governmentality and technologies of governance, unpacks the way in which citizenship discourse constitutes and governs the subject, rather than a normative ideal to which we should all aspire (Cruikshank 1999: 1). The technologies of governmentality exercised in and through colonial rule predated the existence of the nation-state, and continue to operate in the postcolonial period (Chatterjee 2004). In the context of the nineteenth century colonial encounter, citizenship emerged as a tool to discipline as well as exclude. It was available only to those qualified to rule and thereby entitled to possess certain rights and entitlements. The native was categorised as an object of policy against an array of issues associated with governmental functions such as land, revenue, public health, regulation of religious practices, and education (Chatterjee 2004; Singha 1998). The native was also classified into fixed juridical categories along with the legal recognition of customs. While this categorisation and legal recognition was exclusive, it simultaneously provided space for challenging the colonial masters and the colonial order. In the course of the late nineteenth and early twentieth centuries, the nationalist challenge to the colonial encounter initially emerged as a heterogeneous entity in the public sphere (Chandra 2005). Ultimately, however, it was led by the educated and articulate middle class, which had profound implications for the way in which citizenship came to be conceived and understood as it continued to operate along the axis of inclusion and exclusion.

While at a general level citizenship invokes a set of rights and practices denoting membership and belonging in a nation-state, it is equally about representation, cultural practices, and normative behaviour. Although some subjects may be accorded certain rights and responsibilities within the nation's polity, their full inclusion depends on the ways in which social, legal, and political discourses constitute these subjects to produce inclusion or exclusion. Citizenship has remained a contested site which is constantly reconfigured, and the line between belonging and non-belonging is constantly renegotiated. The figure of the citizen as a free autonomous self has been put into question, given the racial, religious, sexual, and gender exclusions against which citizenship has been constituted. This 'otherness' is integral to the idea of citizenship, an essential ingredient and a source of its power (Balibar 2003: 38–39; Mezzadra 2006). The otherness is thus constitutive of citizenship and is not merely that which is excluded from its ambit.

This book argues that the spectre of the migrant is constantly present within the shadows of citizenship and deeply implicated in the ways in which citizenship is defined in law. While citizenship promises the embrace of the universal, it also takes on the garb of the particular in its specific articulations. In India, the zone of citizenship is constantly disturbed by the migrant, which enables it to also be productive (Chatterjee 2003: 142). The very foundations of citizenship as an inclusive concept are challenged and there is a constant renegotiation of the terms on which recognition is bestowed or access to services and resources enabled. Citizenship law in India demonstrates the propensity of oscillation at various moments, and the migrant has been integral to the way in which this history has evolved.

The migrant subject is not separate and apart from the citizen. As I illustrate in some of these chapters, a citizen who is also a migrant is tangled in the field of power and knowledge that both enables citizenship but also limits its realisation due to the normative assumptions on which it is based. The distinct perspective I bring is to analyse how these assumptions, which operated in the course of the colonial encounter, continue to operate in the postcolonial present in the context of the legal regulation of the migrant subject. The citizen as well as the migrant subject is always in a state of becoming as well as unbecoming. Such a reading affords space to the migrant to critically engage with citizenship when it is useful to her and abandon the project once it is no longer useful or productive.

THEORETICAL FRAMEWORK

Postcolonial feminism constitutes the theoretical framework for this book. Although there are innumerable legal studies addressing the issue of rights from a 'third world' or 'developing world' perspective, there is relatively little research that pursues a postcolonial analysis. Postcolonial theory has emerged through a complex interdisciplinary dialogue in the humanities and through the incorporation of theories as diverse as Marxism and poststructuralism. Postcolonial scholarship together with subaltern studies has exposed how the identity of the West and the European has been constructed in opposition to an 'Other'. In the context of the migrant, this opposition exposes an incommensurable tension between claims to universality and inclusion, which continue to inform traditional assumptions about law, and the politics of exclusion of the 'Other' from the project of universality (Darian-Smith and Fitzpatrick 1999: 1–2). These exclusions, whether based on gender, sexual status, race, ethnicity, or religion, are constructed along what are perceived to be 'real differences'. The law produces the binaries of 'us and them', 'here and there', and 'civilised and uncivilised' by representing the migrant subject as distinct and different. These distinctions become the lynchpin for determining who to include and who to exclude when it comes to formulating legal responses to migration as well as determining the lines of citizenship.

Postcolonial theory, much like postmodernism and feminism, draws attention to how Eurocentric social theory is based on otherness and difference which it needs to assert its own centricity. It constitutes itself through and in opposition to the 'Other'. Postcolonial theory is a critique that emerges from within and in relation to postcolonial contexts. It is directed against the European hegemony of knowledge and centres the agency and epistemology of the non-European world. Postcolonialism is not simply a reference to territorial decolonisation or merely a temporal description. It is also invested in the decolonisation of knowledge. It deconstructs and contextualises knowledge and accepts that all knowledge is relative.

Postcolonial theory draws on the subaltern studies project, which regards hegemonic history as part of modernity's power/knowledge complex, and as deeply implicated in the 'general epistemic violence of imperialism' (Otto 1999; Spivak 1985: 251). Subaltern studies reads the official archive against the grain and focuses on 'listening to the small voice of history', including the subaltern voices of peasants, women, and even religious, sexual, and racial minorities (Guha 1996: 1). I use the term subaltern' as a theoretical device. While its function was initially to give voice to those who had been left outside of historical narratives produced by colonial or nationalist writers, one stream of the project has come to challenge all traditions and disciplines that were defined within the logic and rationale of the Enlightenment project. The project has unmasked the universal subject of liberal rights discourse, and brought into critical consideration a host of other categories, including gender, religion, and sexuality (Guha 1980; Sarkar 1997: 82–108).

In the context of the migrant, the subaltern project provides a perspective for challenging the traditional assumptions about universality, neutrality, and objectivity on which legal concepts are based, exposing how the exclusion of certain subjects are produced in and through legal discourse. It is important to distinguish a subaltern position from one that simply foregrounds the marginal voice or which merely seeks inclusion. It is a perspective that critiques the universal as being historically based on particular European experiences, which were consolidated to constitute the foundational categories of Enlightenment thought. It is not sufficient to merely draw attention to that which is excluded, but also to challenge the reference that frames that which is excluded. Focusing on voices that have been left out and privileging the reality of the margin does not topple the idea of a single centre as the location of power. In order for any dialogue on global issues such as migration and women's rights to occur, the centre needs to be deflated, and space acknowledged for the production of several universals through the staging of alien insurrections, that is, an insurrection of knowledge by those subjects who have been relegated to its borders or externalised. Such a staging also draws attention to how the production of any such universals requires constant reflection on what constitutes a universal and how any single universal comes to be constructed as pre-existing, rather than simply accepting and asserting its intrinsic universality. What comes to be constituted as the universal occurs through a historical process, such as imperialism. Thus, while it is important to recognise the historically specific character of colonial discourse and resist binaries of the West and the East devoid of historical content, introducing dialectical nuances devoid of history and power completely misses the point, as it does not topple the idea of a single centre. Subaltern studies is not focussed exclusively on the essential consciousness of the peasant. It has a political intent and an extensive critique of dominant disciplinary formations.

A debate has raged over whether migrants and minorities constitute the postcolonial subject (Bhabha 1994: 6) or whether postcolonial theory simply offers the space to examine how difference is displaced from Empire and the nation or regarded as excessive of both (Spivak 1993: 77, 78). The chapters in this book oscillate between both positions, at times focusing only on the migrant as the subaltern and central to postcolonial understandings of subjectivity in law, while in the later chapters, I expand the discussion to unpack how difference, or 'otherness', is mediated in the prevailing processes and understandings of the nation-state through law. The commonality lies in how exclusion and 'otherness' is constituted in and through legal discourse, and how the subject that emerged out of Empire and the anti-colonial struggle was not immediately knowable. The deconstruction of legal discourse is of particular importance in postcolonial scholarship and is a central task of this book.

Postcolonial theory also foregrounds agency and resistance, decentring understandings of the 'native' subject as passive, docile, backward, or whose agency is cast as dangerous. This challenge is of considerable relevance to understanding the female migrant, who has been primarily viewed through the lens of victimisation and exploitation in law. It fails to address her agency and choice to move and invites legal interventions that are reminiscent of the colonial encounter, where women were invariably viewed as victims of their culture or a backward, barbaric civilisation, in need of rescue and rehabilitation. Any recognition of the exercise of agency by female migrants is invariably read within the framework of contamination, corruption, or criminality. These assumptions have, in turn, produced assumptions about women as being coerced and lured into crossing borders, as a result of which the focus of the legal interventions have been primarily on criminal justice, law enforcement, and restricting movement.

This book also challenges the way in which the subjectivity of the Muslim is cast as dangerous and threatening to the security of the nation. Muslims crossing the Bangladesh border into the north-eastern state of Assam are immediately cast as infiltrators, and those within the nation-state suspect as their loyalties are perceived as lying elsewhere. It is the constant framing of the Muslim within the logic of the 'Other', as an outsider or migrant that renders her position, even if she is an Indian citizen, as unstable and volatile.

Migration involves more than just economic or material well-being. The migrant's cultural, social, and economic context mediates her experiences of migration and her access to the labour market. While this issue needs to be addressed within the context of neo-liberal economic reforms and globalisation, this book challenges the idea that structural changes alone are producing migrations. I draw attention to how cultural, familial, and sexual norms produce or restrict migration and constitute migrant subjectivity. The migrant's experience, especially the female migrant's experience, is mediated through these norms that impact on the choices she makes and the way in which she experiences the legal regulation of both her movement and subjectivity.

As the following chapters reveal, migration is a story about relations of power, whether these are between states, cities and rural areas, or regions; between migrants and non-migrants; or between individuals within a migrant's household or family. It is also a story about how these relations of power are discursively constituted and how the migrant's subjectivity is not merely determined by her material reality but also in and through discourse. I illustrate how she is constantly negotiating, interpreting, and subverting these relations of power within the process of migration and her engagements with the law.

It is important to understand that there are great differences in different parts of India in dealing with the rights of migrants generally and the rights of female migrants specifically. The focus of this book remains on the normative and discursive aspect of law and the making of the migrant subject. While I draw on different legal provisions from different states and courts in India to illustrate my argument, I do not provide a comprehensive treatment of migration and law.

CHAPTER OUTLINES

This book consists of five chapters and is intended to complicate our understandings about gender, migration, and the power of law from a postcolonial perspective. While there are several common themes that run through all the chapters, it is important to emphasise that each stands as separate and distinct. In Chapter 2, I contextualise the issue of migration, identifying the tensions in postcolonial India that have led to a reconfiguration of law, where bright lines are drawn between belonging and non-belonging, between those who count and those who do not. I highlight how gender and religious difference lie at the core of this tension and inform the current legal framework governing migration and citizenship. I set out the primary ingredients that go into the making of a migrant subject in law in postcolonial India, laying out the context within which the migrant is produced, as well as the cultural, familial, and sexual norms and the sexual division of labour that inform the law. Together these shape our understanding of how law constructs the migrant, in particular the female migrant, and also enables the representation of religious minorities as aliens in postcolonial India. In Chapter 3, I discuss existing formal laws and judicial decisions that impact on the rights of migrant women, and unpack the assumptions about women's roles and identity that inform the legal terrain. My discussion focuses on two aspects: the moral regulation through which migrant women are constructed as, and judged in accordance with, the standards of 'good' women, chastity, heterosexuality, self-sacrifice, dependency and victimisation; and economic regulation through which migrant women are constructed as, and rendered into positions of, economic dependence. In Chapter 4, I examine how female migration is overwhelmingly addressed within the frameworks of anti-trafficking and anti-prostitution. Through a discussion of the legal apparatus, I explore the implications of such a framework on the rights of migrant women and also unpack the assumptions about poor women in postcolonial India, which are reminiscent of the construction of the native woman in the colonial encounter. I further elaborate on how these prevalent assumptions about and representations of female sexual subjectivity intersect with other non-legal, non-state forms of representation, referring to three documentaries that ostensibly deal with the issue of trafficking and female sexual subjectivity in postcolonial India: Zana Briski's 2005 Oscar-winning documentary *Born into Brothels: Calcutta's Red Light Kids* (2004), Andrew Levine's documentary titled *The Day My God Died* (2003), and Shohini Ghosh's *Tales of the Night Fairies* (2002). In Chapter 5, I focus on the relationship between the citizen and the migrant subject in a postcolonial context. I foreground the role of the migrant subject in exposing the more complex and contradictory narrative of citizenship. I discuss how citizenship performs a regulatory function, where acquisition is not equated with freedom or denial with unfreedom. Citizenship has not emerged from within the confines of the modern nation-state or linked to liberal understandings of the subject and cannot always be understood to be either empowering or emancipatory. I examine how the migrant plays an important role in the construction of citizenship, and how citizenship laws regulate and exteriorize the migrant. At the same time, the migrant's selective appropriation of the citizenship discourse to her benefit sets her up as a knowing, willing subject, contrary to accounts that position the subaltern as a victim or less than full subject or autonomous of dominant discourses. I discuss two recent cases decided in the Indian courts dealing with migrants to exemplify how juridical entitlements are tied to normative assumptions that inform citizenship, regardless of formal legal membership. One illustrates how, regardless of citizenship, Indian migrant women can be excluded from their enjoyment of rights because of the transgressive nature of the work they do, such as bar dancing or sex work. Similarly, the second case illustrates how the citizenship laws can operate to exclude the Indian Muslim from access to rights and benefits through ideological and normative manoeuvres that construct her/him as an outsider, a threat, and expendable. I use these examples to illustrate how, through citizenship law, the identity of the postcolonial nation-state constantly struggles to establish a perfect symmetry between its geographical space and the normative boundaries of the social units that inhabit this geographical space. In Chapter 6, I continue the theme of how the insider can be constructed as an outsider through my discussion of the riots that took place in Gujarat, a western state in India, in 2002. I examine how the legal apparatus that seeks to provide remedies to the victims of the riots is itself a product of the normative arrangements that regard the Indian Muslim as an 'Other', foreigner, alien, and migrant. I question whether the Indian Muslim woman can secure effective relief within the context of existing normative structures that position her as an outsider or migrant and deny her belongingness. She continues to be perceived as a dangerous and/or contaminating force, to be excluded either through incarceration or elimination.

The diverse responses to the migrant subject are not clear-cut and distinct: they frequently overlap. These subjects are at times represented as victims and at times as perpetrators capable of the most terrifying violence. The common element in the examples I discuss through each chapter is the pervasive effort to construct migrants as alien subjects, along the rigid binaries of 'us' and 'them', and domination and subordination. These binaries undermine the human rights of the migrant and fail to address the complex, fragmented, and blurred realities of our globalised world. The chapters develop a broader understanding as to who constitutes a migrant, as distinct from a legitimate subject in law, by focusing on the discursive and normative effects that produce inclusion and exclusion.

In *Traffic Signal*, the metaphorical relevance of the traffic light lies in its seeming ability to both enable as well as disable the lives of the entire migrant community. The removal of the signal marks a sense of permanent displacement, a loss of ground that cannot be recovered through mere resettlement. Yet the alien subjects are constantly able to recover their balance, and challenge both the normative and material efforts to render them irrelevant or as permanent 'Others.' As the chapters in this book argue, the legal regulation of migration and the rights of migrants, especially migrant women, cannot be addressed simply within the framework of security, or as a law and order problem, or cultural threat. It needs to be situated within the broader dynamics of economic globalisation, the refashioning of the nation-state and the emerging challenge to the sexual, cultural, and familial norms produced by alien crossings. The migrant is a part of our globalised reality, a necessary subject, who cannot be excised from the body of the nation through the mere felling of a traffic signal. She provides the sorely needed intellectual and political insurrection that follows in the wake of the waning of modernity, and the resulting intellectual gaps produced in our understanding of the subject, history and freedom.

NOTE

1. Hindus are posited as a focus here because of their majoritarian status, role in government, and power to influence law and policy. While I centre the Hindu–Muslim relationship, it is important to recognise how religious identity mediates the experience of the migrant in different parts of India. For example, in Kerala, a large portion of female migrants are Christians. Moreover, while Muslim orthodox voices have demonstrated an equally conservative position on women's roles, their voices are invariably articulated from a minority space. With the increased communalisation of the political space, the voices of orthodox elements within the community are being increasingly amplified.

2

The Making of the Migrant

On a cold December morning in 2006, the police made a ghoulish discovery in Nithari, a small village in the satellite town of Noida, adjoining Delhi, the Indian capital. The body parts of at least 20 young women and children were found in the sewers next to the residence of Moninder Singh Pandher, a well-off city businessman. The villagers, consisting of a sizeable migrant population, had made several complaints over the previous two years regarding the disappearances of their children, but the police took no cognizance of these complaints. When Payal, the 20-year-old daughter of Nandlal, a migrant labourer from north India, went missing, he sought the intervention of the local magistrate. The police were directed to register a case and their subsequent investigations led to the discovery of the sewer where the bodies of most of the victims had been dumped. Almost 40 young women and children had been sexually assaulted, abused, killed, their bodies dismembered and dumped into the local sewage system. There was also evidence of cannibalism. Pandher protested his innocence and blamed Surender Koli, his domestic employee, for the brutal murders. In February 2009, both Pandher and Koli were convicted and sentenced to death for the rape and murder of a 14-year-old girl, the first of 18 cases that have been filed against them.[1]

In public discussions and the media, attention is focused primarily on the issue of child abuse, missing children, and child trafficking. The broader issue of the rights of the migrant population, and of migrant women, is all but sidelined. The Nithari case is symptomatic of the conditions under which migrants live and work and their complete marginalisation from the concerns of the city or the country as a whole. The case highlights the priority accorded by the postcolonial state to its national interests and hence its utter lack of concern for the conditions of migrants. This, in turn, partly explains the absence of any national labour migration policy or law to protect the rights of migrant workers and their families. The case also serves to reinforce concerns over national security, where alien groups within the country are regarded with deep suspicion. Initially, the complaints of the families in Nithari over missing family members were disregarded partly because the community was regarded as politically insignificant, consisting mostly of a transient migrant population. When the children began to disappear, suspicion was almost immediately directed towards migrants from Bangladesh who also resided in the locality (Sethi 2007). The fear and loathing of the 'outsider', the Bangladeshi migrant, circulated even amongst those who were also exteriorised 'insiders', that is, the Indian migrant. The Nithari story is a story about what is not seen or remains hidden in the story about migration. The marginalisation of this subject occurs not solely because of lack of legal rights, but also because of the perception of migrants as marginal, irrelevant, or normatively and materially threatening.

Migration is not a new phenomenon. The current wave of migration is driven partly by the demand for cheap exploitable labour under the contemporary processes of globalisation as well as the search for better economic opportunities on the part of migrants. While globalisation denotes the free flow of capital on the one hand, the flow of labour is not free and is continuously subjected to restraints and restrictions, often to placate other competing agendas. These stem from a sense of panic over the erosion of the sovereign state and the sovereign subject, fears of cultural erosion, and the breakdown of social cohesion. The strengthening of border controls and adoption of stringent immigration policies has also emerged against a back-drop of panic over the threat of terrorism. The rise of new economic global processes and non-state actors such as the WTO, non-governmental organisations, and even terrorist groups as well as the global movement of people crossing borders challenge the idea of traditional state sovereignty and porous national boundaries (Sassen 1996). These challenges are facing stiff resistance from the sovereign state and the sovereign subject, and play out in specific ways in postcolonial India. These include moves to strengthen border controls, restrict immigration, and reduce the possibility of safe, legal passage for migrants at the very moment when their numbers are expanding. These tensions have led to a reconfiguration of law, where bright lines are drawn between insiders and outsiders, between who counts and who does not. In the specific context of postcolonial India, there is a constant tension between trying to create an exclusive and separate national identity carved out of a people who share a common space and history, purified of its heterogeneity, and the fact that India's borders remain porous, and strong national minorities remain present within the nation.

Indian identity is mediated by gender and religion, amongst other identities, such as caste and class (Gorringe 2008). During the colonial encounter, women became the repositories of prevalent sexual, familial, and cultural norms against which the Indian state was subsequently constituted. Simultaneously, the new Indian nation was conceived by Hindu nationalists as a Hindu nation. Religious minorities, especially Muslims, who wanted to belong to the new Indian nation had to assimilate and surrender their distinct religious identity and forego any special treatment on the basis of that identity (Golwalkar 1947; Savarkar [1929] 1971). As discussed in Chapter 1, this historical context has come to influence the tension between belonging and non-belonging that informs the current legal framework governing migration and citizenship. These laws continue to be based on assumptions about religious and gender difference, as well as prevailing sexual, familial, and cultural norms and the sexual division of labour that together constitute the legitimate subject.

While this book is not about citizenship, it is important to address the ways in which the migrant is indispensable for identifying the citizen. Citizenship has not been exclusively tethered to notions of territory or defined only in terms of enjoyment of civil, social, and political rights (Marshall 1950: 10–11). It has been fractured by the history of partition, gender and religious differences as well as by governing sexual, familial, and cultural norms. The migrant draws attention to these fractures and cleavages, and explains how and why the legal definitions of citizenship oscillate between a capacious inclusiveness to more restrictive, exclusive understandings. Formal demarcations of citizenship and inclusion do not serve as either an antidote to exclusion nor do they engage with the complex ways in which the migrant is integral to the shifts in the legal definitions and conceptions of citizenship in a postcolonial context.

In this chapter, I set out the primary ingredients that go into the making of a migrant subject in law in postcolonial India. These include setting out the context within which the migrant is produced, as well as the cultural, familial, and sexual norms and the sexual division of labour that inform the law. Together these makeshift arrangements shape our understanding of how law constructs and deconstructs the migrant, in particular the female migrant, and also enables the casting of religious minorities as aliens or interiorised 'Others' in postcolonial India. While this is not an exhaustive list of the elements constitutive of the migrant subject, and touches only peripherally upon other factors such as race, caste, or ethnicity, it serves as an entry point for further exploration of these issues.

CONTEXTUALISING MIGRATION

In the contemporary period, migration into India is taking place from Nepal and Bangladesh due to a number of international and regional factors. These include the reconfiguration of the global economy and the pull of India's attractive booming economy as well as what the ILO terms as the 'global job crisis'. It also includes the displacement and dispossession of marginalised populations from Nepal and Sri Lanka as a result of civil strife as well as from Bangladesh due to fundamentalism and armed conflict (Heisler 1999: 560–67; ILO 2005a: 14–16; OECD 2005). India, Nepal, and Bangladesh all share long and porous borders. Irregular border crossings between these different borders are thus inevitable and innumerable (IOM 2005: 111). There are regular seasonal movements of Nepali and Bangladeshi migrants into India during the harvest season, and there are family ties that straddle borders. Poverty and demand for workers also drive these irregular movements, and at the same time the open border policy, especially with Nepal, make such crossings easy and less hazardous.

India also serves as a transit country for migrants from Nepal, Bangladesh, and Pakistan on their way to the Middle East or Europe. The global patterns of economics and trade have increased the demand for low wage labour in the more industrialised parts of the world which often cannot be met locally. India serves as a transit country for meeting this international demand. This demand is being partly met by trafficking or migration into sites of forced and exploitative labour that yield high rates of profit, but is also often freely chosen (ILO 2005a: 43). Where the official policy of the destination country does not permit legal migration, the motivations for migration and the demand from sectors of the informal economy can be strong enough to create conditions and structures for irregular migration and trafficking.

Migration is also partly produced by the need of poor countries for remittances from emigrants that can assist in meeting some of the social welfare demands that the state is often neither able nor willing to perform in pursuit of liberalisation (Carling 2005; OECD 2004; Puri and Ritzema 1999). An analysis of the scarce data that is available indicates that migrant remittances have been associated with declines in poverty headcount in several poor countries, for example, nearly six percentage points in Bangladesh. Indeed, the World Bank has stated that increasing migration of low-skilled workers can reduce the poverty, increase wages, reduce unemployment, and underemployment in developing countries (World Bank 2006: xii). The plummet in foreign exchange remittances during the global economic recession in 2008–2009 and the steep increase in domestic unemployment rates coupled with the sudden return of thousands of migrants back to various South Asian countries are all indicative of the significant role that migration has come to play in poor as well as emerging economies. Poorer countries thus have little interest in controlling outward movement, legal or illegal. Indeed, countries such as India encourage labour migration to the Gulf as an important source of foreign exchange. The increased remittances assist in meeting the escalating import bill that cannot be met from commodity export alone (Raju and Sasikumar 2006: 204). At the same time studies reveal that the migration takes place from a few concentrated towns and villages, and remittances tend to benefit only a small segment of the population (Chisti, 2007; Raju and Sasikumar 2006: 205).

The benefits of migration are not limited to remittances. While remittances and financial inflows are beneficial for countries of origin or developing countries, domestic consumption and the generation of wealth for the host country or developed economies also takes place (Buch et al. 2002). The host or developed countries are also interested in the financial inflows into developing countries or sending countries. The General Agreement on Trade and Services (GATS) is an international trade agreement that came into effect in 1995 and operates under the World Trade Organization (WTO). It is a multilateral, legally enforceable set of rules covering international trade in services. Mode 4 of GATS specifically addresses the temporary movement of individuals and deals with the supply of a service 'by a service supplier of one member, through presence of natural persons of a member in the territory of any other member' (GATS Article 1:2 [d]). The WTO highlights the benefits of the movement of natural persons to the country of origin and the receiving country under Mode 4 as a 'source of financial inflows'. Income earned abroad is in large part repatriated and contributes to increasing national wealth (WTO 2004: 47). Apart from meeting labour shortages, the benefits to the receiving country include income from foreign workers, which generates wealth in the host country 'including in the form of domestic consumption and tax revenue' (ibid.: 49).

However, GATS covers only temporary movement of workers and excludes measures regarding citizenship, residence, or employment on a permanent basis. Since temporary or non-permanent status in the host country is not specified in GATS, WTO members have interpreted this notion differently in their schedules of service commitments, varying from three months to five years (WTO 2004). According to R. Skeldon, 'The critical benefit to be brought by the GATS proposals is to increase flexibility in globalising labour markets that will allow a matching of skills at various and stipulated levels with available jobs across international boundaries' (2004: 169). India's stand in the WTO completely ignores low-skilled labour, and the Mode 4 negotiations have focused almost entirely on the highly skilled professional class. Although GATS has the potential to loosen stringent visa requirements, emigration restrictions, and other barriers to movement because it actively encourages movement, it is limited and narrow in scope, with the majority of the members restricting their commitments to the movement of high-skilled workers (Broude 2007: 24–30).

WTO negotiations between the developed and developing world highlight how entry restrictions are implicated in the structures of power between nations, which brings to crisis the idea of 'flows' as operating in a neutral space unmediated by power. The European Union migration policies, for instance, are being streamlined, specifically focusing on labour shortages within the country and filling in the deficit through migration. The idea of circular migration is being evolved to stem permanent immigrants into countries on the grounds that they put pressure on the already scarce resources. In the context of the global economic meltdown in 2008 and 2009, there has been a further crackdown on even highly-skilled migrants.

Migration is one aspect of the processes associated with globalisation and economic liberalisation being pursued by states such as India. However, an understanding of the correspondence between various push-and-pull factors and migration has not evolved. Instead, what is evident is that while there has been an increase in the flow of cross-border movements, the routes for safe legal travel have not simultaneously increased. Arguments in favour of globalisation have mainly advocated the free flow of capital and the elimination of protectionism, deemed as critical to the efficiency of the market. Yet the market also triggers a global flow of labour, which is not addressed within the notion of market management. The scale and vastness of the global flow of human beings in turn has produced new tensions and challenges, including tensions over the survival of the nation-state, sovereignty, and the sovereign subject, cultural and religious identity, definitions of citizenship and who belongs, as well as concerns over social and cultural homogeneity.

Legal responses have tended to focus on increasing border controls, and restrictive migration and immigration policies are being adopted in countries of transit and destination. Restrictive policies only serve to encourage irregular migration. The situation of the migrant has been further aggravated by the 'war on terror' that has produced hierarchies of citizens and drawn the line between belonging and non-belongingness in a more insular fashion. The 'alien migrant' has become one of the primary casualties of this elusive and ill-conceived 'war', the purpose and limits of which remain undefined.

Failing to recognise the need for marginalised groups to migrate *on the one hand* and the demand for cheap, exploitable labour *on the other* has forced migrants to continue to move through illicit channels. This demand has produced a growing market for clandestine migration services, which consist of the facilitation of smuggling, illegal migration, and underground travel, as well as the provision of false documents. Clandestine migration leaves the migrant stigmatised, illegitimate, and vulnerable to exploitation. It increases the risk of trafficking and is a primary indicator of migration 'gone bad'. The failure to establish mechanisms and policies designed to secure the rights of migrants renders them prone to abuse and exploitation (Chammartin 2005).

While arguments in favour of state sovereignty are frequently advanced to justify harsh immigration and migration management policies that deter illegal entry, concern over security should be one, and not the exclusive consideration in the formulation of migration policies and laws. People will continue to move clandestinely if the legal means are not made available to them. This fact cannot be ignored nor countered by ever more stringent immigration laws, boundary controls, and exclusive measures targeting vulnerable migrants. Addressing the needs and rights of this besieged subject can maximise the benefits and reduce the risks of migration to the destination and origin countries as well as to the migrant.

The right to free movement is an internationally recognised human right. But this right is restricted or curtailed in light of two contradictory forces that are confronting the nation-state today. As discussed below, the first is economic globalisation and the denationalisation of economies and the second is the aggressive assertions of sovereignty, nationalism, and national identity in the face of increased migration. While the Indian state is voluntarily surrendering sovereignty to enable capital flows, it is simultaneously preserving the right to control borders to ensure its national identity. This right is being carved along the axis of gender and religious differences, including assumptions about women's mobility and the foregrounding of religious identity of the state as primarily Hindu. These differences operate with governing sexual, familial, and cultural norms that are resulting in the imposition of greater restrictions on women's right to mobility through anti-trafficking laws as well as the drawing of rigid boundaries between the 'insider' and 'outsider' along religious divides. The chapters in this book build on this discussion, unpacking the normative and discursive features that inform the construction of the migrant subject, where formal legal status as a citizen is not enough to claim the status of an insider or legitimacy.

Economic Liberalisation and Globalisation

In the early 1990s, India initiated a range of policy and neoliberal economic reforms designed to introduce a regime of greater competition with a more open, market-oriented economic structure. There have been significant changes in the industrial policies of the country to eliminate the 'licensing raj' that has plagued the growth of industry and manufacturing and discouraged foreign investment. All the procedural rules have been simplified and investment encouraged in areas that were previously the preserve of the public sector. The aim of the reform measures has been to open up the economy and encourage export promotion through the setting up of special export zones (SEZs). Studies indicate that liberalisation affected growth in a positive way during the 1990s (Srinivasan and Bhagwati 1999). At the same time, while there has been increased visibility of consumer products and brand names, there has been a simultaneous withdrawal of the state from its welfare responsibilities towards the poor.

Throughout the 1980s, there was greater emphasis on diverting domestic production towards export industries, on increasing competitiveness through cost reduction, particularly through a reduction of labour costs. In the 1990s this process accelerated at an unprecedented pace. The neoliberal economic reforms, which took the form of liberalisation of trade, deregulation of investment, privatisation of industry, and devaluation of the currency fundamentally transformed the Indian economy, increasing export-oriented production and decreasing state spending (ILO 2004: 28). The fiscal and monetary restraints introduced together with devaluation, which reduced real incomes and thus demands for imports, have constituted part of the stabilisation policies designed to affect the demand side of the economy (Bhalotra 2002). On the supply side of the economy, there has been an expansion and diversification of exports to help tackle the balance of payment problems (Pederson 2000).

The Indian state has radically cut back on social spending. Subsidies on food, clothing, and public transit are being curtailed. Government expenditure on welfare activities, including health, education, rural employment, and anti-poverty programmes is being cut down, as expenditure on these is relatively easy to cut compared to the ongoing infrastructural expenses (Chandrasekhar and Ghosh 2004). Indirect taxation is being increased, so that the prices of several essential goods are also increasing. More and more attention is being given to production for exports, and the task of producing necessities at cheap rates for the local consumers is being subordinated to the objective of stepping up exports. In particular, farm exports are being boosted while not enough food is grown for the home market (Patnaik 1999: 3). At the same time, the restructuring of the labour market is resulting in higher unemployment and lower wages. The emphasis on increasing international competitiveness through cost reduction is resulting in the further casualisation of the labour market, that is, a decreased reliance on a permanent workforce and a greater reliance on a casual workforce that works for lower wages and no benefits.

The neoliberal economic policies being pursued by India have impacted differently on men and women. Increase in competition and the need to reduce production costs resulted in the expansion of the informal sectors of the economy (Portes et al. 1989). While women have generally made up a large percentage of the workforce in the informal sectors of the economy, the new economic regime fostered an increase in the labour force participation of women (Cagatay et al. 1995; Sinha et al. 2000). It also intensified the demand for women workers, especially in the reproductive sphere, indicating a redistribution of reproductive labour, and challenging the very construction and identity of the nation as well as class relations. However, such processes have not necessarily lead to a reconstitution of gender relations between sexes (Banerjee 1999). Women are being delegated the tasks of reproduction that more well off-women are unable to do as they increasingly enter the labour force, especially in the urban centres.

The neoliberal economic reforms are having a paradoxical impact on women as producers, consumers, and household managers. While they have offered new opportunities for women in terms of employment and education, these reforms have also had an adverse impact on poor women (Ganguly-Scrase 2003). Economic liberalisation has operated to accentuate the sexual division of labour and women's economic vulnerability and dependency. Restructuring and deregulation has resulted in the deterioration of working conditions and withdrawal of benefits for women. There has also been a simultaneous increase in their workload in the family as the state has steadily withdrawn from a significant number of its welfare obligations. These policies have intensified the conditions that have created women's economic dependency and vulnerability, and further undermined the ability of law to address these conditions.

Women's responsibilities within both the public and private spheres are being expanded at a considerable pace. Within the home, women fulfil the largest share of the daily responsibility and care for family members (Khullar 1999). Women are responsible for the welfare of children and often of parents, in-laws, and the elderly. As home managers, the bulk of the responsibility for managing and budgeting household consumption, especially basic needs in good and bad times, falls on women. As mothers, women play a critical role in human resource development. For example, healthcare and education are a primary responsibility of women in the home.

Cutbacks in government spending in social programmes, healthcare, education, and other basic needs are dramatically increasing women's responsibilities with regard to these activities within the household. The assumption within macroeconomic policy, however, is that women's labour in the home is elastic, and the cost of their unpaid time remains invisible (Bezanson and Luxton 2006: 5). At the same time, the continuing integration of women into an increasingly deregulated economy has substantially multiplied the demands on women's time outside of their families. The increasing costs of basic necessities are forcing women who did not already do so to work outside of the home to help finance the costs of the family. The increasing casualisation of the labour force, that is, a shift from a permanent to a casual labour force, has specifically gendered dimensions. It is women who are being increasingly integrated into the labour market as casual labour (Elson 1999; NCEUS 2008: 100).

The process of restructuring can be seen to be intensifying the problems that women workers already faced in the labour market. Gender segmentation is increasing and the conditions of employment are further deteriorating. Casualisation of the labour force means that more and more women are working in the manufacturing sector, at the same time as this sector is coming to be characterised as 'unorganised', that is, outside the purview of protective legislation and trade union organisation. Restructuring is further reinscribing sex segregation as well as the low wages and poor working conditions already associated with women's work. Increasingly, the need for a free and flexible labour market is casting a negative shadow on legislation that protects women workers (at least in the organised sector), which is viewed as inimical to this particular growth path. The cuts to the public sector employment are eliminating one of the few sources of good jobs for women and simultaneously resulting in an increase in the use of women as cheap and unorganised labour in the export processing zones, where non-implementation and ad hoc exemptions, mainly to industry, from certain protective labour legislation are being granted. The reduction in the size of the public sector and the consequent loss of jobs, as well as the shift in the manufacturing sector to increasingly casual labour, has resulted in fewer women getting access to maternity benefits and other laws passed for their protection. As per a report by the National Commission for Enterprises in the Unorganised Sector (NCEUS), women, who are assumed to be willing to work for lower wages, quite specifically migrant women, are being further entrenched in the informal sector, with deteriorating working conditions, restrictions on trade union organising, and less legal protection (Deshpande and Deshpande 1998; NCEUS 2008: 99–100).

Neoliberal policies are accentuating the conditions of labour market segmentation that have constituted women's economic vulnerability, and in turn reinforcing the effects of the sexual division of labour on women. But the impact of the economic liberalisation and globalisation on women will likely not be measurable in economic term alone. The new economic regime is resulting in the renegotiation of the public and private distinction. This restructuring is seeking to 'shrink the public — the realm of political negotiation — and, at the same time, expand and reassert the autonomy of the private sector and the private sphere' (Brodie 1994: 47, 1995). Services once provided by the state are being reprivatised. The public sphere is being contracted, as the private sphere is expanding. This renegotiation of the public and private, and the process of privatisation, is resulting in the reconstitution of the domestic, in which the normative family and women's roles within it are being reaffirmed as the fundamental building block in society.

In India, the emerging development discourse is to let the needs of the middle class be met by the market and continue some level of state protectionism for the poor. At the same time, the state needs to reduce costs of public spending and thus is also reconstituting the domestic sphere to help facilitate the retraction of the public sphere. The state can justify its reduction in social services by redefining the family as the place where these services ought to be provided. As the state increasingly withdraws from the provision of healthcare, education, and child care, the responsibility for these basic needs is transferred to the private sphere of the family and the market. The reconstitution of the domestic and the revalorisation of the family helps to re-naturalise the idea that these are the sites where these basic needs ought to be provided. This revalorisation of the family seeks to deploy and reinscribe familial ideology and its naturalised and universalised roles for women as wives and mothers. At the same moment that women are being called upon to assume more responsibility within the labour market, women's roles as wives and mothers are being intensified. These contradictory pulls on women's labour and identities are being negotiated through the powerful discourse of familial ideology, discussed in greater details later in this chapter. The revalorisation of the family thus operates to both naturalise the privatisation of state services, and contain the increasingly contradictory demands on women. Rather than displacing dominant understandings about women as good and dutiful wives and self-sacrificing mothers, the new economic policies are drawing upon and reinscribing the same set of norms and values of women's gendered identities.

The legal responses to female migrants reflect this tension, where the state is willing to offer greater security for workers more generally in the unorganised sector, recognising how the demands of the market are producing the demand for more casual and migrant labour. The National Rural Employment Guarantee (NREG) scheme, introduced in 2005, which guarantees 100 days of work in rural areas as a measure to address unemployment and prevent distress migration, is but one such measure (Dreze and Khera 2009). At the same time, there is a shoring up of the normative boundaries that constitute the markers of Indian identity which is deeply embedded in the construction of female subjectivity. Thus women's roles as wives and mothers as reproducers of the nation's identity are constantly reproduced in legal discourse. The female migrant sits on the precipice of the global encounter with national identity and definitions of sovereignty. Far from being unhinged by globalisation, national identity is being reconstituted through greater attention to identity and belonging. As R. Oza argues, 'Women, because they bear the burden of being cultural repositories, subjectively resolve the balance between the old and the new' (2006: 8). While the nation has surrendered a part of its sovereignty to the rules of free trade, the nation's identity remains anchored in the construction of gender and the metaphorical and material ways in which they produce the boundaries of the nation (Kaplan et al. 1999; Mayer 1999). Any breach of these boundaries is cause for alarm and the reassertion of moral and national order.

NORMATIVE BOUNDARIES OF BELONGING

Sexual Normativity

Issues of sex and sexuality have been sites of controversy and contest in the subcontinent since the nineteenth century, often being regarded as a threat to cultural and national identity. The fear factor needs to be understood against the backdrop of the nineteenth century colonial encounter and the relationship between culture and sex negotiated during this period. In the late nineteenth century, Hindu nationalists and revivalists in the subcontinent reconstituted the 'home' — along with sex and sexuality — as a 'pure' space of Indian culture, uncontaminated by the colonial encounter (Kapur 2005: 53).[2] The modern nation-state was fashioned in the home for want of any public space or institutions to construct a modern national identity and culture.

Partha Chatterjee has argued that as there were no public spaces or institutions available to nationalists for constructing a national culture, the modern nation was fashioned in the autonomous private domain of culture (1989: 236). The 'official' culture of Indian middle-class nationalism was elaborated in the private domain — 'the home' — that had important implications on the role of sexuality in nationalist discourse. The home as the repository of national identity had to be protected from colonial intrusions concerning women by using their virtues of 'chastity, self-sacrifice, submission, devotion, kindness, patience and the labours of love' as a cultural defence to such intrusions (ibid.: 287). Chatterjee links this transformation of the woman through nationalist ideology with the disappearance of social reform in the late nineteenth century. The cultural nationalists of that period were completely opposed to social reform, as it would open the door to the colonial power to act in the domain where the nationalists regarded themselves as sovereign. Thus, the issue of female emancipation disappeared in the late nineteenth century precisely because of the refusal on the part of the natonalists to allow any political negotiation of the women's question with the colonial power (ibid.: 250).

But the teleological narrative that informs Chatterjee's position does not take account of the fact that the 'subaltern woman' was not a passive, docile recipient of the interactions between the social reformers, cultural nationalists, and the colonial power. Gender cannot be delinked from issues of culture, nor are issues of gender resolved when issues of culture or nationalism are resolved. The public and private spheres were not two neat categories, where the public was exclusively defined and determined by the imperial power and the private by the anti-colonial nationalists. Indeed, as many scholars have revealed, both were highly contested and segmented spheres (Bhattacharya 2005; Chandra 1998; Mayaram et al. 2007;

Sinha 1995). As T. Sarkar argues, the reinforcement of a static understanding of culture and gender identity stood in contrast to evidence that the home was in fact a highly contested cultural space where there were tensions over women's role as preservers of cultural identity (2001: 191–225). The controversies over the age of consent for marriage gave rise to a plethora of medical and administrative literature, attesting to the extent of violence experienced by girls married off at the age of puberty, challenging the view that the home was in fact a space of honour, dignity, and purity. These internal cultural contests were marginalised in the broader contests between the cultural political nationalists and the colonial power.

Recent scholarship indicates women were also active in the public sphere and the political debate that implicated their identities and roles as upholders of the emerging national identity. For example, as Mrinalini Sinha has argued, the controversy over the issue of child marriage did not block the enactment of the Child Marriage Restraint Act, 1929, the first legal measure that was universally applicable to all communities regardless of religious affiliation (2006: 9). Women were pivotal in the campaign around the legislation, prizing the issue from being merely a community-based concern to a political concern relevant to all women. While their political collectiveness was short-lived in light of the tensions that continued over their existence as 'symbolic insiders' and reflective of their community identities, it nevertheless represented an important moment of active agency and political participation by women. The instance also illustrates that, in contrast to Chatterjee's view, the contest did not remain purely confined to one between the cultural nationalists and the imperial power. Yet women's identity as political activists was constantly in tension with their relationship to their community. This tension over the 'disavowal and constitution' of communities in the claims that were made for and by women remained a central feature of women's political participation and construction of their identities in the emerging nation-state (ibid.: 12). This tension continues to inform women's political belongingness/nonbelongingness in the contemporary period.

The discussion provides an understanding of the ways in which culture and sexuality were reshaped and reconstituted through the colonial encounter. Women's sexual purity confined to and safeguarded within the home and representing in turn the purity of Indian culture was a constituting feature in the emergence of the

Indian nation even while women constantly sought to transgress that boundary. The paradox is that both sexuality and nationalism as they emerged were western (but not). Anti-colonial forces invoked nationalism to draw a distinction between the 'East' and the 'West' but it was a concept grounded in the typology of knowledge production of the 'West' (Said 1978). The reconstituted space of Indian sexuality bore more than a slight resemblance to Victorian sexuality. The idea of sex and sexuality as a dangerous corrupting force, to be carefully contained at all costs within family and marriage, was as Victorian as it was Indian. But, within the emerging fantasy of the nation, the chastity and purity of Indian women, by which this dangerous and contaminating force was controlled, came to represent not only the purity of Indian culture but also its superiority to the culture of the Empire. The home was not an 'uncontaminated' space. It was as much a product of the colonial encounter as the contests in the public sphere. The underpinnings of the assumptions about Indian women's sexuality were both Victorian and Indian. These assumptions were absorbed through the colonial encounter into a litany of laws regulating sexual conduct, and refracted through the gaze of the colonial subject, in particular, the Indian nationalist, to construct a puritanical image of Indian women's sexuality (Nair 1996: 145).

In the context of the legal regulation of migrant women, time and time again, the issue of sex and sexuality is cited as the threat, the risk, and the enemy. Whether the controversy involves bar dancing, sex work, or trafficking, the responses to each underscore how sex is regarded as something that threatens dominant cultural values, the way of life and very existence of the nation (Bose and Bhattacharya 2007; Kapur 2005). The suturing of culture and sexuality into the fantasy of the nation continues to set the discursive stage on which the emerging debates on the rights of migrant women are emerging. The migrant subject is bringing a challenge to what has become over the years a naturalised and universalised set of ideas about sex and culture — the core ingredients in the making of national identity. She is making rights claims while at the same time disrupting prevailing assumptions about sex, culture, and gender that inform the law and the legal regulation of migrant subjects.

Normative sexuality regards sex as a natural force and something that is sinful and dangerous. It is something that will be subjected to unduly harsh penalties unless it falls within the parameters of normative sexuality, which in its purest form is heterosexual, marital, monogamous, reproductive, and non-commercial. In India, motherhood, wifehood, domesticity, marriage, chastity, purity, and self-sacrifice are all integral attributes of normative sexuality. Normative sexuality is accorded the maximum legal and social benefits while practices that fall outside of this dominant sexual ideology, such as sodomy or commercial sex work, bear the greatest social and legal stigma (Bose and Bhattacharya 2007; John and Nair 1998; Puri 1999; Rubin 1992). It is impossible to understand these features outside of the colonial encounter, which set the stage for engagements with sexuality in law as deeply implicated in the constitution of the nation and national identity. These features of normative sexuality were also cultural constructs used to mark the distinction between the colonial power and the colonised subject. It is this history that distinguishes normative sexuality in postcolonial India from that which has emerged from western liberal traditions (John and Nair 1998: 11). Female sexuality was either controlled or bounded within the institution of marriage or it was to be subsumed to the spiritual. Normative sexuality was incorporated into the nationalist agenda, where the discourse of purity and chastity produced a sexuality that was distinct from the contaminating, corrupting (imperial) West. It was a thoroughly modern construct. These assumptions about sexuality that came to inform the law were products of the nineteenth century colonial encounter and remain prevalent in the contemporary moment.

Familial Norms and the Sexual Division of Labour

The family is asserted throughout national and international human rights documents as 'the basic and fundamental unit of society'.[3] It is a term the meaning and importance of which is more often assumed than examined. The concept of family is not simply descriptive of kinship and household structures but rather is a discourse through which these structures are given meaning. The discourse of family is a set of ideas that evokes 'truth' claims about the family, about what it is, and how it works among the different members that constitute the family. It is a way of giving meaning to a particular grouping of individuals who are related by blood and marriage. Further, 'family' is a dominant ideology through which a particular set of household and gender relationships are universalised and naturalised. Although women in the subcontinent live in diverse family forms, there is a dominant ideology of family that shapes and informs the legal regulation of the family.

The term 'family' has often been conflated with the term 'household'. In India, these terms have been used interchangeably. For example, as stated in the Census of India from 1881 to 1941: 'The household or family consisted of those who lived together and ordinarily cooked at the same hearth including their servants and visitors' (Census of India 2001: paragraph 4; Rao 1992: 58–59). In 1951, the Census dropped the term 'family' and used only the term 'household' (Rao 1992: 61).[4] The National Sample Survey Organization and the Department of Labour used similar concepts of household in their data collection (Conklin 1976; Rao 1992: 66–69). In both these legal and public policy definitions as well as in academic literature, 'household' generally refers to those persons with a common residence and some degree of economic cooperation (Jain and Banerjee 1985; Wilks et al. 1984).[5] The head of the household can be either a man or a woman, or a younger member. If the head of the household is absent, then the person who is responsible for managing the affairs of the household is regarded as the head regardless of whether that person is a male or female (Census of India 2001: paragraph 7). Family, on the other hand, is defined as 'those kinship based relations that are located within co-residential groups and to the particular ideological forms taken by kinship structures within the [particular] context' (Shah 2005: 119–23; Standing 1991: 3). Family is not simply descriptive of these kinship and household structures, but rather, is a discourse through which these structures are given meaning (Gubrium and Holstein 1990, 1999). Family, then, has an additional ideological dimension: it is a discourse through which certain relationships are naturalised and universalised, and through which unequal power relations are obscured and legitimated. The ideology of the family consists of all those values and norms that instruct us on how 'ideal' family life should be lived (Gavigan 1993, 1997). The ideology of family provides a justification for how family is understood in a particular context. The ideology is regarded as part of common sense, as something that is natural and hence rarely questioned.

Familial ideology further operates to naturalise particular gender relations within the household arrangement, based on a sexual division of labour. This sexual division of labour allocates roles and responsibilities within the family on the basis of gender. Women are responsible for child rearing and domestic labour, whereas men are responsible for the financial welfare of the family (whether through subsistence agriculture, wage labour, or managing family property). Within the family, identities are gendered: women are daughters, wives, and mothers; men are sons, husbands, and fathers. The sexual division of labour further assigns to women the status of economic dependency on the men in families. In capitalism, the wage is the dominant mode of distribution for the working class. This wage is distributed in and through the sexual division of labour and in so doing, the work that women perform within the family is rendered invisible and valueless. Familial ideology operates to naturalise and universalise these household and gender relations so as to cast such relations as both inevitable and self-evident, and assume that women are in situations of dependency. It is in and through familial ideology that the roles accorded to women as wives and mothers, as caregivers and as economic dependents, come to be seen as natural, universal, and inevitable. The idea that women are 'naturally' wives and mothers becomes a self-evident product of women's biological role in reproduction; simply a part of our collective common sense.

The sexual division of labour has also been used to explain the way in which women have been integrated into the labour market. The labour market is characterised by a gendered segmentation. Women are concentrated into certain sections and occupations, which are seen as particularly well-suited to women's 'natural' skills. These occupations are low paying and often characterised by a very low degree of unionisation. Women's participation in the labour market has been structured around the assumption that women are economically dependent on men and thus do not need a family wage. Women's work has often been assumed to be temporary, as young, unmarried women would only work until such time as they got married. Women's participation in the labour market has been further shaped by the idea that women's skills are analogous to the skills they perform without financial compensation in the family. These skills are thereby constructed in and through familial ideology as less valuable than men's skills.

Familial ideology and the sexual division of labour operate in historically and materially specific contexts. Chandra Talpade Mohanty has argued that this sexual division of labour and the economic dependency of women are often applied in universal and problematic ways, that is, 'without their specification in local cultural and historical contexts'. If such concepts

> ... are assumed to be universally applicable, the resultant homogenization of class, race, religious, and daily material practices of women in the third world can create a false sense of the commonality of oppressions, interest and struggles between and among women globally. (Mohanty 1991: 67)

Mohanty further writes

> ... the existence of a sexual division of labour in most contexts cannot be sufficient explanation for the universal subjugation of women in the work force. That the sexual division of labour does indicate a devaluation of women's work must be shown through analysis of particular local contexts. ... Concepts such as the sexual division of labour can be useful only if they are generated through local, contextual analyses. (1991: 68)

The sexual division of labour and the economic dependency of women are thus assumed as explanations for the subordination of women rather than established through local and contextual analyses. It is important to consider the applicability of these concepts in the materially specific context of Indian women's lives, and examine the ways in which women's position in the family and the labour market is mediated through their class, caste, religious, ethnic, and other historically and contextually specific locations (Patel 2005: 95–146).

While familial ideology and the sexual division of labour within the family has been developed and analysed largely in relation to the nuclear family, this is not the dominant form of family in India. The predominant legal definition of family is that of the joint Hindu family (Bharat and D'Cruz 2001). Although there is no absolute consensus on its form, its features are generally listed as three or more generations, related through the male line, living in a common dwelling or in close proximity, sharing property, income, and various rights and obligation. In composition, it consists of parents, sons, their wives and children, and unmarried daughters (Dhruvaraja 1989: 36). The authority structure is patriarchal, succession is patrilineal, and living arrangements are patrilocal. In terms of cross-cultural familial forms, it has been identified as 'the asymmetrical community family', characterised by equality between brothers laid down by inheritance rules and cohabitation of married sons and their parents (Todd 1985: 155).

This legal definition does not necessarily represent the ways in which people actually live, but represents the understanding of family popularised by Orientalists and Indologists as well as lawyers involved in suits for the partition of joint family property (Desai 2005: 81–95; Patel 2005: 25–26 ; Shah 2005: 159–60). It represents part of the broader invention of Indian tradition that took place during the course of the colonial encounter (Chakravarti 1989; Uberoi 2005: 32–33). This joint family has quite a different meaning in law than in other social discourses. Until recently, the joint Hindu family in law comprised only of males who, by birth, had an interest in joint or coparcener property. The enactment of the Hindu Succession (Amendment) Act (2005) now permits a daughter to become a coparcener at birth in the same way as the son of a coparcener and she also has the same rights in the coparcener property as a son. While there remains a prevailing assumption that the joint Hindu family is culturally embedded and is largely male-centred, there is a general consensus that this definition of a joint Hindu family is a legal construct to regulate property ownership, and not an attempt to codify in law how people live as family (Desai 2005: 115–16). Nevertheless, this legal presumption of joint family status may be seen to reflect and reinforce the ideology of the joint family as the ideal within Indian society — an ideology that has a very different definition of family.[6]

There is considerable evidence to suggest a change in household structures in India (Census of India 2001; Kapadia 2005: 172). For example, there has been an enormous increase in female-headed households, in which a woman and her children (and possibly other relatives) live apart from the husband and father. This increase is due partly to globalisation-related economic changes that are impacting on the family, producing migration for employment, abandonment, or widowhood (Patel 2005: 30; Rao, 1992: 62–66). Notwithstanding these important demographic changes, the joint family continues to be the prevailing conception of family and the dominant way in which people define their family, regardless of its lack of correlation to their own domestic arrangements. The subjective attitude towards family bonds and responsibilities continues to be informed by the dominant discourse of the joint family. This disjuncture between household and family further underscores the argument that family is not simply descriptive of kinship and household structures but is a discourse through which these structures are given meaning.

The dominant familial ideology in India continues to be informed by the joint or extended family. Despite the changing demographics in the family form, the joint family continues to operate as the dominant conception of the family and the dominant way in which people envisage their own family. Any discussion of familial ideology in India must therefore take this idea of the joint family into account. It is also important to consider the particular manifestation of the sexual division of labour within the ideologically dominant joint family. In this joint family, women are not simply assumed to be economically dependent on their husbands. Rather, the joint family structure spreads this economic dependency more broadly: as daughters, women are economically dependent on fathers until their marriage, as wives they are economically dependent on their husbands and their husbands' joint family; and finally, as mothers, they are economically dependent on their adult sons. Further, within this joint family, women are wives, mothers, and daughters, but are also ascribed identities and roles as mothers-in-law, daughters-in-law, sisters-in-law. In these families, work is not only divided along gender but also along a generational axis, in which some women have more status and power than others. For example, a married woman is not considered a full member of her husband's family until she has produced a child, preferably a son.

Second, it is important to recognise that familial ideology and sexual division of labour do not accurately describe the way in which vast numbers of Indian women live in families. Poor, rural women have long been involved in subsistence farming within the family. Their unpaid work on the family farm has been and continues to be essential for the subsistence food production. Further, implicit in the analysis of the sexual division of labour within the labour market is the fact that many poor and working-class women — urban and rural alike — are employed as wage labour outside of the home. Many women may in fact be the sole wage earners within the household. At the time of the last census, women-headed households constituted 10–11 per cent of rural households, either because of male migration or abandonment (Census of India 2001: 5). State-wide, the numbers were as high as 22 per cent in both the north-eastern state of Meghalaya and the south-western state of Kerala. In urban areas, poor women are likely to be employed in domestic service. Further, the last decades have seen a tremendous increase in middle-class women's participation in the labour market, a process that is only intensifying with the opening up of the market.

Familial ideology is not a concept that can be unproblematically applied to describe the way in which all Indian women live in and are subordinated in families. Many women work as wage labour outside of the family and as unpaid but productive labour inside the family. In both contexts, women may make important, and often essential, contributions to the financial provision of the family. The nature of women's work both inside and outside of the family is mediated by relationships of class, caste, religion, regional location, and other materially specific contexts. There are many other material specific contexts that may affect women's position within their families, and the ways in which they are affected and constituted in relation to familial ideology.

In order to be effective, ideologies must have resonance with individuals' experience of the world. Familial ideology continues to have resonance because it is partially constitutive of individuals' identities within their families. It is in and through this familial ideology that women's and men's gendered identities within the family are constructed. It is through this ideology that women, despite their differences, are constituted as mothers and wives. Familial ideology operates to obscure women's differences of class, caste, and ethnicity, and to constitute women as homogeneous. It is through this familial ideology that unequal gender relations are constituted and sustained, naturalised, and obscured. Women are not only constructed as economic dependents, but this dependency is presented as a 'natural' consequence of their 'natural' roles.

In the context of migrant women, familial ideology continues to operate in influencing policy as well as demand. For example, the focus on women in the service sector, especially nursing, reinforces gender and sexual stereotypes where women are assumed to be natural caregivers. Servicing the aged, children, and the sick and taking care of domestic chores are non-threatening tasks typically performed by women and therefore encouraged. In the context of Indian nurses, one scholar observes how '… in Kerala the models of a perfect nurse that … are constantly referred to are two women: Florence Nightingale and Mother Teresa. Humility, dedication to suffering human beings and feelings of fulfilling religious duty by being so are expressed as "natural" feminine virtues' (Percot 2006: 157).

While it is important to examine the particular ways in which the sexual division of labour operates in particular women's lives, familial ideology resists such historically and materially specific analysis. Law, which simply assumes the homogeneity of women's experiences, is particularly resistant to such historically and materially specific analysis. These assumptions about the family continue to inform the legal regulation of women more generally and migrant women in particular. The law plays an important ideological role in shaping and questioning the understanding of women generally as possessing certain natural attributes that makes them suitable for a life of domesticity as mothers and wives. In so doing, those women who trespass these normative boundaries are denied the benefits and also subjected to punitive sanctions.

Familial ideology and the sexual division of labour shape and inform the legal regulation of migrant women. The construction of women as wives and mothers, sexually contained, and economically dependent on their families, has been partially constitutive of women's subordinated position and has informed the legal and policy responses to migrant women. Sometimes familial ideology operates to protect women. When women have been good wives and mothers, when they have lived up to the normative expectations, the law can operate in their favour. But, by the same token, a migrant woman whose life has deviated from the roles allocated to her by this familial ideology may often find herself on the losing side of the law. Female migration sits in tension with familial ideology and the attempt to confine women to a male-regulated private sphere.

Cultural Norms

Several complaints were filed in district courts in India against Richard Gere under the obscenity clauses of the Indian Penal Code for giving Bollywood actress Shilpa Shetty a sweeping embrace and kiss on the cheek at a public AIDS awareness event in New Delhi (BBC News 2007). Movements against public displays of affection as well as increased surveillance of female sexual conduct in public have emerged. The harassment of couples celebrating Valentine's Day or of homosexual men under legal provisions that until recently criminalised sodomy and other 'unnatural' sexual offences is justified in the name of cultural purity and salvation. Hysteria about culture is sweeping the country. Everywhere, cries of Indian cultural values being in danger are heard. The threat, the risk, the enemy, time and again, is cast as foreign, as the 'Other', as dangerous. This contest over culture is being played out in the context of migration and the legal contests being waged in the courts over the rights of migrant workers, especially female migrants.

The legal regulation of migrant women has invariably been informed by prevalent assumptions about culture, about what constitutes 'authentic' Indian cultural values, and about who conforms to these ideals and who does not. Indeed, rights and benefits, while determined along the access of formal legal citizenship, are also mediated by normative assumptions about culture. The line between the legitimate and illegitimate subject is drawn along a cultural boundary, which has a direct impact on the rights of migrants generally, and on the rights of migrant women more specifically. Migrant women who transgress certain sexual norms experience serious erosion of their rights to citizenship, mobility, equality, and livelihood. Their entitlement as well as access to rights is often contingent on the nature of the work they do. For example, while migrant women arriving from Nepal into domestic work in India may be entitled to work and limited rights protections, those who work in the sex industry have been subject to police raids, rescue operations, and repatriation. The transgression of sexual and cultural norms, such as engaging in sex work or bar dancing, renders migrant women subject to harsh bans and at times they are rendered nearly destitute in the process. A hierarchy of rights is produced contingent on cultural and sexual conformity.

In the context of the colonial encounter in the late nineteenth century, cultural debates were integral to political discourse and the competing positions which emerged over the conceptions of national identity. For example, the relationship between culture and national identity in the colonial encounter of the nineteenth century was played out in the debates between the cultural nationalists and liberal social reformers over how the nation was to be defined and the citizen subject to be constituted. Nationalism and the struggle to forge a national consciousness were deeply embedded in culture during this period. One view, articulated by social reformers such as the Derozians and the Adi Brahmo Samaj (First Society of God), wanted to restructure Indian society along the lines of western modernity, based on the values of the Enlightenment and liberalism (Chaudhuri 2000; Roy 2005: 83–94, 95–110). This position was advocated by those who had been primarily products of the English educational system and its emphasis on liberalism, rationalism, and utilitarianism. It was an appeal to the Enlightenment's tools of modernity, based on rational, scientific thinking as the basis for social transformation.

A second view sought to resurrect ancient scriptural practices and traditions and forge a national identity in the shape of a Hindu identity. This was a position developed in opposition to the anti-traditional, liberal democratic, and secular concept of the nation. For example, some Hindu nationalists argued in favour of the 'regeneration' of Hinduism through the articulation of a pure 'Vedic' practice and faith. The birth of the nation had to be grounded in a return to the 'Vedic Golden Era' and the bringing about of a national renaissance of early Hindu doctrines. This position simply equated Indian national identity with Hinduism and Hindu tradition and articulated nationalism purely in terms of ethnicity. The Hindus were regarded as the direct descendants of the Aryans and this movement led to the founding of the Arya Samaj (Society of Aryans). The effort was towards establishing a monolithic and homogenous Hindu identity, that is, a Hindu nation, through the propagation of a common religion and culture in India and conversion. In 1909 Lala Lajpat Rai, an Arya Samaj nationalist leader, stated that 'Hindus are a "nation" in themselves because they represent a type of civilization all their own' (Jaffrelot 1996: 19). The idea of 'the nation' was embedded in the notion of a community possessing a certain civilisation and culture. The constitution of the nation could only be achieved through the assertion of a Hindu identity and not just through the idea of an Indian nation. It was the ideology of the Arya Samaj that subsequently impacted on the emergence of Hindu nationalism in the 1920s (ibid.: 17).

These two competing positions on culture continued through the latter part of the nineteenth and the early twentieth centuries. Liberals and social reformers advocated for reforms of Hindu culture, while the cultural nationalists glorified Hindu culture and opposed any kind of reform as providing an avenue for the colonial power to intervene in the private domain, the domain where Hindu national identity was being forged. In the contemporary context, it is the Hindu Right's approach, informed by the colonial encounter, which has been in ascendance. *Hindutva* – the establishment of India as a Hindu state — has become a powerful ideological tool to consolidate Hindu identity and define what constitutes both 'Indian culture' and the Indian nation.

In perhaps what may be a move to complicate understandings of Indian culture and to resist the complete appropriation of its meaning by the Hindu Right, Amartya Sen unpacks how Indian culture has been used to distinguish the Indian nation from the West. He sets out three distinct positions: the 'exoticist', 'magisterial', and 'curatorial'. The distinctions between them lie in their evaluations of Indian culture and the location from which they distinguish India from the West. The 'exoticist' approach focused on the 'wondrous aspects of India' and was 'wowed' by India's exotic ideas and views, its sages, and way of life (2006: 141). The 'magisterial' approach adopted by the colonial rulers presumed that a backward, unwashed nation was being brought into being under the benign and reformist administration of the British Empire. This approach was mirrored in the writings of James Mill, who produced a six-volume *History of India* in 1917 that came to be heavily relied on by British governors in India (ibid.: 147). The 'curatorial' approach focused on systematic and rational curiosity about Indian culture and history, involving neither blind praise nor wholesale condemnation. By way of example, Sen points to the text by Alberuni, the Iranian born historian, who wrote the *History of India* in Arabic in the early eleventh century. Alberuni presents an account of the rich intellectual traditions of India during this period in the areas of astronomy, philosophy, literature, and science.

For Sen, all three approaches emphasise the distinction of India from the West and share the use of culture to make this distinction. Contemporary Hindu nationalism by attempting to retrieve an indigenous cultural past ends up being no different from Mill or the magisterial approach that Sen discusses (2006: 140). For Sen, Indian cultural nationalists have uncritically borrowed from these strands of scholarship. However, 'the special characteristics of Western approaches to India have encouraged a disposition to focus particularly on the religious and spiritual elements in Indian culture' (ibid.). All three approaches use culture to present homogenised representations of India, although they differ in their interpretations.

In the contemporary period, the subaltern studies project has further complicated the understandings of culture in postcolonial India. Sen critiques the subaltern as lacking in the ability to critically reflect upon or understand India's rich intellectual past (2006: 157). This argument is made in the context of his larger argument that curatorial approaches, which focus on the metaphysical traditions of India, are more effective instruments for understanding culture and countering western perceptions about the orient. Similarly, he argues that a project that focuses on peasant consciousness as a strategy for critiquing western enlightenment is insensitive to the lack of formal education and literacy of the subaltern, which is not an instance to be valorised.

In the process, Sen affirms his liberal stance and does not engage with the deeper challenges posed by the project to the foundations of liberalism. Subaltern studies are not merely descriptive narratives driven by the search for an essential peasant consciousness. As discussed in the Introduction, while this search may have initially characterised the project, it did not determine the project. The subaltern studies project eventually bifurcated into those who continued to search for an essential peasant consciousness and story of victimisation, and those who came to be increasingly influenced by post-structuralism (Chakrabarty 2002). The refashioned project adopted a more Foucauldian analysis, focusing on contesting the Eurocentric, metropolitan, and bureaucratic systems of knowledge and how the subaltern subject came to be constituted in and through discourse. The new tradition was concerned with challenging all traditions and disciplines that were defined within the logic and rationale of the Enlightenment project. This challenge included unmasking the humanist subject and bringing into critical consideration a host of other categories, including gender, class, ethnicity, and race.

This scholarship has expanded and begun to address and challenge the neo-imperialism of the late twentieth/early twenty-first century and problems of agency, subject position, and hegemony in an era of globalisation (Bhabha 1994; Chakrabarty 2002; Ludden 2002; Mignolo 2002). While the subaltern studies project unmasks the power–knowledge relationship embedded within the terms of liberalism, it also challenges the monolithic and essentialist assumptions about culture, exposing its hybridity (Hall 1996). The techniques of critique and dialectics have characterised Indian intellectual thought, which is not fearful of interrogating the metaphysical foundations of knowledge (Balagangadhara 1994; Burton 1999). Subaltern studies go beyond merely distinguishing India from the West using different interpretations of culture. It strikes at the very foundation of liberal thought as an emancipatory mission and exposes the relationships of power and the binaries of 'us and them', 'here and there' along which it has operated.

Competing understandings of culture characterise the legal regulation of migrant women. In several chapters in this volume, I expose the ways in which culture is deployed to reaffirm sexual normativity by those in positions of power and view it as static and immutable. I also examine the ways in which cultural arguments are being made by migrant women attempting to challenge these familiar narratives of culture, sex, and nation. At first glance, these arguments appear to deploy static assumptions about culture in the same way as those in positions of power, but at a deeper level, they can be seen to be based on cultural hybridity, countering stagnant, fixed, unmoving approaches to culture.

Migrants are challenging assumptions about sexuality, about who constitutes the subject of the nation-state, and the assumptions about culture as static and immutable. These categories are not separate and distinct, but invariably converge and remain integral in law. For example, Indian cultural values are often linked with sexual conduct as well as marital status. Any transgression of sexual norms produce fears that the very fabric of Indian culture and ethos is under threat of erosion, if not collapse. The laws and judicial decisions discussed in the following chapter illustrate the ways in which assumptions about family, sex, and culture come to be embedded in the law as well as the challenges that are made by migrants to these assumptions.

CONCLUSION

Cross-border movements have become a feature of the contemporary moment and an integral aspect of globalisation. While the right to freedom of movement is a well recognised human right, it is restricted and curtailed in light of a broad array of historic factors and contemporary changes. In the current period of neoliberalism and economic globalisation, a new legal order has emerged to deal with and facilitate the cross-border movement of capital, goods, services, and ideas. However, there has not been a similar response to accommodate the concomitant cross-border movement of people and labour demand produced by this new reality. Instead, states have sought refuge in traditional notions of nation-state identity and sovereignty to resist cross-border traffic (Beneria and Bisnath 2004: 2). This assertion of national identity is being deployed in and through law and the reproduction of the register of sexual, familial, and cultural norms that draw the line between insider and outsider, those who shore up the nation's identity, and those who are suspected of threatening or betraying it. The construction of the migrant subject in law is integral to demarcating the normative as well as material boundaries of the nation, while at the same time she remains expendable.

Returning to the brutal slayings that took place in Nithari in 2006, the case provides a stark example of how the migrant remains almost entirely expendable and can never entirely belong. While some of the migrants in Nithari had lived and worked in the area for years, they remained outsiders, confined to the borderlands of law, citizenship, and society. Repeated attempts by the inhabitants to access the state machinery for their 'protection' remained unsuccessful. Nandlal, the father of the girl whose case ultimately led to the gruesome discovery, was rebuffed by the police on several occasions when he tried to lodge a complaint. After approaching the court which directed an investigation into the case, the police responded by accusing Nandlal of running a call girl racket and his daughter of being a prostitute (Dubey et al. 2007). In the period between the disappearance of his daughter and the ultimate discovery of the skeletal remains of the victims, seven more young people went missing. It was only when the media focused attention on the 'pathological' or aberrational acts of the perpetrators that transgressed normative assumptions about sexuality that the state was compelled to respond to and assist the migrant subject. Nithari is an example of how the migrant is first ignored and then accommodated, but on terms that relegate her to the frontiers of sexual normativity. The migrant finally becomes visible, but through violent and aberrational acts that transgress all sense of normativity. In the process, the liberal state attempts to retain its self-proclaimed role as protector and upholder of the law, and is in no way implicated in producing the horrific violence that took place in Nithari. Yet, as the following chapters illustrate, the migrant refuses to remain passive or silent. In the process of demanding rights from the very mechanisms that render her mute or threatening, the migrant is able to disrupt the self assuredness of the nation-state, display the edginess of its borders, and expose the role of law in producing the very zones of inclusion and exclusion that constitutes the liberal project of justice.

NOTES

1. The Allahabad High Court subsequently acquitted Pandher of the murder. He still has 17 other cases of murder pending trial.
2. There is a focus on Hindu nationalists because of their majoritarian position. This is not to suggest that religious minorities had no influence on the political or legal agenda, or that they were exclusively victims. But religious minorities have not been situated in the same way to influence the shaping and construction of dominant norms and the making of the majoritarian (Hindu) nation-state.
3. For example, Article 23 of the *International Covenant on Civil and Political Rights* states: 'The family is the natural and fundamental group unit of society and is entitled to protection by society and the state.'
4. In the 1961 survey, the household was treated as an economic unit separate from the individuals within it. In 1971, the 'household' was defined in greater detail: 'there may be one-member households, two member households, or multimember households' (Rao 1992: 63 quoting from Census of India 1971). It further made a distinction between the household of blood relations and unrelated persons or 'institutional households' (ibid.: 63). In the 2001 Census, the 'household' continues to be defined as a group of persons who normally live together and take their meals together in a common kitchen unless the exigencies of work prevent them from doing so. If the group is unrelated and do not take their meals in a common kitchen then they are not a part of a common household. The data also provides separate definitions for an institutional household, which include boarding houses, hotels hostels, orphanages or ashrams, and houseless households, where people do not live in a concrete shelter, but on pavements, roadsides, under flyovers, in ashrams, or on railway platforms.
5. D. Jain and N. Bannerjee define the 'economic household' as 'the entire group of persons who commonly live together and take their meals from a common means.'
6. There are also considerable regional variations and diversity in family formations and legal rights to property. For example, in the south-west Indian state of Kerala, matriliny is allowed for children born before 1976, which means that property can pass unequally to female children and their children. Boys have to be given an equal share if born after 1976. The children of daughters no longer get a share of the land. Family formations are also influenced by this matrilineal notion of the family. The Kerala example is just one example of the regional differences. As a result, the rights that women have and their migration paths and legal status can vary greatly.

3

Victims, Whores, and Wives: Migrant Women and the Law

In this chapter I focus on laws and judicial decisions that have impacted on the rights of migrant women, examining the assumptions about women's roles and identities that are deeply embedded in the law, including those laws that have ostensibly been designed for women's benefit. I direct my discussion to two aspects: the moral regulation through which migrant women are constructed as, and judged in accordance with the standards of 'good women', chastity, heterosexuality, self-sacrifice, dependency, and victimisation; and economic regulation through which migrant women are constructed as economic dependents or exploited victims. Each of these is in turn informed by the register of sexual, familial, and cultural norms that are used to legitimise or delegitimise the migrant subject. I argue that the law is intensifying the conditions that have both created women's economic vulnerability and also undermined the law's ability to adequately address such vulnerability. It is further reifying assumptions about Indian cultural values and the defining attributes and identity of the nation, as well as who constitutes the legitimate sovereign subject.

MORAL REGULATION OF MIGRANT WOMEN IN AND THROUGH LAW

Women's sexual purity confined to and safeguarded within the private domain, that is, the home, represented the purity of Indian culture and was a constituting feature in the emergence of the Indian nation (Kapur 2005: 54). This assumption continues to inform the ways in which women's rights are taken up and addressed in law in the contemporary period. To a large extent, judicial decisions and law still rotate around the belief that sexual promiscuity and premarital sex go against the tenets of model Indian citizenship and national integrity.[1]

The ways in which the register of sexual, familial, and cultural norms shape and inform the moral regulation of migrant women is most readily apparent in the anti-sex work and anti-trafficking laws that have operated to increasingly restrict women's mobility. I reveal the extent to which these norms inform the laws in India and the construction of women's subjectivity. They naturalise and universalise the construction of women as good wives and mothers, as passive, dutiful, and self-sacrificing. Any transgression of these normative standards frequently results in the victimisation or criminalisation of the migrant woman. These laws obscure the reasons why women move as well as the multiplicity of differences between and among migrant women, and the very different ways in which women experience migration.

Sex Work and Anti-trafficking Interventions

Assumptions about what constitutes appropriate sexual conduct for women continue to inform the legal regulation of migrant women. The increased focus on strengthening anti-trafficking laws and policies over recent years has resulted in sex workers and migrant women being faced with evictions, forced rehabilitation/repatriation, mandatory HIV testing, and police searches, all ostensibly in the interests of protecting women. Several judgments illustrate how sex workers are portrayed as less than ideal citizens, as illegitimate inhabitants who do not qualify for national belonging. Or they are regarded as contaminants originating from elsewhere who must be contained. In most instances, however, they are portrayed almost exclusively as victims, to be protected through limited incarceration, juridically deprived rather than empowered through the conferment of rights. In many cases, sex workers are categorised as victims of trafficking who need to be rehabilitated and repatriated back, either to their home state or country of origin.

In 1997, the Bombay High Court took *suo moto* (on its own initiative) notice of two newspaper articles about several minor girls who had been trafficked from outside of the western state of Maharashtra and ostensibly forced to work as sex workers in Mumbai.[2] Based on these reports, the High Court directed the state to organise the rescue of such girls from all brothels, repatriate them to their home states, create a cell involving social workers for the rescue and rehabilitation of minor girls, and form a scheme for conducting HIV tests in the brothels. It also directed that regular raids be carried out in the area where sex workers operated and that homes be set up for the 'rehabilitation of rescued sex workers including children so as to enable these rescued sex workers to acquire alternative skills in order to enable them to have alternative sources of employment' (*Public at Large* 1997: paragraph 32).

At the same time, the court observed that:

> Periodical raids pursuant to the directions of this Court and/or well meaning citizens raising their voice is no answer to the duty cast on the State by the Immoral Traffic (Prevention) Act to weed out the obnoxious trade. It is to be stated that even till date in spite of social reformers like Raja Ram Mohan Roy, Mahatma Gandhi, Jyoti Phule and others, our inability to educate and inform our citizens is a national shame. Let our attitude towards women be slightly changed by not considering them as only an explosive material of sex-stimulation. (*Public at Large* 1997: paragraph 21)

Further, with regard to the repatriation of the women, the court stated,

> The survey conducted in respect of the girls rescued from Mumbai shows that the girls hail from Maharashtra, Karnataka, Andhra Pradesh, Tamil Nadu, West Bengal, and Eastern parts of India, including, Nepal and Bangladesh. The reports submitted by the organisations working under the State government as well as the various NGO's reveal that by and large the rescued women on proper counselling would prefer to go back to their homes. (*Public at Large* 1997: paragraph 19)

According to the court, the model Indian citizen should condemn brothels and the purchase of sexual services, and casts a duty on the state to eradicate this 'obnoxious' trade. The state is allocated the role to reform men who view women only as 'explosive material of sex stimulation' to become better citizens of India. The reference to nineteenth century social reformers such as Raja Ram Mohan Roy exemplifies how the state's role as social reformer is pre-eminent. Rights are cast in opposition to sex work, which is referred to as a 'national shame' while at the same time reproducing a conservative sexual morality and defining the appropriate role of the Indian woman. The court's comments are embedded in dominant assumptions about family, culture, and sexuality.

The court also fails to distinguish between adult women and girls, stating that the main objective of the anti-trafficking act is to take effective steps to prevent the 'exploitation of women and children hailing mostly from rural areas, who are lured into the trade by unscrupulous elements taking advantage of the socio-economic backwardness of women' (*Public at Large* 1997: paragraph 19). Such statements assume that women are victims, forced into the sex trade, and are in need of rescue. According to the High Court, 'One should not forget that these rescued girls are also fellow human beings who require some support and treatment for getting out of immoral activities' (ibid.: paragraph 32). Although somewhat patronisingly considered human, migrant women who become sex workers are denied any agency and deemed incapable of making choices and informed decisions about whether or not they want to be rehabilitated or repatriated. Moreover, the court's support for police raids contradicts empirical evidence which indicates that raids have adversely impacted sex workers and their families (*Vamp News* 2002). Not only do such raids result in women being incarcerated in unsanitary and uninhabitable conditions, several women have also died while in custody (ibid.).[3]

In a separate case concerning a settlement of migrant workers, the legal responses were once again couched within the framework of anti-trafficking interventions and the protection of public morality. The case concerned a challenge by Savera, an NGO, to the eviction of 5,000 residents of Baina beach in Goa, a western coastal state in India. Baina was a residential area where the settlements dated back to the 1960s, and consisted largely of migrants from other states who worked as daily wage labourers at the port or as garbage collectors or in other types of manual labour (Bailancho Saad 1997).[4] Some women amongst these workers were engaged in commercial sex work and carried on their work from 250 cubicles located amongst the many other small residential units, businesses, and NGO offices in the area. Their clients included sailors, shipyard workers, and tourists (Desouza 2004: 3341).

The municipality sought the eviction of the residents in 1997 to accommodate the demands of the tourist industry for the construction of luxury resorts along the beach as well as the needs of the port authority to expand the port facilities given the increase in maritime traffic. The resulting property boom produced a developmental conflict that facilitated the push for the evacuation of the residents of Baina beach. The rationale of state-led development justified the violation of human rights through the discourse of public interest (Desouza 2004: 3342). Prior to this conflict over development, when the land market was not so buoyant in the 1980s, migrants and sex work were tolerated. The evictions were partly justified on the grounds that the beach needed to be 'cleaned up' as it was overrun with sex workers who allegedly posed an HIV threat to the local population. Proponents of the eviction were intent on ridding the area of all 'criminal activity' including prostitution, and reclaiming the beach for the local citizens and tourists (ibid.).

The High Court directed that a committee be set up to examine the issue of rehabilitation of the residents who were to be evicted. The Committee focused mainly on the sex workers and recommended that a detailed socio-economic profile of the women in prostitution be prepared, including the feasibility of repatriating them to their states of origin (Kamat Committee Report 1998). The National Human Rights Commission (NHRC), which was also approached by the residents and some local NGOs, stated that the women had the right to be treated humanely and if they were to be evicted, they had to be provided with reasonable alternate accommodation.

The Kamat Committee's report as well as the language of the court and Savera's petition are replete with references to sex work as a demeaning trade, sex workers as 'poor', 'unfortunate', or 'fallen' women, and promoters of the sex trade as 'human vultures'. While the Kamat Committee and the High Court sympathised with the sex workers' fear of eviction, and loss of livelihood, they did not question the order of eviction nor address the broader question of the rights of the migrants to remain on the beach. In fact, the overwhelming focus of the Kamat Committee's report as well as the court decision was on the rehabilitation of the sex workers, and not on the other migrants in Baina, who were merely clubbed together in the Committee's recommendations as well as the High Court's judgment. The fact that the programme for rehabilitating the sex workers was not based on any empirical evidence either that the women were being forced, trafficked, exploited, or abused when engaging in their trade or that young girls were being forced into prostitution in the area also did not impact on the Committee's recommendations (Bailancho Saad 1997: 7).

The High Court ultimately directed that the 250 cubicles being used for sex work be closed down or demolished if found to be illegal and operating on government land. The court gave considerable weight to the objections from the local population to the presence of the sex workers and stated that measures needed to be taken to prevent commercial sex workers from being brought into Goa — 'The need to protect the rights of the law abiding citizens at the same time has to be asserted. The sex workers cannot cause inconvenience to other citizens and their right to life to live in a surrounding free from amoral activities' (*Savera* 2003: paragraph 9). The citizen's right to livelihood and residence was rendered conditional upon the type of work in which she was engaged. Her expulsion from the beach did not result in her expulsion from juridical control. She was transformed from a worker, with some sense of entitlements, to an expelled contaminant or victim to be contained within the territory for her own protection as well as the protection of the remaining uncontaminated citizens. What is striking about the response to the Baina beach residents is how the inhabitants, in particular the sex workers, are constantly viewed as either victims or sexual contaminants (Bailancho Saad 1997: 6). For example, the police cautioned visitors to the area, especially tourists, of the potential health risks on entering the beach, alleging that a 'large number of persons and commercial sex workers are affected by venereal disease' (ibid.).

Ultimately, while the sex worker teetered on the brink of being exteriorised, the entire habitation of Baina beach was simply obliterated. In June 2004, the municipality ordered the demolition of the entire habitation. The government initially claimed the demolition only affected the cubicles of the sex workers but subsequently justified the demolition of the habitation, arguing that the demolished structures were in any case illegal and that the evicted persons were 'non-Goans', that is aliens from the southern states of Karnataka and Andhra Pradesh. The complete demolition of the habitation rendered all the migrants of Baina beach as outsiders and cultural contaminants. They were transformed from subjects living and working in Baina beach, with a sense of incipient entitlements, into jettisoned subjects with little or no sense of entitlement. While they no longer retained any political status in terms of equal citizenship, they were exposed to the brutality of political power that rendered them into non-citizens, or lesser citizens, because they were found to be culturally and morally wanting. The residents of Baina beach were discursively constituted through the field of power, that is, they were re-made into migrants, and at the same time juridically deprived (Butler and Spivak 2007: 31).

In another High Court case, sex workers in Surat, a large city in Gujarat (a western state in India), filed a public interest litigation challenging several provisions of the Immoral Trafficking Prevention Act, 1956 (ITPA) as violating their fundamental rights to equality, livelihood, and mobility (*Sahyog Mahila Mandal and Another vs. State of Gujarat and Others,* (2004) 2 Gujarat Law Reports 1764) (hereinafter Chakla Bazaar). The ITPA is intended to combat trafficking in women by targeting brothel owners, but it is largely used against women who solicit for sex (Nair and Sen 2004: 313). The sex trade had been carried on in Chakla Bazaar for over 400 years. While the bazaar was initially located outside the city limits, the area was engulfed by Surat as a result of urban expansion and the influx of labour. The women and their customers were mostly migrant labourers who had migrated from Nepal and other states in India in large numbers to Surat in search of work.

The case involved a challenge by sex workers to orders promulgated by the local police prohibiting the conduct of prostitution in the Chakla Bazaar area on the grounds that it was situated near places of public worship and educational institutions and hence violated the provisions of the ITPA. The police also prohibited landlords from allowing women to return to the rooms that they had leased as residences effectively rendering them homeless. The sex workers alleged that they were constantly subjected to police abuse, raids, harassment, and arrests both within their homes as well as on the streets, even when they were carrying out simple daily tasks such as buying vegetables from the vegetable vendor. The women also objected to the government's proposals to send them into protection homes and their children to orphanages or remand homes as well as to police proposals to repatriate the women to their places of origin.

The sex workers relied on a decision of the Bangladesh Supreme Court to support the argument that sex workers as citizens had enforceable fundamental rights (*Bangladesh Society for the Enforcement of Human Rights vs. Government of Bangladesh,* reported in Volume LIII 2001 Dhaka Law Reports). The Bangladesh case involved the legality of the wholesale eviction of sex workers from Tanbazaar and Nimtali, well-established red light areas for over 200 years. The sex workers argued that the eviction violated their rights under Articles 31 and 32 of the Constitution of Bangladesh, 1972, which guaranteed their rights to protection of law as well as to life and liberty.

The Court upheld the rights of the sex workers not to be deprived of their livelihood or right to life, and declared the eviction as illegal. The sex workers of Chakla Bazaar also relied on a decision of the Indian Supreme Court, which stated that women in sex work should not be regarded as moral offenders of society, but victims of adverse socio-economic circumstances (*Gaurav Jain vs. Union of India* (1997) 8 Supreme Court Cases 114). Ultimately, the Gujarat court held that the Indian Constitution prohibited prostitution. It stated:

> Article 23 of the Constitution of India prohibits traffic in human beings, begar[sic] and other similar forms of forced labour. The victim of prostitution is the prostitute herself who is placed in a slave-like condition and subjected to virtually unlimited authority of others in the trade for rendering distinctly personal service. (Chakla Bazaar 2004: paragraph 8)

The court further stated that:

> The most potent rejoinder against recognition of the degrading practice of prostitution, which undermines womanhood itself, comes from Article 51–A (e) of the Constitution, which ordains that it shall be the duty of every citizen of India to renounce practices derogatory to the dignity of women. (Chakla Bazaar 2004: paragraph 8.2)

The court stated emphatically that 'It is never right for a man to be able to buy a woman and recognition of prostitution would be an undesirable phenomenon in a civilized modern society' (Chakla Bazaar 2004: paragraph 8.5). Where `the vice of prostitution' was endemic and degraded the lives of the women in the trade and demoralised those who came into contact with them, then it was perfectly justifiable to impose 'severe restrictions' on the rights of the sex workers to move about and live in a house of her own choice. And if the 'evil' was rampant, then the women could be deported from the place where they worked. 'The magnitude of the evil and the urgency of the reform may require such drastic remedies' (ibid.: paragraph 9.5). The court cited various provisions of international law in its holding including Article 6 of CEDAW as well as the UN Trafficking Protocol, and stated that 'To recognize prostitution as a legitimate means of livelihood would be an open invitation to trafficking in women which is shunned internationally and in all the civilized nations of the world' (ibid.: paragraph 8).

The decision illustrates how prostitution is erroneously conflated with trafficking, treating all women in prostitution as trafficked women. Such a position ends up taking a stand on the legality or illegality of prostitution rather than attending to the rights violations of the sex workers, failing to realise that rights are a critical tool for fighting the abuse, violence, and exploitation that may occur within the trade. The broader fundamental rights implications for the migrant sex workers, including their loss of livelihood and shelter, remained unaddressed. Instead, the court adopted a paternalistic stance robbing the women of any subjectivity, rendering them as lifeless, helpless objects. They were simultaneously deemed as threatening and immoral for transgressing sexual boundaries. The reasoning is couched in explicit statements about appropriate sexual conduct for women and their roles in the family. The court characterises commercial sex work as the public and impersonal display of the most intimate of human activities. A distinction is drawn between prostitution and sex. The latter takes place in the private realm, 'where the expression of sexuality, not the commercial aspect, is at the core'. Prostitution involves acts that are both 'indiscriminate and loveless'. What is being punished is not the privacy of the individual but 'sex which is both indiscriminate and for reward', which empties the act of sex of its private and intimate character (Chakla Bazaar 2004: paragraph 10.1). The sex worker is not involved in 'nurturing relationships or taking life-affirming decisions about birth, marriage, or family', but only making money. This aspect places her 'far away from the inner sanctum of protected privacy rights' (ibid.). Prostitution is aligned to a host of criminal, illegal activities and health risks, including trafficking, child prostitution, the risk of spreading sexually transmitted diseases, including HIV/AIDS, drug abuse, crime, assault, rape, and murder, as well as being a public nuisance. Thus the removal of the women from the area was held to be consistent with the provisions of the ITPA and also for ensuring the 'moral hygiene' of the locality (Chakla Bazaar 2004: paragraph 12.2).

As in the *Savera* case, the rights of sex workers to earn a livelihood and have a place to reside are trumped by the rights of other citizens to a sexually sanitised environment that confines legitimate sex within the home, the sanctity of heterosexual marriage, and as primarily for the purpose of procreation. The status of the Indian woman, civilisation, and morality are all invoked to deny the rights of migrant sex workers. The push-and-pull factors that have produced her migration remain unaddressed and the normative criteria of culture, family, and sexuality are centred to effectively deny her her fundamental rights.

These normative proscriptions regarding sexual conduct do not apply exclusively to sex workers, but also to their clients. In 2008, the Indian government proposed amendments to the ITPA seeking to penalise 'any person who visits or is found in a brothel for the purpose of sexual exploitation of any victim of trafficking ...'[5] The amendment would have effectively penalised all clients found visiting brothels, as no criteria was set out for distinguishing between clients who visited trafficked victims and those who did not. The assumption once again was that clients of sex workers were sexual deviants as they failed to conform to the normative criteria of monogamy and sex within marriage. As stated by Geetanjali Gangoli, 'Isolating and humiliating clients may serve the interests of some patriarchs that seek to preserve marriage and the conventional family. The very knowledge that men use the services of prostitutes is shameful within this discourse ... Ultimately, however, the shame and humiliation is vested with the prostitute, as she is considered so stigmatised that by association the client is also stigmatised and degraded' (2006: 226).

The moral regulation of female migrants remains present even in determining the rights of those who are not sex workers. In a report on the rights of construction workers, a majority of whom are migrants from other states, the NCW identified four methods of recruitment used to hire daily labour. These include the direct recruitment of workers by labour contractors from rural areas, city slums, as well as the market place (*naka*, *chowk*) (National Commission of Women 2005b: 16). The NCW criticised the method of recruitment from the *naka* or *chowk* on the grounds that it would lead to sexual harassment and sexual exploitation of women workers.

> Women who wait in the *chowks* often find themselves leered at by prospective employers and subject to various indignities. Contractors prefer younger women, both because they can work faster and because they are more attractive. Sexual exploitation is rife, given the insecurity of a daily wage system. (National Commission of Women 2005b: 21)

The disapproval expressed by the NCW report of soliciting work through *naka*s reflects a deep tension between the demands for migrant women's labour and state regulations over women's rights to solicit their labour. The migrant women have argued that restrictions on *naka*s invite police harassment and an eviction from their spaces by vegetable vendors and auto-rickshaws (National Commission of Women 2005b: 68). Svati Shah has argued that solicitation by migrant women for paid work, that is, the *naka*, 'provides a key income generating space for low wage and unskilled workers in the city' including small scale construction work, building repair work and sex work (2006: 239). Women who solicit for work in public spaces go against governing familial and cultural ideology and sexual norms. According to Shah,

> the signifiers of solicitation for respectable construction work and un-respectable sex work both include having proximity to large groups of men, being un-chaperoned by a family member in public areas, and visibly using a public space to seek out paid work. All of these are also signs of transgression of gendered norms of propriety for these communities. (2006: 244)

The cases discussed in this section illustrate how the rights of female migrants are mediated in and through moral regulation. Migrant women who do sex work are invariably classified as either victims of trafficking or as sexual deviants but in either case their rights are inferior to the rights of other citizens. Therefore evictions, forced rehabilitation/repatriation, mandatory HIV testing, and arbitrary police searches are justified to protect the rights of those who conform to sexually and culturally normative behaviour. The cases illustrate how prevailing assumptions about sex and culture shape and inform the legal regulation of migrant women. Women's roles and identities are constituted in and through familial ideology, the roles that women are assumed to play within and outside of the family, and then judged according to their adherence to these norms and standards. Women who deviate from their allocated roles of obedience, self-sacrifice, and loyalty to their husbands are often judged as bad women and are thereby accorded less protection. Invariably, the migrant woman is assessed as transgressing these very boundaries that are installed for women's protection and is therefore undeserving of such protection.

ECONOMIC REGULATION OF MIGRANT WOMEN IN AND THROUGH LAW

The Directive Principles of State Policy of the Indian Constitution provide for the protection of women workers (Articles 39 and 42). Special provisions are made in various labour laws protecting and promoting the rights of women.[6] These legislative provisions have been widely criticised as failing to adequately protect women's rights, including migrant women's rights (Bhatt 1988). Women workers suffer from the under-enforcement of labour legislation in general, as well as from the under-enforcement of legislation specifically designed to protect and promote the interests of women workers. The problem with these legislative provisions, however, does not lie in their under-enforcement alone. I explore how the sexual division of labour and assumptions about women's economic dependency have shaped women's participation in the labour market and the ways in which the very legislative provisions designed to address discrimination against women have been undermined by the continuing sex segregation of the labour market. I examine both the organised and unorganised sectors and unpack how law (or the absence of laws) reproduces gender roles and the sexual division of labour in the labour market.

In discussing the legal regulation of women's work, it is important to recognise the distinction between the organised and unorganised sectors of the economy. This distinction was recognised very early on in the 'Report on the Status of Women in India' which stated:

> The difference between these two is not functional, as between agriculture, industry and services because these functions can be found in both the sectors. The real difference between them lies in the organisation of productive relations, the degree of penetration of public control and regulation, and recognition by data-collection agencies and scientific investigators. The organised sector is characterised by modern relations of production and is regulated by laws that seek to protect the security and working conditions of labour as well as by labour organisations that can engage in collective bargaining. This includes the entire public sector ... as well as that part of the private sector which is regulated. The unorganised sector, which includes agriculture as well as various industries and services, is characterised by the absence of all the protective measures and machinery. (Government of India 1975: 63)

The Report found that 94 per cent of women workers were in the unorganised sector. In 1988, a government study on the status of women reported that 'approximately 90% of women workers are engaged in the unorganised sector. Of these over 80% are in agriculture and allied occupations. In the organised sector, women constitute only 13.3% of all employees' (Government of India 1988). This distinction between the organised and unorganised sector persists into the present day and is an important factor in explaining why working-class women are more affected by the gap between formal rights and their substantive under-enforcement (Sharma and Piush 2001). Women employed in the organised sector have more direct access to labour regulations. The lack of access to rights by women in the unorganised sector is recognised in the 'National Policy for the Empowerment of Women', 2001 (paragraph 1.10).[7] Moreover, women employed in the organised sector of the economy have primarily been middle class. In contrast, the overwhelming majority of women workers are working class and employed in the unorganised sector which is characterised by low pay, long hours of work, low productivity, low skills, and low job security (National Perspective Plan for Women 1988–2002). It is a sector that is effectively outside the purview of most labour legislation. This distinction between the organised and unorganised sectors is in turn related to the gendered segmentation of the labour market. The resulting segmentation of the labour market has two main consequences for women: it results in wage differentials between men and women and discrimination in terms of concentration of women in particular sectors and certain types of jobs such as domestic work and agricultural labour.

Many rules, regulations, and practices that impose restrictions on women's employment have been challenged as violating the equality guarantees in the Indian Constitution. Women who have been denied employment on the basis of these restrictions have overwhelmingly brought in these challenges. There are no specific laws in India governing the rights of migrant women or their working conditions. There are, however, gender-specific laws governing the rights of women in the organised sector, and some laws addressing the rights of interstate migrant workers. I evaluate some of the existing laws that impact on the rights of women workers, including migrant women, in both the organised and unorganised sectors. I unpack the assumptions about gender and the sexual division of labour that inform these laws. I also discuss some of the sex discrimination challenges that have been brought to rules that restrict the employment of women workers and impact on the rights of migrant women as well. While some of these challenges have been successful in striking the restrictions down, the decisions in this area are not entirely unproblematic. First, some of the rules and practices which restrict women's employment, including migrant women's employment, have been upheld. Second, the approach to equality and gender difference informing these decisions is often problematic and tends to reinforce traditional assumptions about gender roles.

Organised Sector

In this section, I briefly discuss two laws that govern the organised sector relevant to female workers: the Equal Remuneration Act, 1976 and the Maternity Benefits Act, 1961. Given that the vast numbers of migrant women take up employment in the unorganised sector, these two acts have little relevance or application to such workers, although there are some exceptions. Yet the analysis exposes how assumptions about women's familial roles and the sexual division of labour inform the legal regulation of the female worker.

The Equal Remuneration Act, 1976 (ERA 1976)

The ERA, 1976 provides for equal pay for equal or similar work (section 5). Such work is defined as that performed by a man and a woman, where the skills, efforts, and responsibilities required are the same, and performed under similar working conditions (section 2 [h]). Work will be considered to be the same or of a similar nature if any differences in skill, effort, and responsibility between women and men 'are not of practical importance in relation to the terms and conditions of employment' (section 2 [h]). The Act also prohibits discrimination in the recruitment of workers and, since its amendment in 1987, further prohibits discrimination in promotions, transfers, and training (section 5).

However, the practice of paying women lower wages for equal or similar work persists. First, there is no institutional procedure for determining if work is of a similar nature and the decision rests entirely with the employer. Such evaluations are invariably made against assumptions about gender roles and the sexual division of labour, that is, women workers are simply assumed to be less skilled.

The Act provides for the appointment of inspectors, who are empowered to review whether employers are in compliance with the law. But, in the absence of a duty on employers to examine whether the work of women and men is not of a similar nature, enforcement through individual complaints and/or government supervision will be, at best, uneven. Second, as a result of labour market segmentation, women continue to be employed in lower paying occupations. Since the work is not the same as that being performed by men, there is no violation of the Act. In fact, this approach was expressly adopted by the Supreme Court in *Mackinnon, Mackenzie & Co v. Audrey D'Costa* (*All India Reports 1987 Supreme Court 1281*), one of the few cases to reach the Supreme Court under the ERA, 1976. The Court, while finding that the female and male stenographers in question did the same work, and that the female petitioner was thus entitled to equal pay, went on to state:

> We do not suggest that there can be no discrimination at all between men and women in the matter of remuneration. There are some kinds of work which women may not be able to undertake. Men do work like loading, unloading, carrying and lifting heavier things which women cannot do. In such cases there cannot be any discrimination on the ground of sex. (paragraph 7)

The sameness test has overwhelmingly determined the subsequent challenges brought to court under the ERA, 1976. In a Delhi High Court ruling, women workers who were working as packing cleaners in an industrial unit complained that they were being paid a lower rate than their male counterparts who were doing the same kind of work but were called packers (*The Cooperative Store Ltd. (Super Bazar) vs. Bimla Devi and Ors (MANU/DE/0731/2005)*. The Court following the D'Costa decision held that the nature of the work being performed by the women was similar to the work being performed by their male counterparts. The different designations of the workers could not be held to be a determining factor for fixing the different pay scales if the nature of the work was the same. The court upheld the right of the women workers to be paid the same as their male counterparts.

While the outcomes in these cases were favourable to the women workers, the court appears to have rejected a comparable worth or equal pay for work of equal value approach, contrary to the provisions of the Equal Remuneration Convention, 1951, adopted by the ILO and ratified by India in 1958. The continuing sexual division of labour within the labour market can and does continue to preclude any increase in women's wages and justifies differential treatment. In one case, the Supreme Court overruled the decision of the Bombay High Court that struck down a rule by Air India making it mandatory for air hostesses to retire at the age of 50 with the option to take up ground duties after 50, up to the age of 58 years (*Air India Cabin Crew Association v Yeshawinee Merchant, All India Reports 2004 Supreme Court 187*). The Supreme Court held that the job of flight pursers, who were mostly men, was entirely distinct from that of airhostesses and that the difference in retirement age between them was not exclusively on grounds of sex. The Court stated that in the context of employment on an aircraft, gender-neutral provisions of service would not necessarily be beneficial for women. The nature of duties and functions on board deserve at times different and preferential treatment of women compared to men (paragraph 41). The Court stated that the retirement age of 50 coupled with the option to take up ground duties accommodated the family and marital obligations of the hostesses.

There are no cases dealing with the payment of wages to migrant workers under the ERA, 1976 as it is applicable only to the organised sector. However, cases have arisen concerning the regularisation of casual workers, a large segment of whom are migrant workers, which would make them eligible for all the rights and benefits given to ordinary workers (*Union of India v. Dharam Pal and Ors All India Reports 1996 SC 3234*). The Supreme Court has held that workers who have not been regularised even though they have worked in the same place for 10 years are entitled to be regularised and given equal pay for equal work if they are doing the same work under the same conditions as ordinary or regular workers (*Dharwad District Public Works Department Literate Daily Wages Employees Association vs. the State of Karnataka, All India Reports 1990 Supreme Court 883*). While the case moves towards placing casual workers on the same legal footing as regular workers, it does not impact on the sexual division of labour. Equal pay for equal work continues to be informed by a sameness standard, where female causal labour are paid the same wages as men provided they are doing the same work as men rather than work which is different though it may have the same value.

Maternity Benefits Act (MBA), 1961

The MBA, 1961 provides for 12 weeks maternity leave and benefits (section 5). Women are prohibited from working for six weeks immediately following childbirth (section 4). Pregnant women are also entitled to take up to six weeks paid leave of absence prior to their expected date of delivery, entitling women to a total of 12 weeks paid maternity leave (section 4). The Act further provides for nursing breaks twice a day when the woman returns to work, until the child is 15 months old. In order to qualify, women must have worked a minimum of 30 days within the 12 months prior to childbirth. The MBA, 1961 prohibits the employer from discharging a woman during her maternity leave or otherwise changing her conditions of employment (section 12).

Within the unorganised sector, women often are unable to work at the same place of employment for the required qualifying period. Employers frequently manipulate women's working conditions to ensure they do not qualify. The most significant weakness in the Act is the very limited response provided to deal with the widespread problems of discrimination faced by female workers during and immediately after pregnancy. Employers refuse to hire pregnant women, demote them, deny them promotions or pay hikes, or force them to terminate their pregnancy. The Act does not provide any in-built protections to women, encouraging employers to discriminate against them and also to hire men over women in order to avoid payment of such benefits. Although penalties have been levied through several amendments to the Act, they have not been stringent enough to discourage employers from evading the provisions of the Act.

Further, the nursing provisions of the Act are in many respects contingent upon the availability of on-site childcare facilities. Labour laws specifically provide for crèche facilities for children of working mothers in factories and plantations.[8] But these laws are rarely enforced, and in many work sites, employers actively discourage women from bringing their children, particularly in the unorganised sector. When women do bring their children, they are often prohibited from tending to and nursing them by their supervisors. Further, where crèche facilities are available, these facilities are well below the prescribed standards and level of supervision.

In the context of the construction industry, which is made up largely of migrants, the specific problems faced by women include a denial of maternity leave, non-provision of crèches, frequent relocations, and payment of wages to the husband, except in the case of single women (Government of India 2002). The Supreme Court has upheld the right of women construction workers to be given maternity leave in *Municipal Corporation of Delhi vs. Female Workers (Muster Roll) and Another* (All India Reports 2000 Supreme Court 1274). The Municipal Corporation of Delhi granted maternity leave only to its regular female workers and not to the female workers on the muster roll (daily wages). The daily wage female workers demanded that they be granted maternity leave, stating that the nature of their responsibilities and duties at work were the same as those of regular employees. Denial of leave required that the woman work relentlessly until the very end of her pregnancy and resume work shortly after delivery. The Court held that

> Not long ago, the place of a woman in rural areas had been traditionally her home; but the poor illiterate women forced by sheer poverty now come out to seek various jobs so as to overcome the economic hardship. (paragraph 6)
>
> *To become a mother is the most natural phenomenon in the life of a woman.* Whatever is needed to facilitate the birth of child to a woman who is in service, the employer has to be considerate and sympathetic towards her and must realise the physical difficulties which a working woman would face in performing her duties at the workplace while carrying a baby in the womb or while rearing up the child after birth. (paragraph 33) (emphasis added)

The Court extended the application of the MBA, 1961 to women employed on daily wages. While the judgment was favourable to the women workers, the Court's reasoning revolved around two normative constructions of women — one, as economically helpless victims, and two, as willing, self-sacrificing mothers.

Limiting the cause of migration solely to poverty victimises the migrant woman subject. According to S. Arya and A. Roy, '... it is not the poorest who migrate, but those who have some means to invest, or an available network enabling them to migrate' (2006: 24). Further, according to M. Thapan, 'Migration is ... undertaken with the aim of betterment, in terms of employment and economic gains, and as an escape from cultural and societal constraints in terms of achieving greater autonomy and independence' (2005: 12). The approach adopted by the Supreme Court is contradictory insofar as it affirms migrant women's rights to the same benefits as other regular female workers, while at the same time reinscribing women's roles as mothers in the family and the underlying assumption that she would be better off at home.

Second, honouring women at the workplace and making childbirth the most 'natural phenomenon' in the life of a woman reinforces traditional assumptions of women as reproducers. According to A. Roy, 'Tradition has invariably lent itself at various historical moments to bridge the contradiction in time that the nation epitomises, with women represented as the atavistic and authentic body of national tradition' (2005: 211). By declaring motherhood as the 'most natural phenomenon' in a woman's, the Court reinforced the prevailing familial and sexual norms, where women possess certain natural attributes that make them suitable for a life of domesticity as wives and mothers.

Unorganised Sector

Women are relegated to the unorganised sector of the labour market in part because they do not have the opportunity to acquire the skills and training that could help them to improve their employment situation (Rajan 1990: 127). They continue to work in the home and bear the burden of domestic work, which is time consuming, particularly in poor households. Family obligations keep women out of the paid labour force for considerable periods of time and their skills atrophy in the process. Their domestic chores do not afford them the time to develop their skills and train for better jobs, and thus restrict the opportunities and incomes available to women when they enter the paid labour force. Familial obligations and the sexual division of labour work together in reinforcing women's unequal position in the labour market. There is a link between the fact of female wage labour being advantageous as a cheap and flexible source of labour power to capital with the presupposition of a particular form of the family. Women's wages need not cover the costs of their reproduction because of the assumption of a position within the family of financial dependence on their husbands or cohabitants. Payment of wages lower than the value of labour power is thus justified. This wage discrimination is related to women's economic dependency within the family not only in terms of reflecting the assumption of this dependency, but also in reinscribing the material conditions of dependency. Even migrant women who work outside of the home and have access to independent income may not achieve a substantial level of economic independence. One reason is that there is an assumption that they are less skilled and that their wages are supplemental, which is regarded as a legitimate basis for payment of a lower wage. A woman's standard of living even at the subsistence level may be dependent on the assumption that her husband is the primary wage earner, despite the fact that she has migrated and works outside of the home.

I examine some of the laws as well as the absence of laws that are relevant to the rights of women in the unorganised sector that specifically impact on the rights of migrant women. These include the Interstate Migrant Workers Act, 1979, the Building and Other Construction Workers (Regulation of Employment and Conditions of Services) Act, 1996, the legal regulation of the domestic work sector, as well as the Unorganised Workers Social Security Act, 2008, which covers benefits for unorganised agricultural workers and non-agricultural workers.

Interstate Migrant Workmen (Regulation of Employment and Conditions of Services Act (ISMWA), 1979

The ISMWA, 1979 is the only legislation dealing with the rights of internal migrant workers. It provides such workers a number of facilities, including equal pay for equal work irrespective of sex, suitable conditions of work, residential accommodation, medical facilities, and protective clothing (section 16). The Act applies to every establishment in which five or more interstate migrant workers are employed and to every contractor who employs five or more interstate migrant workers on any day of the preceding 12 months (section 1 [4]). The Act essentially provides for the registration of establishments employing interstate migrant workers and the licensing of contractors. It also prohibits establishments from hiring migrant workers, unless the establishment is registered (section 6). According to Arya and Roy, the ISMWA, 1979, has 'substantial possibilities' of safeguarding the rights of migrant labour (2006: 42). However, apart from mentioning equal pay for equal work, the Act does not address any other rights for women specifically.

While there are a number of significant court decisions dealing with the fundamental rights of migrant workers and compliance with the provisions of the ISMWA, 1979, there is no decision specifically addressing women's labour migration.[9] The NCW has proposed certain amendments to be made to the ISMWA, 1979, including the incorporation of a provision stating that women who are recruited should be permitted to be accompanied by a family member to the state of destination at the employer's expense (National Commission of Women n.d.: section 25). The NCW has further recommended that each district from where the worker is migrating should maintain an office for the registration of migrant workers, providing contact and employment details. Both measures have been proposed in the bid to stop the possible trafficking of migrant women. The first proposal reinforces a protectionist approach towards women, and it may operate against women it if it is interpreted as a mandatory prerequisite for women's interstate migration.

Building and Other Construction Workers (Regulation of Employment and Conditions of Services) Act (BCWA), 1996

The BCWA, 1996 provides benefits for building and construction workers and applies to every establishment which employs 10 or more construction workers (section 1 [4]). All such establishments have to be registered (section 7) and it is mandatory for employers to provide for drinking water (section 32), first aid (section 36), establish a safety committee when more than 500 workers are employed (section 38), and constitute state welfare boards to look into building and construction workers' welfare (section 18). The employers are also required to provide crèche facilities where more than 50 female construction workers are employed (section 356), and the state welfare board *may* make payment of maternity benefits (section 22 [g]) though this is not a mandatory requirement. There are no other rights specifically for women construction workers stipulated in the Act.

The NCW has noted that only six states have made serious efforts to implement this Act and most women construction workers are unaware of the laws enacted for their welfare (National Commission for Women 2005b). While this is a generic problem common to all labour laws, the Act in itself is deficient, as the only benefits provided to women workers are the provision of crèches and voluntary payment of maternity benefits. The provision of crèche facilities has undoubtedly alleviated the problem of women construction workers from being compelled to bring their small infants to the construction site or leave them in the care of older siblings. At the same time, these provisions are once again based on an assumption of women as primary caregivers, ideally suited for the private realm. While a sizeable number of construction workers are migrants and women, there are no other legal provisions directed towards their specific conditions of work, including safety and protection, provision of living accommodation for female migrant workers, or provisions for workers who are victims of distress migration.

Legal Regulation of Domestic Work

Domestic work is one of the largest job enclaves for female migrant workers, partly due to care deficit produced by increased entry of middle-class women in India as well as globally into the labour force (Ehrenreich and Hochschild 2002; Parrenas 2001).[10] Domestic work is recognised as legitimate work by the Indian state. Recent government reports and judgments on domestic workers in India attempt to give domestic workers labour rights without attempting to regulate their profession in a manner that would conflict with their human rights or diminish their sense of entitlements and citizenship status. Unlike sex work, no official statements have been made seeking the sacrifice of domestic worker's rights in the interest of the larger community or the deportation of domestic workers back to the neighbouring countries from where they have migrated. There are some accounts of attempts to deport Bangladeshi maids, but these fall under the general deportation drives targeted at removing Bangladeshi migrants from India, rather than specifically directed at domestic workers per se (Chaudhuri 2005: 302). Migration for domestic work (cooking, cleaning, washing clothes, etc.) does not tarnish the reputation of the nation-state nor threaten dominant familial ideology and the sexual division of labour. There is space for the domestic worker and the housewife to coexist. As stated by the Second Labour Commission Report, in many houses, the housewife also works with the domestic worker (Government of India 2002).

There is recognition that female domestic workers are performing functions in the domestic sphere as more and more middle-class women are moving into regular paid employment. The absence of women from the home 'necessitates a "replacement", somebody who can be a substitute for her' (Kaur 2006: 198). Male domestic workers prefer to be cooks or graduate to semi-skilled or skilled jobs such as driving and hence to not perform household tasks (ibid.: 196, 199). Women are more willing to work in low status jobs for low wages and hence the demand for women domestic workers is higher.

At the same time, when domestic work is linked to any kind of sexual misconduct or exploitation, it is curtailed. India has imposed tighter restrictions and new mandatory provisions to govern the migration of household or domestic workers to the Middle East. The provisions have been introduced following reports of serious abuse by employers as well as the police, especially in Saudi Arabia. These restrictions apply to 18 countries in the Middle East. The measures pertain to maids, cooks, drivers, and butlers and include a mandatory obligation on employers to pay a monthly salary of 400 dollars as well as to make a security deposit of 2,500 dollars in the form of a bank guarantee with the local Indian mission. Employers are to provide mobile phones to the workers and contracts are to be registered with the mission. The minimum age of hiring is 30 years. The age ban formalises the informal restrictions placed on the deployment of Indian women below 30 years of age seeking to go abroad as domestic workers recommended by the NCW.[11] The ban was imposed partly in response to complaints by women who sought to go to the Gulf as domestic workers, and were forced into the sex trade (*The Times of India* 2006). The government is introducing a hotline to curb the exploitation of female migrant labour as well as a compulsory skills certificate and pre-departure training to workers before issuing an immigration clearance. The measures have been announced primarily for the welfare of India's emigrant women workers who are considered especially vulnerable to abuse and exploitation. India is also proposing to sign bilateral labour welfare pacts with Kuwait, the United Arab Emirates, Oman, and Qatar. While the new policy seeks to address the harms and abuses experienced by female migrant labour going to the Middle East, they produce a double bind. If women below the age of 30 are banned from migrating, it produces a situation where women of a younger age will seek the assistance of traffickers and smugglers to move clandestinely and hence also increase their vulnerability. The new provisions which protect the minimum wage paid to low skilled labour, especially to domestic workers, also stands in contrast to the fact that no such protections exist for workers within the domestic legal context.

The Second Labour Commission Report has pointed out that existing laws do not provide domestic workers with the protections they need and has recommended that domestic workers be brought within the purview of reformed labour laws (Government of India 2002: Volume II, 90). The NCW report on domestic workers also provides an account of some of the rights violations experienced by domestic workers (National Commission of Women 2005a). These include the non-payment of salary, physical abuse and torture, rape, sexual harassment, accusations of theft, cheating by the placement agency, denial of leave, and denial of a range of benefits including a minimum wage, medical allowances, bonus, or a yearly increment. The report also recommends that domestic workers be recognised as workers and provided with labour benefits and protections.

In 2003, the Human Rights Law Network filed a petition in the Supreme Court, requesting it to direct the government to enact comprehensive national legislation to protect the rights of domestic workers (*National Domestic Workers Welfare Trust and Others vs. Union of India and Another, Supreme Court Writ Petition (Civil) 160/2003*). The petition, filed on behalf of the National Domestic Workers Welfare Trust, contended that domestic work was a form of slavery per se under the provisions of the Slavery Convention, 1926. The contention was based on the argument that failure to provide legal protections to domestic workers in turn produced conditions of work that were exploitative and akin to slavery-like conditions. The petitioners alleged that domestic workers were largely made up of women migrating into the city in search of a livelihood as a result of disruption to their lives in the rural area being produced by the new economic policies adopted by the government. Female domestic workers were preferred by employers as they were assumed to be more submissive, polite, loyal, and compliant. The petitioners sought the enactment of legislation that would include penalties against employers who failed to pay wages, give weekly holidays, make provision for medical assistance and a provident fund to domestic workers, as well as a ban on the employment of children as domestic workers.

The government submitted that migration for the purposes of domestic work was permissible unless the worker was exploited or working in slavery-like conditions. The government's position on domestic work contrasts sharply with its position on sex work where there is no distinction drawn between coerced and consensual work and where women in sex work are invariably assumed to have been trafficked and sexually exploited. The government further submitted that it was enacting a bill for the unorganised sector with the aim of providing comprehensive protection for workers in the unorganised sector, including domestic work. The proposed bill would include provisions for the safety, social security, health, and welfare of workers in the unorganised sector. In light of the government's assurances, the petition was dismissed.

While there is a recognition that domestic work needs to be brought within the purview of the labour laws, there is also recognition that domestic work is largely a female occupation. (Government of India 2002: Volume II, 57). The NCW's recommendation in favour of a ban for women below the age of 30 working as domestic workers in the Middle East is linked to its concern over the sexual exploitation of domestic workers. Nevertheless, resorting to a protectionist stand serves to reinforce assumptions about women as weak and vulnerable and in need of state (or male) protection. The ban is not an empowering move as it will not stop women who wish to move from finding clandestine means to do so if legal routes are not available. In addition, while recognising the rights of domestic workers as workers is an important step towards affording them formal legal rights, it does not disrupt the segregation of women into the lower end of the labour market and the sexual division of labour. The demand for female domestic work nationally and internationally reinscribes women's roles within the reproductive sphere as housekeepers, maids, and caregivers.

One aspect of the domestic worker's issue that remains unaddressed is the impact of economic liberalisation on shaping women's work and family life. Women from rural areas are migrating for many reasons, including the search for new economic opportunities. The dynamics between economic production and social reproduction is producing a large pool of 'disposable domestics' who are virtually invisible because of the nature of the work they do and where they do it. Although the demand for domestic workers is produced by public, global economic processes, it occurs in the so-called private sphere, rendering the work and the lives of domestic workers invisible and vulnerable (Chang 2000). While the production of more jobs for women is welcome, it is the new economic policies that are creating the conditions of poverty and unemployment that compel migration in the first place. The disappearance of traditional manufacturing jobs, their replacement with high-tech industries, and the expansion of the service sector in response to the demands of this new high-income workforce provides a ready market for women seeking work (Sassen 1998). Indeed, these policies are producing an exploitable, low wage workforce to staff middle-class homes and the care sector.

Unorganised Workers' Social Security Act, 2008

While India has no formal social security policy, it does have a universal social development agenda emerging from the Directive Principles of the Constitution as well as a number of programmes dealing with the eradication of poverty and deprivation. The drive to create a national social security system is located within the framework of these existing programmes for the poor and the broader universal social/human development programmes (NCEUS 2008: 216). In addition, the recognition of the large-scale of migration within the country and the lack of any support provisions in law for workers in the unorganised sector has also produced a demand for greater social security for workers in the unorganised sector, many of whom are migrants. The Labour Commission was entrusted with the task of drafting umbrella legislation to address the concerns of workers in the unorganised sector and ensure their protection and welfare. The Commission found the existing laws relating to the unorganised sector to be hopelessly inadequate and unable to meet the needs and demands of the workers in this sector. It also recognised that women constituted an important segment of the work force in the unorganised sector and that migrant labour was also involved in some of the sub-sector activities of the unorganised sector (Government of India 2002: Volume I, Chapter IX, 51). These workers were neither very visible nor organised. The Commission further highlighted the fact that debt bondage was a common experience among the employed as well as the self-employed workers in the unorganised sector, and that exposure to health hazards was a common experience amongst the workers in this sector (ibid.: Volume I, Chapter VII, 88). These groups included home workers/home-based workers, domestic workers, sex workers, plantation workers, mines and quarry workers, scavengers, workers in the ship-breaking industry, fishery, bangle industry, brassware industry, street vendors, construction labour, ragpickers, carpet workers, and rickshaw pullers. The report proposed that sex workers should be entitled to the benefits recommended for self-employed workers and that their children should not be denied the opportunity for education. It recognised that labour migration, especially to the Middle East, provided an important safety valve for the unemployment problems at home and was also an important source of foreign exchange (ibid.: Volume I, Chapter 4B, 38). It emphasised the imperative need to 'examine the implications of the contemporary migration flows so as to evolve a more purposeful migration policy framework aimed at the maximisation of benefits from migration in the wider context of economic development' (ibid.: Volume I, Chapter 4B, 36).

The Unorganised Workers Social Security Act, 2008 was enacted to address some of these concerns. The Act provides for the registration of workers and the issuing of social security cards. Workers are categorised into those who fall below the poverty line and those who are just above it. This enables the government to develop specific schemes for each category and to include the establishment of complaint mechanisms in each scheme. The Act is purportedly based on the human capabilities approach developed by Amartya Sen, which focuses on creating and enhancing human capabilities by offering entitlements to all citizens funded by the public exchequer such as literacy, healthcare, schooling, drinking water, sanitation, and technical training (NCEUS 2008: 215). These benefits, based on citizenship rather than work status, function to provide a basis for effective social security policies and schemes. The Act is also partly geared towards market efficiency and demand. A contented and secure workforce is seen as essential for increasing the national income and the capacity of the economy to grow.

However, the Act falls short in many respects. There is no minimum level of social security for all workers set out in the Act, nor has it set out a national minimum wage for workers, which continues to be determined at the state level. The central concerns of workers over non-payment of wages, payment below the minimum wage determined in a state, or unequal remuneration on the basis of gender and the type of work done remain unaddressed in the new Act. There are no provisions dealing with issues of equal pay for women, sexual harassment in the workplace, or provision of decent working conditions. Women continue to be addressed in the Act as dependents, that is, as mothers and wives, or helpless, such as widows. They remain beneficiaries of government schemes rather than workers entitled to rights and hence the paternalistic approach to workers in the unorganised sector continues to objectify them (Goswami 2009: 18).

The sexual division of labour and familial ideology can thus be seen to affect the legal regulation of women's labour in complex ways and quite specifically impact on the rights of migrant women who work in the unorganised sector. It underlies labour market segmentation according to which women are relegated into sex segregated, low paying, unorganised sectors of the economy. This segmentation also operates to undermine the substantive rights of women in the organised sector set out in the ERA, 1976 and the MBA, 1961. Women's location in sex-segregated occupations effectively precludes the operation of any rights under the ERA, 1976. Similarly, their location in the unorganised sector operates to preclude the enforcement of their rights under the MBA, 1961. The result is that the very problem that these laws were intended to address — discrimination against women in the labour market — continues. And, in turn, women's precarious position in the labour market only further reinforces their socio-economic inequality and thus their economic dependency within the family. The discrimination that women continue to experience in the workplace remains unresolved in the new social security act for unorganised sector workers. There is minimal recognition that women make up a significant number of the workers in the unorganised sector, let alone attention given to their very specific issues. The law continues to assume that men remain the primary wage earners and that the worker is invariably male. Yet, within the growing context of migration, this myth remains fully exposed, though the enfranchisement of female migrant workers nevertheless remains largely unaddressed.

NATIONALISM, NEW ECONOMIC POLICIES AND FEMALE MIGRANTS

The increased encounters with global capital have resulted in a sense of loss of sovereignty, somewhat similar to the loss experienced during the colonial encounter. In many respects the migrant subject comes to represent all that comes with globalisation — the sense of a loss of sovereignty and national identity. This sense of loss is not merely experienced by a hegemonic state but also by the different actors in civil society including non-governmental organisations, feminist and human rights groups. The nation-state is re-establishing its sovereignty through these various actors and discourses of culture, family, and sexuality. Globalisation is not resulting in the unilateral demise of the nation-state as argued by some scholars, but is producing a reassertion of its identity (Hardt and Negri 2000; Kofman 2005). The nation is no longer understood exclusively in terms of space or geographical area. 'Old territorial units such as nation-states are no longer sufficient spatial mechanisms to demarcate the world, given the flows of capital, electronic signals, refugees, and migrant labour that traverse the boundaries of the nation-state' (Oza 2006: 4). Although the nation-state remains central in the formulation of laws and policies, the forces of the WTO and global economics reduce the space of manoeuvrability to do what it likes.

These processes may be opening up spaces for women by producing new possibilities in terms of economic opportunities, while at the same time producing new anxieties in terms of the resistance they may experience when taking advantage of them (McDowell 1996: 31). While there is a withering of national sovereignty in terms of space and territory, there is at the same time a redeployment of sovereignty at the level of constructing notions of identity and belongingness. The re-suturing of the nation-state is taking place partly through the refortification of the register of norms in relation to gender, culture, family, and sexuality as well as through the strengthening of borders and anti-terror laws.

As discussed in Chapter 2, one of the manifestations of the new global economic order is to trigger the global flows of people. Women are amongst those seeking new opportunities in the market, finding clandestine means to cross borders where legal means are not available. The migrant woman produces anxieties in the postcolonial nation, whose identity has been forged partly in and through women's bodies. The mobility of women is welcomed insofar as it brings much needed foreign remittances and contributes to the increased prosperity of the nation. Yet, in crossing borders, she also disrupts the normative criteria that are integral to the identity of the nation-state — she transgresses familial, cultural, and sexual boundaries. The re-regulation of female migrants in law reflects one effort to restore the nation's sense of integrity, sovereignty, and control. The legal engagements illustrate how there is a constant effort to reinscribe women in their roles as wives and mothers and as economically dependent. Women's identities remain tied in both discursive and material ways to these dominant normative assumptions that partly constitute the borders of the national sovereign state

(McClintock 1995). Those who seek to emigrate face a number of normative obstacles that seek to keep them at home or confined within the parameters of who and what constitutes the 'good Indian woman' and the Indian state. The strong bonds between gender and nationalism are essential to the survival of national identity (Bannerji et al. 2001; Parker et al. 1992). At the same time, an effort to secure the nation against the outsider or that which is foreign is a concomitant response to labour flows into India. The women inside the nation-state need to be protected from flows from outside. Globalisation has thus given way to a nationalistic rhetoric that plays out in and through the discourse of gender, culture, family, and sexuality.

The contemporary discourse of the Hindu Right relies heavily on the language of tradition, of respecting and honouring women, and returning women to their rightful place of honour (Bhatt 2001: 137). This discourse bears more than a slight resemblance to the debates throughout the nineteenth century of the women's question, where women became the site of the rearticulation of tradition, and the re-construction of Indian history and identity (Mani 1998; Sangari and Vaid 1989; Sarkar 2001). At one level, the Hindu Right's discourse is reminiscent of the discourse of women's uplift used by the social reformers in the nineteenth century and one faction of the women's movement in the early twentieth century. The discourse of women's uplift was deeply imbued with familial ideology and adherence to familial, cultural, and sexual norms. The discourse emphasised women's roles within the family. Campaigns to improve women's conditions were justified in the name of improving women's ability to perform their roles as wives and mothers, thereby strengthening the family. But the emphasis on culture and tradition, and on the important role of women in upholding this tradition, bears a stronger resemblance to the gendered discourse of the cultural revivalism and nationalism of the nineteenth century. The language within which the Hindu Right is appropriating and articulating women's issues draws on many of the same discursive elements: the need to restore respect for women in their roles as wives and mothers within the family, and the focus on women as the site of Hindu culture and tradition more generally (Bhatt 2001: 136–40; Chakravarti 1989).

This discursive continuity lies not only in the rhetoric of tradition, but perhaps more significantly, in the extent to which the rhetoric of tradition represents a selective and modern reinterpretation of history. Feminist historians in India have examined the extent to which the discourses on women in the nineteenth century, imbued with the rhetoric of tradition and culture, were in fact thoroughly modern discourses (Chakravarti 1989; Mani 1998; Sarkar 2001). As Lata Mani has argued in relation to the nineteenth century discourse on sati:

> ... it was a modern discourse on tradition. It exemplifies late eighteenth century colonial discourses that elaborated notions of modernity against their own conceptions of tradition. I suggest, in other words, that what we have here is not a discourse in which pre-existing traditions are challenged by an emergent modern consciousness, but one in which both 'tradition' and 'modernity' as we know them are contemporaneously produced. (Mani 1998: 116)

Feminist historians, and others, have persuasively demonstrated the need to subject the discourses of tradition to historical interrogation to reveal the extent to which these discourses are reflections of the period within which they are articulated. Historians have similarly attempted to reveal the extent to which the contemporary discourse of the Hindu Right, and its emphasis on tradition, are selective and thoroughly modern reinterpretations of the past (Thapar 1989, 2002 : 60–88). The contemporary gendered discourse of the Hindu Right is similarly one in which both 'tradition' and 'modern' are, as Mani suggests, 'contemporaneously produced'.

Notwithstanding the discursive continuity of the language within which the Hindu Right is articulating women's issues, there are important ways in which the discourse represents a break from its historical antecedents. First, the appropriation of the language of equality marks a significant departure from the language of Hindu revivalists in the nineteenth century. The claim that women are equal was not one that was characteristic of the cultural revivalists or early nationalist discourse. Even well into the twentieth century, Hindu nationalists rejected the language of equality as western (Golwalkar 1966: 16). In the discourse of the cultural revivalists, women were seen to represent the spiritual domain far removed from the material influences of the public sphere (Chatterjee 1989).

Second, the contemporary discourse on women can also be seen to mark a significant departure from past discursive practices in its attention to women's employment. In the past, women's identity was constituted as exclusively within the private sphere. Debates over women's education in the nineteenth century extended this sphere somewhat, as social reformers advocated schooling for girls. Yet, these debates over education remained firmly located within women's roles as wives and mothers within the family. Those who supported women's education argued that such education would only strengthen women in their familial roles (Chatterjee 1989: 245–47). Education was not supported as a means of changing or challenging the private, familial sphere as women's appropriate domain. In contemporary discourse, however, women's identity includes their roles in the labour market and the context of globalisation. While these new roles continue to be framed within the discourses of tradition and familialism, women's identity is moving beyond the private sphere of the family and into the public sphere of work.

This emphasis on the need for women to attain equality and to work outside of the home has been absorbed within the rhetoric of the Hindu Right to meet the challenge of modernisation and globalisation. For women, modernisation is posited in opposition to westernisation. A central discursive component of Hindu communalism for women has become one of constituting the identity of 'modern, but not western'. Women must play a political role without compromising on their 'basic nature' (Kandiyoti 1993: 36). The theme of 'modern but not western' is directed specifically at women. The economic reforms are projected as compromising on the Indian women's cultural and sexual integrity, while the government opens the 'Indian economic womb to the West' (Hansen 2004: 303). It is women who must guard against losing their cultural traditions and identity. This message is directed specifically to women's roles in the family. As is common to many nationalist movements, women are identified not only as biological reproducers but as cultural reproducers, with the special responsibility of transmitting tradition and heritage to their community, especially the younger members. It is in their roles as wives and mothers, as guardians of the tradition to be passed on to younger generations that women of the Hindu Right must guard against encroaching westernisation.

This identity of 'modern but not western', which recurs throughout the rhetoric of the women's wings of the Hindu Right, corresponds to what Rajeswari Sunder Rajan has described as 'the new Indian woman', 'perennially and transcendently wife, mother and homemaker, who saves the project of modernisation — without westernisation' (Sunder Rajan 1993: 133). She is a liberal woman who is rich, independent, and fashion conscious — what Oza describes as the 'mimetic trope of the nation in globalization' (2006: 18). She embraces the emergence of the nation onto the global arena and she is modern, but not too modern, as her identity remains anchored in the bedrock of Hindu tradition. Simultaneously, she is being reconstituted as a highly consumerist subject in and through neoliberal economic processes, which does not necessarily associate modernity with a commitment to universal liberal values (Gupta 2000: 89).

This emphasis on 'modern but not western' also has parallels with the nineteenth-century revivalist discourse on women. Much like the earlier discourse, women continue to be posited as the site for retaining and reconstituting Hindu tradition and culture. In the contemporary discourse of the Hindu Right, culture is again designated as a sphere distinct from material life. Women's identity continues to be constituted through the discourse of tradition and culture, in which women are the site of the opposition to the crass materialism of westernisation. The discourse of tradition is very similar, insofar as it posits culture as a separate sphere. At the same time, much like the discourse of tradition in the nineteenth century was a response to nineteenth century conditions, this discourse of tradition is a thoroughly modern discourse, responding to the materially and historically specific context of the late twentieth/early twenty-first century India. In much the same way as revivalist discourse in the nineteenth century disguised the fundamental social, economic, and political changes that were taking place, *Hindutva* discourse in the contemporary period is also operating to 'disguise, mitigate, compensate, contest' fundamental transformations in the social, economic, and political landscape and the role of women therein.

This significant transformation is in the form of globalisation and the neoliberal project of the market that it sustains. The need to reinforce the boundaries of control over women becomes all the more imperative in the context of these fundamental economic transformations in contemporary India. The increased demand for women's labour is being met with a tightening of the construction of women's identities within the governing frameworks of family, culture, and sexuality. The new identity of 'modern but not western' is providing legitimacy not only for the increasing political role of women, but also for their increasing economic role, that is, the increasing demand for women's work within the labour market.

This identity, which recognises women's role in the public sphere, while protecting their cultural integrity as the guardians of culture and tradition, is in many respects the perfect ideological companion to neoliberal economic restructuring. Women may work outside of the home, but their identity remains first and foremost as wives and mothers. As wives and mothers, women are the guardians and purveyors of Indian tradition and culture. The Hindu Right is attempting to reconstitute an identity for women that firmly reinscribes their roles within the family while embracing the demands of contemporary consumer capitalism and global economic restructuring.

This new identity of 'modern but not western', of the new Hindu woman is all the more useful in the context of the renegotiation of the public and private spheres engendered by neoliberalism, as discussed earlier. Neoliberalism is resulting in a reduction of the public sphere and an expansion of the private. It is a process within which services provided by the state are being reprivatised, and in which the role of both the market and the family are being expanded. This renegotiation of the public and private spheres includes a formidable increase in women's roles, not only within the economy but also within the family, as the family is called upon to provide more and more of the services once provided by the state. The identity of the new Hindu woman, as strong wife and mother, is an identity that corresponds to the call for women to perform more work, both inside and outside of the family. The new Hindu woman is a woman who can respond to all of the demands of contemporary consumer capitalism — she can rise to the call of modernisation, yet she can continue her role as the guardian of culture within her family. This renegotiation of the public and private is evident in the increasing emphasis on the family and family values within the political rhetoric of the Hindu Right. Women are called upon to safeguard the values and culture in the family and in so doing, to protect Hindu society from moral degeneration.

The issue of employment is taken up in recognition of the new economic role of women within the context of neoliberalism and the opening up of the market. At the same time, their participation is controlled and constantly justified in the name of the family. For example, while supporting women's employment, violence against women must be addressed as women come more and more into the public sphere.

> Thrust into public and mixed spaces for the first time, women encounter yet new forms of overt or covert sexual discrimination and violence. It is no wonder that the physical training programmes of the shakhas prove extremely attractive to such women, with the promise of a powerful body and the attendant self-confidence. That body and that mental attitude that it generates would be a vital shield against gender oppression within domestic as well as public. (Basu et al. 1993: 84–85)

It is the violence that women experience within the public sphere that is the easiest for the Hindu Right to address. Violence in the public sphere operates as an obstacle to women's employment and constitutes a threat to their identities as wives and mothers.

In the nineteenth century, it was women and women's bodies, which, as Tanika Sarkar has described, operated as a pure space that escaped the transformative effects of colonisation, 'ruled by our scriptures, our custom' (2001: 203). Similarly, in the contemporary moment it is women — and women's bodies — who are the cultural signifiers of the opposition to westernisation. The need for the protection of women is heightened with the increasingly visible role of women within the public sphere. It is part of the 'modern but not western' identity that is being constituted for women.

The reconstitution of women's identity hardly requires a radical disjuncture with prevalent representations of women. Rather, the very ideological power of the Hindu Right's discourse on women lies in its reliance on dominant cultural, familial, and sexual norms that I have discussed in Chapter 2. The image of women as wives and mothers is one that remains firmly embedded in legal regulation as well as in a broad range of social relations. Women, whose subjectivities and life experiences are shaped by these norms, are taking up issues that affect them, and articulating these issues in ways that make sense to them. Women experience the world in large part through their roles as wives and mothers — it is in and through this lens that these women are articulating the issues that concern them. The register of sexual, familial, and cultural norms which underlies the women's rights agenda of the Hindu Right is effective precisely because it is not being imposed by fiat, but rather, because of the way in which it shapes the subjectivity of women within the movement, who, in turn, are shaping the discourse within which these issues are being articulated.

The Hindu Right is playing into an image of women that continues to be part of the collective common sense. It is doing so by taking up contemporary issues such as globalisation and women's increased participation in the workspace in ways that do not challenge the governing ideological construction of women as wives and mothers. Issues of employment are articulated within the legal discourse of rights, without fundamentally challenging or displacing these dominant norms. Women continue to be constructed as naturally different — as dutiful wives and self-sacrificing mothers — and these differences must be respected and celebrated. Women's issues can thereby be recognised and addressed in ways that not only do not challenge the family, but which ultimately reinforce its ideological hegemony.

At the same time the Hindu Right continues to preserve and protect the ideological hegemony through a deployment of the Other — an alien who continues to gnaw away at this normative arrangement. The migrant is cast as the foremost threat and includes not only the Muslim who is reconstituted as a migrant in the discourse of the Hindu Right, but also migrant women who are disrupting the normative framing of women's cultural and sexual conduct. This strategy has been partly pursued through a rewriting of Indian history as a narrative divided into three periods — the Hindu Golden Age, the Muslim Dark Ages, and the colonial period. The Hindu Right's focus on the Hindu and Muslim periods attempts to cast the Muslim as a foreign oppressive and tyrannical power. Muslims were migrants descending from Turks and Arabs who settled in India. At the same time, those who were not migrants were simply victims of the proselytising campaigns of the foreign invaders. This version of history ignores how all Muslim migrants were not invaders, but also came as pastoralists, traders, and associates of Sufis and other sects (Thapar 2007: 198) and that conversion did not mark a break with the previous way of life and many continued to live according to the cultural ways of their earlier identities. Female migrants also become marked as 'Other' because of the insurrections they are staging at borders of sexual normativity. Female migration is invariably associated with prostitution partly because of the anti-trafficking rhetoric that views nearly all women's movement as forced and for the purpose of prostitution. Her wanderings in the public domain trespass her bodily integrity as well as the cultural lines that keep her tethered to one space and location.

It is not coincidental that the rise of the Hindu Right in politics in contemporaneous with the induction of India into the global economic process. The aspirations of the middle class and the sudden affluence of some segments of the population are increasing the disparity between social classes. The breakdown of earlier forms of community living has led to a turn towards narrow identities and the culture of violence (Thapar 2007: 206). These new identities are forged through religion and an appeal to the nation's glorious past through the representation of both Indian women as enjoying a place of honour and respect as well as assertions of virile Indian masculinity through events such as the showcasing of its nuclear weapons capability in 1998. The protection of women discourse is intensified and Hindu nationalism consolidated through the reification of gender boundaries (Oza 2006: 13). The boundaries of the nation are contingent on the construction of the desexualised woman and a distinction from the 'Other', who is a transgressor, foreign, and suspect.

Migrant women represent a challenge to this sanitised construction of the female subject. The response to this challenge is to fortify the nation against such intrusions, not merely physical, but cultural and sexual as well. The perforation of the nation's boundaries is partly performed by the migrant woman and must be repaired and women resituated within the dominant canvass of appropriate familial, cultural, and sexual behaviour. While there is a continuous recognition that more women are migrating as a result of new economic opportunities and change in market conditions, there is also a constant fear over the infringement of gender roles that require increased control and surveillance. This control is partly exercised through the legal regulation of migrants generally and migrant women specifically.

NOTES

1. *Phul Singh v. State of Haryana*, 1979, 4 Supreme Court Cases 413, paragraph 5; *Sudhansu Sekhar Sahoo vs. State of Orissa*, 2002,10 Supreme Court Cases 743.
2. *The Public at Large vs. The State of Maharashtra*, 1997, (4), Bombay Criminal Law Reports 171.
3. See also *Lucy R. D'Souza v. State of Goa and Others*, 1990, *Maharashtra Law Journal*, 713.
4. *Savera vs. the State of Goa*, MANU/MH/0888/2003.
5. Section 5C, Immoral Trafficking Prevention Bill 2006.

6. See, for example, the Factories Act, 1948, the Plantations Act, 1951, the Mines Act, 1966, and the Bidi and Cigar Workers Act, 1966.
7. In the NPEW, 2001, the government recognised the difficult circumstances of migrant women and the need for special treatment of 'women in difficult circumstances' (paragraph 6.12). This category includes 'women in extreme poverty, destitute women, women in conflict situations, women affected by natural calamities, women in less developed regions, the disabled widows, elderly women, single women in difficult circumstances, women heading households, those displaced from employment, migrants, women who are victims of marital violence, deserted women and prostitutes'.
8. For example, the Factories Act, 1948 provides that every factory in which more than 30 women workers are ordinarily employed must provide suitable rooms for the care of children less than six years of age.
9. See, for example, *People's Union for Democratic Rights v. Union of India*, All India Reports, 1982, Supreme Court 1473; *Bandhua Mukhti Morcha v. Union of India*, All India Reports, 1984, Supreme Court 802; *Salal Hydroelectric Project v. State of J and K*, 1984, 3 Supreme Court Cases 538; *Mahabubnagar District Palamoori Contract Labour Union v. M/S Nagarjuna Construction Company*, 1998 (1), *Karnataka Law Journal* 639; *Dhanurjaya Putel and Another v. State of Orissa*, 2002, (II), Orissa Law Reports 412.
10. B. Ehrenreich and A. R. Hoschschild's volume addresses the demand for nannies, maids, and sex workers in the context of the care-deficit in developed countries which is in turn creating a similar deficit in communities from which the women are migrating.
11. Ministry of Overseas Indian Affairs, Guidelines for Emigration Clearance System.www.moia.gov.in/services.aspx?id1=102&id=m6&idp=100&mainid=73. Accessed 17 November 2009.

4

Sexual Restraints: The Construction of Female Sexual Subjectivities in Anti-Trafficking Discourse

> Like many other occupations, sex work is also an occupation … we systematically find ourselves to be targets of moralising impulses of dominant social groups, through missions of cleansing and sanitising, both materially and symbolically. If and when we figure in political or developmental agendas, we are enmeshed in discursive practices and practical projects, which aim to rescue, rehabilitate, improve, discipline, control or police us. Charity organisations are prone to rescue us and put us in 'safe' homes, developmental organisations are likely to 'rehabilitate' us through meagre income generation activities, and the police seem bent upon to regularly raid our quarters in the name of controlling 'immoral' trafficking. Even when we are inscribed less negatively or even sympathetically within dominant discourses we are not exempt from stigmatisation or social exclusion. As powerless, abused victims with no resources, we are seen as objects of pity.
>
> — Durban Mahila Samanwaya Committee
> (The Unstoppable Movement for Women's Equality) (1997: 2–3)

In this chapter I elaborate on a concern briefly touched upon in Chapter 3, about the ways in which female migration is overwhelmingly addressed in and through the international and national legal discourses of 'prostitution' and trafficking. This discussion is written at a time when reaffirming sexual purity, cultural cohesion, and national security are sweeping through public discourse and entering the courts and the legislative arena. The battle over the labelling of certain desires, pleasures, sexed bodies, and sexual acts as either illicit or licit has always been contentious. But it has been particularly contentious in the current moment, when sexual transgressions are being coupled with cultural othering and rendering the female migrant subject as a threat to the very constitution of the nation-state and normative sexuality. Intersecting with emerging discourses of the religious and conservative right, as well as the focus of some feminists on issues of sexual violence rather than on sexual rights, female migrants are becoming a favourite target for majoritarian surveillance and discipline sanctioned by law. Paradoxically, the legal interventions focussed on criminality, surveillance, and border controls are producing clandestine migrant mobility regimes that facilitate the movements of sexual subjects rather than stopping trafficking.

In this chapter, I explore the contours of female sexual subjectivity as constituted in and through anti-trafficking interventions in law. In the first part I discuss the global context within which anti-trafficking laws have emerged, and their focus on sex trafficking. I then provide a brief overview of the domestic anti-trafficking laws in India. The intention is not to conduct an extensive evaluation of these laws, but rather to set out the framework for my subsequent discussion on how the constitution of the female migrant's subjectivity in anti-trafficking laws intersect with assumptions about female sexual subjectivity and the discursive interventions of the conservative or religious right as well as some strains of feminist and human rights advocacy and scholarship. I argue that these interventions operate as sexual restraints and are partly reminiscent of the colonial encounter and its representations of the 'native' woman as a victim or part of a backward culture. I elaborate on how this understanding of female sexual subjectivity came to be constituted in and through the colonial encounter in the late nineteenth century, building on the analysis set out in Chapter 1. I then illustrate how these representations of female sexual subjectivity inform the contemporary positions on trafficking, focusing on the arguments of the religious right, liberals, as well as some feminists. Throughout this chapter, I elaborate on how these assumptions about female sexual subjectivity intersect with other non-legal, non-state forms of representation. I refer to three documentaries that purport to deal with the issue of trafficking and female sexual subjectivity in postcolonial India: Zana Briski and Ross Kauffman's 2005 Oscar-winning documentary *Born into Brothels: Calcutta's Red Light Kids*, Andrew Levine's documentary entitled *The Day My God Died* (2003) and Shohini Ghosh's *Tales of the Night Fairies* (2002). I explore what each film reveals about female migrants' subjectivity as well as trafficking in a postcolonial context and how such representations intersect with legal discourse in ways that produce meanings and constitute subjects that are not altogether progressive or emancipatory.

THE EMERGENCE OF THE ANTI-TRAFFICKING LEGAL REGIME

The legal regulation of female migrants has received a great deal of momentum over the course of the past decade — with a flurry of laws being enacted at the domestic level, and protocols and conventions being adopted at the regional and international levels. Since 2000, we have witnessed the adoption of the UN Protocols on Smuggling and Trafficking, as well as the entry into force of the Migrant Workers' Convention in July 2003. At the domestic and regional levels, some significant initiatives include the adoption of the SAARC Convention on Preventing and Combating Trafficking in Women and Girls for the Purpose of Prostitution, 2001, the U.S. Trafficking Victims Protection Act of 2000 (with its extra-territorial reach), and proposed amendments to India's Immoral Trafficking Prevention Act, 1956 to address the issue of trafficking, primarily within the framework of criminal justice and law enforcement.

'Sex trafficking' has become a major focus of women's human rights campaigns in the contemporary period. It is an issue that has also appeared on the agendas of right-wing, conservative groups, as well as human rights groups and other well-intentioned social justice movements worldwide. The issue is represented in alarming terms, with advocates citing statistics that are invariably anecdotal (Botti 2000; Laczko et al. 2002; Sung 2001), and presenting scenarios that reduce trafficking to descriptions of brutality and violence inflicted by organised criminal networks, the rape and abuse of innocent, thoroughly victimised women, who are kidnapped or dragged away from their homes or duped into prostitution or sexual slavery (Smith 2000). There exists a 'discursive verbosity' in the area of trafficking that emanates from the very different and even opposing political and ideological positions (Berman 2003; Block 2004; Human Rights Watch 1995: 1–2; Raymond 2005; Foucault quoted in Stoler 1995:180). This concern has led to a startling proliferation of laws and policies at the domestic and international level.

International Law

The issue of human trafficking, especially trafficking in women, is neither new nor unfamiliar. The legal regulation of trafficking has been developing over the course of the past century. The issues of sex and violence, evil traffickers and innocent victims have appealed to the religious right, conservatives, and human rights activists alike since the early 1900s when the issue of 'white slavery' was first addressed by the international community.[1] Invariably, the legal responses were based on tales of abuse of young women taken to foreign lands by force, fraud, or false promises, and used for 'immoral' purposes (Demleitner 1994: 165–67; Doezema 1999; GAATW 2001: 26; Roberts 1992; Walkowitz 1982). The early responses to trafficking grew out of the anti-prostitution movement, which focused primarily on the trafficking of white women and children for the purpose of prostitution or sexual exploitation (Article 3, IASWST).[2] Little attention was given to issues of forced labour or keeping workers in slavery-like conditions. The early legal responses had weak enforcement mechanisms, focusing on warning possible victims, restricting or discouraging migration, emphasising law enforcement and criminalising the conduct of traffickers, and international cooperation. However, there was essentially no discussion of the rights, needs, or interests of the trafficked women themselves or of trafficked men.

In the contemporary period, there has been a refocus on the issue of trafficking as a result of the numbers involved and the enormous profits that it generates. In the area of anti-trafficking legislation, the UN Trafficking Protocol epitomises how the trafficked subject is constituted in and through international human rights law.[3] The definition of trafficking under the UN Trafficking Protocol is intended to cover instances such as the case of a woman from a developing country who ends up enslaved at a garment factory in the USA; or a man smuggled from a North African country into Europe and then forced to harvest crops under threat of beatings or death; or a Nepali woman who is taken across the Indian border and held against her will to work as a prostitute. However, in popular discourse trafficking has invariably been conflated with women who are duped, forced, or deceived with the promise of legitimate jobs, kidnapped, and then sold into prostitution. Unfortunately, the broad arrays of situations of abuse and exploitation that constitute trafficking have been overshadowed by a focus on 'sex trafficking'.

Sex trafficking is presented by nearly all players in the human rights arena as an overwhelming problem. This focus is produced through constant and repeated reference to alarming statistics,[4] a sensationalised rhetoric that speaks in terms of 'supply of flesh', 'duped women', and horrifying journeys as well as the reiteration of the victim's innocence and vulnerability. The issue is presented simultaneously as an issue of protecting women's rights while also securing the destination country from contamination through sexual immorality or threats of criminality. While it needs to be stressed that cases of trickery, fraud, and forced sex work do take place, unfortunately many of the legal interventions have done little to protect women's rights (GAATW 2007). In fact, these issues have often served as a metonym for using the criminal law to intensify border security, lobby for the abolition of sex work, restrain the female sexual subject, and view gendered migrations primarily in terms of victimisation and violence. The complex processes of migration and constitution of subjectivity, including sexual subjectivity, are flattened and replaced with simplistic, linear narratives about 'sex trafficking' and women's subjectivity.

While the definition of trafficking in the UN Trafficking Protocol extends beyond the specific issue of prostitution, it retains its focus on prostitution and violence against women in the broader public arena. States throughout the world have enacted legislation pursuant to the anti-trafficking campaign that has invariably lapsed into moral surveillance techniques over women as well as a visceral concern over border security that has neither advanced women's rights nor solved the problem of trafficking.

South Asian Regional Initiative

The South Asian Association for Regional Cooperation Convention on Preventing and Combating Trafficking in Women and Children for Prostitution, 2002 (SAARC Convention) was ratified by all the member countries in 2006. It represents significant progress within the region insofar as the problem of trafficking is recognised. The Convention was adopted to promote cooperation for the prevention of trafficking, the rehabilitation and repatriation of victims, and to trigger change in domestic laws (Bharti n.d.). Trafficking is defined as the 'the moving, selling or buying of women and children for prostitution within and outside a country for monetary or other considerations with or without the consent of the person subjected to trafficking' (Article I [3]). Member states are encouraged to adopt measures to ensure the proper treatment of trafficked victims. The Convention also seeks to build the capacity of the law enforcement officers and treats trafficking as an extraditable offence.

The SAARC Convention reproduces nearly all the limitations and assumptions about trafficking found in the international legal arena. It does not adequately distinguish between voluntary migration and trafficking. As a result, women who have moved consensually within or outside of their country of origin could also be covered by the Convention. And it is limited to trafficking for the purposes of prostitution. Thus, it not only imperils the rights of voluntary migrants, but also ignores the rights of persons trafficked for purposes other than prostitution. There are no adequate mechanisms for ensuring that member states comply with the obligations imposed by the Convention, such as a reporting body or rapporteur to monitor compliance and receive complaints.

The SAARC Convention is concerned with eliminating 'the evil' of sex work rather than with restoring the human rights of trafficked persons. It conflates trafficking with sex work and seeks to criminalise prostitution-related activities that do not necessarily involve coercion or harm. Seemingly inspired by the now largely defunct 1949 UN Convention for the Suppression of the Traffic in Persons and of the Exploitation of Prostitution of Others (hereinafter the UN Convention 1949), the preamble of the SAARC Convention condemns 'the evil of trafficking in women and children for the purpose of prostitution [because it] is incompatible with the honour and dignity of human beings and is a violation of basic human rights'. It conflates trafficking with sex work; deals only with the trafficking of women and children, making relatively little distinction between the two; deems consent irrelevant and thereby encompasses voluntary sex work; fails to consider the consent or safety of trafficked persons in relation to repatriation; and lists a host of prevention mechanisms that encourage the surveillance of a broad range of female workers and do not require the involvement of trafficked persons, vulnerable groups, or the community. Even the prevention measures aimed at creating awareness of the underlying causes of trafficking are more concerned with reducing temptations for traffickers than empowering and educating people who are vulnerable to being trafficked. The consequence of such initiatives has been to undermine the rights of migrant women and render them even more susceptible to exploitation.

Domestic Law

In the domestic context of India, the contemporary focus on anti-trafficking interventions has been driven by two concerns. The first includes a concern over the spread of HIV in India and the second, with the concern over the exploitation and trafficking of minors, in particular young girls, into sexually exploitative situations, quite specifically, prostitution.

In the early 1980s, state officials denied that AIDS could be a problem in India because of the 'moral values' of Indian men and women (AIDS Bhedbhav Virodhi Andolan 1993: 25). According to the 2008 UNAIDS report, in India nearly 2.5 million people are now living with HIV (UNAIDS 2008). Within the South Asian region, AIDS could easily emerge as the largest cause of adult mortality in this decade. As regards the concern over the trafficking of young girls into prostitution, while there are almost no reliable statistics or data available on the number of children or women who are trafficked into this form of exploitation, there nevertheless seems to be a sense of urgency over producing a response to this 'problem', usually in the form of strengthening the criminal law (Asia Foundation and Horizons Project Population Council 2001: 17; Gallagher 2002: 70).

The AIDS crisis and concerns over trafficking of minors have produced different responses by the government. A principal response includes increased surveillance of so-called 'at-risk populations', including sex workers. The crisis over HIV in particular has sparked a plethora of research with an emphasis on 'knowing and measuring sexual practices of "at-risk populations", such as the youth, college students, and sex-trade workers' (Puri 1999: 283). The concern over trafficking in young girls, in particular sex trafficking, has also led to an overwhelming focus on sex workers.

While the Indian Constitution prohibits 'traffic in human beings, *begar* (sic) and other similar forms of forced labour' (Article 23), the Immoral Traffic Prevention Act, 1956 (ITPA) is the primary act that addresses the issue of trafficking. The ITPA was initially enacted in compliance with India's obligations under the UN Convention, 1949, ratified by India on 9 January 1953. As such, the aim of the Act is to eliminate the recruitment of women and girls for the purpose of prostitution. The Act targets brothel keepers as well as those who live off the earnings of prostitution and prohibits soliciting for prostitution. The ITPA grants police officers and magistrates broad powers in relation to the rescue and rehabilitation of victims. Police officers are permitted to search premises without a warrant if accompanied by two or more female police officers or by two or more 'respectable inhabitants' of the community (section 15), and 'rescue' any person found in a place where it is believed that prostitution is occurring (section 16). Rescued persons are then supposed to be subjected to mandatory health checks and can be placed in a protective home for up to three years if they are deemed to be 'in need of care and protection' (section 17). The law focuses primarily on treating trafficking as a law and order problem, a problem of moral turpitude, and sex workers as either victims, 'evil doers', or vectors of immorality and criminality.

In 2005, the Indian Cabinet approved proposed changes to the ITPA that were scheduled to go before the Indian Parliament in 2007 (CFLR 2006: 2). These changes included: raising the age of majority from 16 to 18; adding a new offence prohibiting the purchase of the services of prostitutes; de-criminalising solicitation for prostitution; and allowing police officers of a lower rank to conduct raids and arrests (ibid.: 22 and 26). The Bill was resubmitted for further discussion in a parliamentary committee after extensive lobbying against it primarily by sex workers as well as some migrant groups and human rights activists.[5] Neither the existing law nor the new proposals consider sex workers as having rights to healthcare, a family life, or access to education without discrimination, nor are they entitled to safe and non-exploitative working conditions.

The ITPA primarily targets trafficking and exploitation linked to commercial sex, and does not address any other form of trafficking. Although there is no specific definition of trafficking in the Act, the focus on prostitution has narrowed the focus of the Act to women and children trafficked into prostitution. The ITPA is based on the assumption that the main victims of trafficking are those who are forced into prostitution by procurers, pimps, brothel-keepers, and madams. Its primary aim is to punish 'immoral trafficking' and traffickers. It pursues this objective in two ways: first, by criminalising activities such as trafficking and the keeping of brothels, and second, by introducing welfare measures for the rehabilitation of sex workers. The provisions aimed specifically at criminalising the activities of persons engaged in the sale and procurement of women *for the purpose of prostitution* focus on the purpose for which the woman is being sold or procured rather than on the use of force, fraud, violence, or deception. Where the purpose does not qualify as illegal, such as in the case of domestic labour, then the manner in which the procurement occurs, no matter how violent, would not fall under these provisions.

The consent of the trafficked person is relevant only for the purpose of sentencing and not at the stage of defining the offence. Excluding consent perpetuates the assumption that women are victims who are invariably forced into the sex trade against their will. Where the use of force, fraud, coercion, or even sexual violence is manifest, but the woman is or has been a sex worker, is unmarried or not a minor, then she may be less able to take advantage of these provisions. In fact, there is a risk that an adult woman can become vulnerable to prosecution as a co-conspirator. The law provides no remedy to a woman who willingly agrees to enter into sex work but is subjected to sexual abuse by her procurers. Although the issues of force, fraud, deception, and violence are specific concerns behind the anti-trafficking provisions, these are not addressed in the ITPA, nor are remedies provided for these criminal acts in other legal provisions. The primary focus of the ITPA provisions is on whether or not the trafficking is 'immoral', which deflects attention from the main concerns, namely the use of *force, fraud, deception, coercion, and sexual exploitation*, which may have been used on a woman in the process of being trafficked or at the point of arrival.

Recent evidence suggests that the provisions of the ITPA have been used overwhelmingly against women and children engaged in prostitution and have invariably harassed the women rather than prevented trafficking (Nair and Sen 2004: 397). There are provisions that assume that children found on premises where sex work is carried on are being used for sex work. Such provisions place a burden on the sex worker to establish that her child or children have not been used for sex work, making her vulnerable to police harassment. In some cases, this leads to the removal of the children from the premises and their placement in a government home or shelter. In addition, if a sex worker uses her residence for the purpose of sex work, she can be charged under the ITPA. The Act also makes it an offence for a sex worker to support her family from her earnings where her children and other family members are not minors. These provisions appear to betray the ITPA's objective of not targeting the sex worker. They also effectively undermine the rights of children to be with their families, if they so choose, assuming such an option would not be in the child's best interest.

The anti-trafficking law as well as the overall approach by the state focuses on the method of rescue and rehabilitation of the women and girls assumed to have been trafficked for the purpose of prostitution. Brothel raids are regularly carried out by the police with the assistance of information provided by NGOs and have been the primary and most problematic of the strategies pursued under the provisions of the ITPA. The raids are justified in order to 'rescue' women and children forced into prostitution, yet there is evidence that these raids have occasioned abuse by the police and are also counter-productive (McGill 2002: 32; Terre des homes and Partnership Nepal 2004).

The raids and rescue operations are frequently followed by the detention of the woman in a protective home or a corrective institution. Such detentions are approved by the anti-trafficking scheme adopted by the Ministry of Women and Child Development and seen as appropriate treatment for those considered victims of trafficking into the sex trade (Ujjwala 2007). Once incarcerated, a woman has no right to privacy or bodily integrity and is subjected to invasive medical examinations and inquiries into her personal background. The conditions in corrective and protective homes have been documented and have been shown to be barely habitable (Coomaraswamy 2001: 8). Indefinite incarceration, loss of liberty, forced medical examinations, and appalling living conditions drive the young girls and women placed in these institutions back into sex work. Frequently, they incur huge debts to cover the cost of legal fees, bail, and sureties, which reinforces their debt bondage status. Rehabilitation has the limited objective of providing the victim with temporary shelter and safeguarding her from the abusive and exploitative aspects of her work. However, these homes serve to restrain rather than reintegrate the sex worker (ibid.: 18). Nor are women entitled to leave the homes of their own free will. They are regarded as being in protective custody and can only leave through an application to the court. This procedure denies victims the rights to which ordinary criminals are entitled, namely, due process and the right to liberty. This omission is particularly problematic given that the women are ostensibly the victims of criminal conduct and not actual criminals themselves. These institutions also provide few options for self-employment and alternative income generation. Marriage is promoted as the primary mechanism for the reintegration of such women into society.

As briefly discussed in Chapter 3, the courts have engaged in high-level judicial activism in the interpretation and implementation of anti-trafficking legislation, often reproducing and reinforcing the assumptions about women who are targeted by the law. The sex worker has become the primary target of such laws and courts have constantly reproduced the stereotype of sex workers as simultaneously helpless and vulnerable, as well as sexually unrestrained, corrupting and contaminating. In one well-known case involving a public interest litigation, the petition argued for the removal of children from mothers who were 'prostitutes' or 'fallen women' and their placement in segregated schools set up specifically for such children (*Gaurav Jain vs. Union of India* [All India Reports 1990 Supreme Court 292]). The Supreme Court held that 'children of prostitutes should not be permitted to live in the inferno and the undesirable surroundings of prostitute homes' and that the human rights of such children had to be protected (Gaurav Jain 1990: paragraph 1). In a subsequent order, the Court, while drawing attention to the impact on human rights of some anti-trafficking provisions, reiterated that the 'eradication of prostitution is integral to social welfare and the glory of womanhood' (*Gaurav Jain vs. Union of India*, All India Reports 1997 Supreme Court 3021: paragraph 15). The Court stated that it was in the interest of the children of sex workers and of society that they 'be segregated from their mothers and be allowed to mingle with others and become part of society' (Gaurav Jain 1997: paragraph 1). The Court was opposed to the establishment of separate hostels and schools for the children of sex workers. However, it was of the view that 'accommodation in hostels and other reformatory homes should be adequately available to help segregate these children from their mothers living in prostitute homes as soon as they are identified' (ibid.). The Court also observed that the capacity of a woman in prostitution to pay for her child's education would not relieve the child from social trauma and that it would always be against the interests of the child to permit the child to remain in her custody or in a brothel. 'So, they should be rescued, cared for and rehabilitated ... the three Cs, namely, counselling, cajoling and coercion of the fallen woman to part with the child or child prostitute herself from the manager of the brothel is a more effective, efficacious and meaningful method to rescue the child prostitute or neglected juvenile' (Gaurav Jain 1997: paragraph 20).

Anti-trafficking initiatives in India have emerged almost exclusively from within the debates around the legality or illegality of prostitution. Existing legal and policy initiatives, judicial decisions, and proposed reforms on trafficking have invariably been displaced onto debates about whether or not prostitution constitutes violence against women, is against Indian cultural values, and compromises the nation's integrity. The push-and-pull factors that compel unsafe movement, the various sites into which trafficking takes place, and the larger issue of migration all remain largely unaddressed within the debates on trafficking in India (Kapur 2005:143). As a result of the narrow focus of the debate, the legal and policy responses focus almost exclusively on regulating sex work, strengthening border controls, and prosecuting brothel keepers and those who profit from the sex work industry. Legal discourse continues to collapse concerns over violent crimes committed against women with the complex phenomenon of migration in the current period of globalisation (ILO 2001). It further conflates distinctions between trafficking and sex work, despite evidence that trafficking exists in ways that are completely disconnected from sex work. The contemporary legal responses to trafficking continue to reproduce the flaws of earlier legal responses, focusing on the victimisation of the trafficked person and linking trafficking to sex work.

There is a vast network of laws in place designed to regulate cross-border movements. This legal web is overwhelmingly informed by assumptions of female migration as invariably forced and sex workers as invariably trafficked into the trade. While rights to migration, freedom of movement, and equality exist in international and domestic laws, such rights do not in and of themselves disrupt the normative assumptions about female migration and the female migrant subject. She continues to be constituted either as a victim to be rehabilitated and protected or a sexual and cultural contaminant to be cleansed, removed, or expelled. These constructions of the female migrant in legal discourse continue to reproduce the logic about the 'Other' that has informed the colonial project (Banerjee 1998). As discussed in the following section, this logic regarded women as victims in need of rescue from an inferior or barbaric people and culture and justified the processes of Empire as a means to civilize the 'native' (Kapur 2005: 142–50).

FEMALE 'OTHERS' AND THE ORIENTAL FANTASY

> To the Women of Hindu India: Your culture, it is true, is under no necessity to satisfy our Western judgment. But until it satisfies that judgment in what we consider essential points of common humanity, it must do without our respect. Until you change the facts, therefore, the verdict [on a cruel and barbaric culture] cannot be different. . . . The liberty afforded to American women for example, is as great as your thraldom. (Mayo 1929: 212)

In 1927, Katherine Mayo, an American feminist, wrote about the condition of Indian women. Her views were published in *Mother India*, a furious invective against the unhappy condition of Indian women. The text is primarily an inventory of the brutishness of Indian men, horrors of different cultural practices, such as child marriages, the treatment of widows, as well as the unsanitary habits of the Indian (Albinia 2005; Sinha 2000). Women were presented as atavistic slaves to their husband's whims and fancies. The text served as both an exoneration of as well as justification for the continuation of imperial rule, and the view that these appalling conditions were not the consequences of Empire, but of native backwardness and barbarism. It was designed to subvert the national agitation for self-rule, claiming that given the condition and treatment of women in the subcontinent, Indians were unfit for self-rule.

While Mayo considered herself a far-sighted liberal feminist, her arguments were deeply embedded in the imperial project. Her arguments set the stage for a vitriolic attack on her writings by prominent male Indian nationalists (Lajpat Rai, 1985; Mukherji 1928; Ranga Iyer 1928). Many commentators dismissed Mayo's analysis as foreign, inapplicable to the Indian context, and also demonised western feminism. This nationalist trepidation of western liberal feminism continues in the current period. The elite nationalists, responding to Mayo, resorted to cultural authenticity arguments — that the emancipation of Indian women had to be sought in indigenous practices and idioms. *Mother India* was regarded suspiciously as imperialistic and provoked an indigenous or relativist response, which served merely to polarise positions around women's rights. It is nevertheless a representation that has continued to resonate in the work of 'First World' as well as liberal feminists in postcolonial India.[6]

Mayo's work epitomises how the 'Other' was an entity that was central to the logic and project of Orientalism (Said 1978: 3). While a full mapping of Orientalism is beyond the scope of this chapter, I highlight its major attributes as set out in Edward Said's work. He argued that Orientalism was a 'Western style for dominating, restructuring, and having authority over the Orient' (ibid.). It was grounded on an ontological and epistemological distinction between the 'Orient' and the 'Occident' (Said 1978: 2). While Orientalist discourse lacked any correlation with 'reality' and was concerned primarily with the making of the West and locating it in a position of superiority to the 'rest', it remained internally consistent and highly attractive (ibid.: 5–7). It was a discourse that influenced scholars both in the West and in the 'Orient' itself.

Said's work has been criticised for providing a totalising account of the nature of western power–knowledge as fully constituting the Orient, according no space for the subjectivity or history of the 'Other' outside of this construction. Not only is the colonised subject rendered into the exclusive position of the victim, this subject is exonerated from any complicity in constructing structures of exploitation and subordination (Sarkar 2001:192–93). Through the work of Indian historiography, the Orient no longer remained an 'inert object', but was an active participant.[7] Indian historiography was able to unmask the colonial discourses that enabled the self-constitution of the West as liberal and civilised in contrast to the 'Other' as inferior and uncivilised.

Colonial discourses were also quite specifically influenced by Darwin's theories in the late nineteenth century to construct a science of gender and race. All women were associated with the faculties of 'the lower races … and of a past and lower state of civilization' (Darwin [1871] 1971: 275). The actual brain size of women was considered smaller to that of men; this was used to assert that men and women belonged to two different species and that the female skull resembled that of an infant, and to a greater degree, that of the lower races. Like the 'darker races', women were unreliable, irrational, passive, and inferior to the white man. In addition, the 'lower races' were perceived as sexually deviant

(Gilman 1985). White women were still more civilised and morally pure than their darker racial counterparts (Burton 1994). These assumptions about women fused with those about the lower races to reinforce the argument that neither women nor colonial subjects were capable of self-rule, whether in the home or in politics, and needed to be constantly subjected to the control and governance of the white man.

The gender and race theories of nineteenth-century Europe were transposed onto the colonial context to produce Others. Thus, the Hindu was considered superior in intelligence, but simultaneously as effeminate and lacking in manliness, while the Muslim was regarded as lustful and aggressive (Sinha 1995). Somewhat contradictorily, the Indian was also constructed as being obsessed with sex — sex that was vile, ritualistic, and ever sadistic. The presence of female and male sexual symbols, sexual sculptures and erotic temples, worship of dark erotic goddesses, together with the practice of child marriage in some parts of the subcontinent rendered the Indian as lewd and lascivious, and perceived as evidence of the native's depravity (Oman 1973: 246). This fantasy was reinforced in the context of interrelations between 'native' women and the coloniser, which were often sexual in nature. The native woman was initially essentially regarded as a sexed subject. While the concubine system was prevalent in the colony until the middle to the nineteenth century, from the 1860s onwards, there was a marked shift in preference for a self-contained English type of society and family arrangement (Sen 2002: 44–45). Sexual liaisons with native women were regarded as a matter of shame and disapproved. The major cause of the shift was the 1857 mutiny that brought about a rift between the races as well as the subsequent consolidation of a distinct imperial identity that required distance from the local natives. The distance was enforced through an increased policing of interracial sex (Strobel 1992: 6–7). At the same time, the 'native' sought to control the sexuality of their women through confinement in zenanas (harems), where they were sequestered away from the colonial gaze. The native woman's body thus became the site of contest over the meaning of culture and identity, and played out most significantly over the controversy surrounding the Age of Consent Act, 1891 (Chandra, 1998; Sarkar 1996).

From the middle of the nineteenth century, the focus of the colonial power in the area of social reform was on the elimination of social practices that were identified as oppressive and barbaric.

These included the oppression of widows, female infanticide, child marriage, and the practice of veiling or purdah. Their responses were cast as chivalric, while those of native men were regarded as degrading and oppressive. The position of women within Hindu tradition was symbolically deployed by the British to legitimise colonial rule. Attention was directed at the most extreme of cultural practices as evidence of the 'barbarity' of Indian society and of its resulting need for foreign rule. What is important is that the ultimate objective was not to produce a free, strong-minded, liberated, fully active native woman. It was to endorse the ideals of self-denial and the idea of a gentle subservient wife (Sen 2002: 65–67). The native man was constituted by the colonial power in terms of his opposition to women's equality. At the same time, the colonial interventions retained the assumption that women were different from men and needed to be protected from native men. As G. Spivak has stated, such interventions were based on the idea of the white man protecting the brown woman from the brown man (Spivak 1988: 296). The discourse of equality was invoked at one and same time to reinforce the idea that all women are or should be the same (Indian women should be treated the same as English women) as well as the idea that women are not and should not be the same as men. Thus, the colonial power was able to delegitimise the recognition of cultural differences without challenging the assertion of natural gender difference. It was at best a form of intervention that would bring about the 'Victorianisation' of the Indian woman (Sen 2002: 70).

Social reformers in India also sought to reform traditions and customs to improve the status of Indian women. While they appealed to the use of law to promote such reforms, their appeals were also embedded in references to Hindu scriptures. In the same manner as the colonial power, their interventions in relation to women were informed by a protectionist approach. Women were not assumed to be equal to men; indeed, the discourse of equality was strikingly absent from the debates, as were the voices of women themselves (Kosambi 1988: 46; Sinha 1995: 33–68). Social reformers sought to eliminate customs and practices that they considered to be evils perpetrated on women through the enactment of protective forms of legislation prohibiting these practices. The discourse within which legal reforms were sought was heavily embedded within the familial. Women were assumed to be wives and mothers by nature, and the social evils had to be eradicated in order to protect women in these roles. Even the campaigns for women's education, which gathered support from the mid-nineteenth century and which would bring women out from the confines of the family, were justified in the name of the family (Roy 2005). Educated women would be stronger in their roles as wives and mothers.

At the same time, social reformers were wary of legal reforms for fear of being cast as colluders with the colonial power. In the last decades of the nineteenth century, the contradictions of engaging on the legal terrain came to the fore as Hindu nationalists entered the fray and sought to undermine the project of legal reform (Chandra 1998; Kapur and Cossman 1996: 43–50). The conflict between social reformers and the nationalists reached a peak in the age of consent controversy at the end of the nineteenth century. For the nationalists, law was an ineffective means of changing behaviour and practices within the family. While there was some agreement that marriages should not be consummated below the age of puberty, law reform was not regarded as an effective instrument for eliminating child marriage. Not only was the familial sphere resistant to reform imposed upon it but more significantly, within the colonial context, law was seen as an instrument by which the British intended to legitimise their rule. The nationalists rejected the legitimacy of the colonial regime and thus flatly refused to engage in projects of law reform. In these debates, law was again a site on which the much broader visions of the social reformers and the Hindu nationalists were fought out. In this contest, the very legitimacy of law was at issue. While the social reformers were ultimately successful insofar as their demand to raise the age of consent was passed into law, the nationalists were enormously successful in their efforts to rearticulate the domestic sphere as beyond the reach of the colonial intervention.

The role of law was in effect contradictory. For example, while legislation was ultimately passed to increase the age of consent for child marriage, the controversy succeeded in mobilising a resistant discourse that insisted on non-intervention in the realm of the private sphere (Bannerjee 1998). The legislation condemned the practice of child marriage by further raising the age of consent, but the outcome of the discursive struggle was to very effectively mobilise the Hindu nationalists and undermine the legitimacy of the efforts of the social reform movement in seeking legislative change from the colonial state. The Hindu nationalists sought to redefine Hindu conjugality and renegotiate the public/private, the domestic realm of the family, the home, as beyond the reach of colonial intervention. The family was reconstituted as a 'pure space' of Hindu culture and tradition, uncontaminated by colonial intervention. Women who occupied this space, in turn, came to represent all that was pure and untouched by colonialism. Social reformers, who were attempting to redefine Hindu tradition to exclude child marriage, were thereby trying to introduce changes into the very sphere that in the eyes of the Hindu nationalists was most representative of Hindu culture and tradition. The contest between the social reformers and the Hindu nationalists was not simply over the legitimacy of engaging with the colonial state, but was also a contest over the power and authority to define Hindu culture and tradition and the constitution of women's sexuality (Roy 2005).

The representation of the native woman as incapable of decision making, whose body is a site of contest over the meaning of cultural and national identity, continues to haunt contemporary legal discourse in the context of anti-trafficking. This representation continues to inform the discourse of both the religious right as well as the work of some liberal advocates, feminist activists, and scholars. In the next section, I illustrate how these divergent voices consolidate around the image of the battered victim subject of trafficking and produce unusual alliances and a common missionary zeal. I discuss several documentaries to illustrate the point and put into question the meaning of progressive politics.

INTERSECTING DISCOURSES AND UNLIKELY BEDFELLOWS

'Sex Trafficking', Female Morality, and the Religious Right

I use the term 'religious right' to refer very generally to groups in different countries who use orthodox, conservative, or even deeply fundamentalist visions of their religions and defend a very strict understanding of family and women's roles within that unit. I refer specifically to two such organisations or networks — the Christian Evangelicals in the USA and the Hindu right-wing nationalists in India.[8] These groups have a specific international agenda of supporting women's equality with men, but in a way that either promotes 'harmony' within the family or supports women's formal rights to equality. Thus, they can and do support women's right to work or to be educated while simultaneously recognising and celebrating women's natural differences from men, including their role as caregivers, in the interests of preserving the family.

During the Bush presidency, the Christian evangelicals in the USA exercised considerable influence on the human rights agenda of one of the most religious White Houses in US history. They were responsible for the extensive remarks made by George Bush on sex trafficking in 2003 and 2004 at the UN General Assembly meetings.[9] Such human rights issues appealed to the white evangelical base of the Republican Party, which historically belongs to denominations such as the Southern Baptists and the Assemblies of God. The evangelicals believe that the Bible is the truth, that members have a duty to proselytise and convert, and that the only way to salvation is through Jesus Christ. The embracing of human rights by Christian evangelicals produces an interesting alliance with liberals and human rights groups. Although human rights groups work on a broad range of issues on which they disagree with the evangelicals, such as abortion, school prayer, or homosexuality, on the issue of 'sex trafficking' they appeared content to forge alliances with the orthodox right which during the Bush years was closely aligned with power at the White House.[10]

In 2000, Richard Cisik, vice-president for government affairs of the National Association of Evangelicals, forged together a coalition of groups, that included representatives from Equality Now, Ms Magazine, as well as B'nai B'irth, to lobby for the enactment of the US Victims of Trafficking and Violence Protection Act, 2000 (hereinafter the US Act, 2000). A primary concern was over the trafficking of women from the 'Third World' to industrialised countries, through force or coercion.[11] The focus on 'Third World' women resonates with the 'charitable' instincts of evangelicals and their do-good notions of saving the 'wretched of the earth'. Although this instinct is not to be derided, it is the deeper political agenda of the evangelicals that is a cause for alarm. This includes their views on sexual integrity and the role of women in the family. Sex for them must be non-commercial, preserved exclusively within marriage, and only between a man and a woman. A woman's primary role is in the home, as a caregiver and domestic provider.

Feminist organisations such as the Coalition Against Trafficking in Women (CATW) and Equality Now who supported the Act argued that there was no such thing as consent to sex work and every woman who crossed borders to work in prostitution was a victim of trafficking. Their concerns were pursued in and through the discourse of human rights. Janice Raymond, a member of CATW, wrote, 'Opposing sex trafficking, the system of prostitution and the sex industry doesn't make you a conservative, a moralist, or an apologist for some political party or group. It helps make you a feminist and a human rights advocate' (Raymond 2005). Similarly, Jessica Neuwirth, director of the New York Office of the United Nations Office of the Commissioner for Human Rights (UNOCHR), is uncompromisingly of the view that an abolitionist stand on sex work is critical to combating trafficking (Farley and Neuwirth 2008: 24). The views of Neuwirth and others of her ilk have come to overwhelmingly inform the position of faith-based organisations, orthodox groups, US policy, and legal interventions on issues of trafficking around the world (Hertzke 2006: 316–35). The troubling alliance of some feminists with the Christian evangelicals was reconciled by a former anti-porn activist, Laura Lederer, who was an appointee to the US State Department's anti-trafficking office. She stated that faith-based groups brought 'a fresh perspective and a biblical mandate to the women's movement. Women's groups don't understand that the partnership on this issue has strengthened them, because they would not be getting attention internationally otherwise' (Crago 2003: 1).[12] J. Neuwirth, J. Raymond, and CATW do not represent the views of all feminists on the issue of trafficking. In fact, as K. Kempadoo argues, there is a growing body of literature that has analysed the impact of the colonial encounter on contemporary feminist conceptions of sex work, including trafficking. The need for feminist theory to engage with racialised sexual subjectivities in tandem with the historical weight of imperialism, colonialism, and racist constructions of power has only been raised recently in the context of feminist theorising on prostitution (Kempadoo 1998: 13).

While the US Act, 2000 was intended to concentrate on labour abuses across all industries such as debt bondage and use of force, it was drafted as part of a package on violence against women. Conservatives supported the Bill as it did not threaten their business constituencies. The Bill was also consistent with the evangelicals' concern over moral turpitude and sex, as well as the positions of one segment of the feminist lobby, which was determined to link prostitution with trafficking and violence in the law (Freeman 1996). In practice, the US Act, 2000 has placed undue emphasis on commercial sex work rather than focus on exploitation in a broad range of jobs and industries. The Act was reauthorised in 2003 and amended, calling for increased cooperation between governments, assistance for the family members of the victims of trafficking, as well as enhanced prosecution of traffickers. The amendments permitted victims to sue their perpetrators in criminal court and for the government to terminate contracts with companies or individuals found to be engaged in trafficking. The Act was reauthorised yet again in 2005, seeking to combat trafficking by addressing the needs of victims of trafficking in post-conflict settings, as well as to address domestic trafficking for the first time. It further expands the US criminal jurisdiction for felonies committed by US government personnel or contractors abroad to ensure they are held accountable if they are involved in human trafficking. Despite these amendments, the Act authorises programmes which are primarily geared toward reducing the demand for prostitution in the USA, and thus continues to conflate trafficking with prostitution or sexual wrongs. An appeal to faith-based groups is central to this pursuit. After signing the 2005 reauthorisation of the Act, George Bush stated, 'We're attacking this problem aggressively. Over the past four years, the Department of Homeland Security has taken new measures to protect children from sexual predators, as well as pornography and prostitution rings. The Department of Health and Human Services has partnered with faith-based and community organisations to form anti-trafficking coalitions in 17 major cities across our country.'[13]

The Act provides for countries to be annually assessed in terms of their efforts to combat trafficking. Through annual tier placements, which grade countries according to the strength and sincerity of their efforts, the US has appointed itself as the global policeman for monitoring anti-trafficking interventions (Chuang 2006). These annual tier placements announced in the US Department of State's Trafficking in Persons Report (TIP Report) are regarded with considerable suspicion by some state and non-state actors, as they are frequently based on criteria that has little to do with trafficking. The impact of the US Act, 2000 has at best been questionable and at worst, harmful to the rights of the very constituency it is intended to help (Katayama 2005; Shapiro, 2004). For example, India has been placed on the Tier 2 Watch List for the fourth consecutive year because of its apparent failure to comply with the minimum standards for the elimination of trafficking (US State 2009). While India has a range of laws on trafficking, kidnapping, and slavery, and one that regulates the sex industry, it does not have a law outlawing prostitution. The threat of sanctions pressurised the Indian government to draft a new law focusing on trafficking for prostitution, targeting a broad range of consensual sexual relationships where some exchange takes place, as well as women in the sex industry, at the expense of their human rights.

The proposed Immoral Traffic (Prevention) Act (ITPA) Amendment Bill, 2006 ignored trafficking in other sectors and sought to criminalise clients, omitting employers or companies that use trafficked labour. The proposed amendments to the Indian law would have done little to control trafficking and would actually have increased trafficking, as sex workers would be unable to unionise or monitor the entry of underage girls or women into the profession, as is currently done through the self-regulatory boards set up by a union of sex workers in Calcutta (Durbar Mahila Samanwaya Committee 2007: 17–18). The sex workers mounted a very successful public and vocal campaign opposing these reforms, supported by some feminists, community-based migrant groups, and those aware of the US pressure. Partly as a result of this mobilisation and pressure from constituencies which were likely to be the worst affected by the new law reform proposals, the Cabinet was forced to direct the bill back to the parliamentary standing committee for the Ministry of Human Resource and Development for further discussion.

In the meantime, the Ujjwala programme of the Ministry of Women and Child Development (MWCD) on the rescue, rehabilitation, and reintegration of victims of trafficking for commercial sexual exploitation was adopted in 2008. The programme acknowledges that India is a source, destination, and transit country for both in-country and cross-border trafficking. It applies to 'women and children who are vulnerable to trafficking for commercial sexual exploitation', and thus covers even consensual sex work. The programme acts as a stop gap to the proposed amendments to the ITPA that have proved so controversial.

The advocacy by the religious right and some feminist interventions are reinforced by representations of the battered sexual subject, especially in the postcolonial world, that dominates anti-trafficking advocacy. For example, a slew of documentaries have been produced on this theme foregrounding such a representation. One such portrayal is found in *Born into Brothels: Calcutta's Red Light Kids*, directed by Ross Kaufman and Zana Briski. The film was awarded the Oscar for the best documentary film at the 77th Academy Awards in 2005. While documenting the experiences of sex workers in Sonagachi, the red-light district of Calcutta, Briski offered the children in the area a chance to record their own lives. The children were provided with cameras to present a portrait of the realities of their world. Although it is not made evident in the film, not all the children are those of sex workers, but are simply poor children excited about participating in a project that is both fun and one in which they can take charge. The children click away happily, though it is evident that not all those who are represented in the portraits consent to the activity.[14] At the end, the film centres more on Briski than the children or the situation of the sex workers. Briski becomes the heroine in the film — she takes on the Indian bureaucracy, teaches the children photography, tries to get them into missionary schools, tests them for HIV, and also takes them to the zoo. Zana 'aunty', who has a master's degree in theology and religious studies, emerges as the real centrepiece and heroine of the film. She endeavours to save the children from their 'dead-end' lives, where the boys have limited prospects and the girls are merely being groomed to 'go onto the line' as prostitutes. In contrast to the representation of Briski as the 'Great White Saviour', the sex workers themselves are mostly represented in the documentary as cruel and uncaring parents. While Briski promised not to screen the film in India, after having won the Oscar, the lives of these women and their families have become a part of global public consumption.

The White House Project gave the Gender Lens Award to Briski's film in 2005. The film reinforces the position of faith-based groups as well as their influence on the trafficking agenda in the international arena. These groups worked with the Bush administration to aggressively link issues of sexuality to morality, using law and rights discourse to advance this link. In January 2003, the USA's international aid agency (USAID) issued a notice that it would not provide any more funding for projects against trafficking in people to 'organizations advocating prostitution as an employment choice or which advocate or support the legalization of prostitution'.[15] The directive is part of the broader US policy to cut funding to projects perceived as supporting trafficking of women and girls, legalisation of drugs, injecting drug use, and abortion. Some feminists have celebrated the move as a way in which to finally deal with the issue of prostitution and to rescue women and girls who are in the trade. As Donna Hughes from CATW stated, 'The challenge now is to implement these landmark [anti-prostitution] policies in order to free women and children from enslavement' (Crago 2003: 2).

In a similar vein, the religious right in other democratic countries have advanced anti-trafficking agendas in and through rights discourse. For example, in postcolonial India, the Hindu nationalists have pursued a women's rights agenda that includes combating domestic violence at home, sexual harassment in the workplace, as well as enacting anti-trafficking laws. As discussed in Chapter 1, the issue of sexuality is integral to the self-definition of the postcolonial nation, informed by the politics of the colonial encounter. Restoring masculinity to the Hindu male and clearly defined borders for the Hindu nation have been overriding concerns in the agenda of the Hindu Right. Hindu nationalism is based on the articulation of a right-wing stance on Indian politics, culture, race, gender, and sexuality and the naturalisation of difference (Breckenridge and van der Veer 1993). A key to the construction of Hindu nationalist identity is the role of women. The Hindu Right's official position on women is filled with commitments to equality, which involves a pledge to restore women to the position of equality with men that was proposed and accepted by the myth of the golden age of Hindu tradition (Bacchetta 2004; Sarkar 2001). Policies such as maternal and natal care, that reinforce women's roles in the family as mothers and wives, are supported as part of women's equality rights as they reinforce assumptions about the natural and essential differences between women and men. Women are mothers and wives — they are different, and these differences must be honoured and protected.

As I discussed in Chapter 3, the Hindu Right's agenda on women's rights is informed by a 'modern but not western' position. While emphasising the need for women to attain equality and to work outside of the home, modernisation is posited in opposition to westernisation (Basu et al. 1993: 85). Women can work, but must also guard against losing their cultural traditions and identity. This message is directed specifically to women's roles in the family. Women are thus identified not only as biological reproducers but also as cultural reproducers. It is in their roles as wives and mothers, as guardians of the tradition to be passed on to younger generations that women must guard against encroachment by westernisation. This 'new Indian woman' is deployed to distinguish Hindu national identity and Indian culture from the West, while at the same time to portray the country as advanced. The Hindu Right argues that the battle for equality cannot be fulfilled by simply imitating western women (Bhatt 2001: 138; Joshi 1995). It must be grounded within the Hindu family.

> In India, social relationships and institutions are patterned in such a manner that an evolving structure of balanced social amity is created. The family is an important institution. It is only through a happy family that an aware society is born. In this society woman has an important role to play. She is not merely a domestic community. At all times she has made an overall contribution to the growth of the social order. (Joshi 1995)

The Hindu Right is attempting to reconstitute an identity for the Indian woman that reinscribes her role within the family while embracing the demands of contemporary consumer capitalism and global economic restructuring (Nanda 2003). This new identity of 'modern but not western', of the new Hindu woman as a strong wife and mother, is all the more useful in the context of the renegotiation of the public and private spheres engendered by the new economic policies. The Hindu Right's discourse on women is an effort to ensure that neither the mass politicisation of women nor their increasing integration into the labour market undermine the patriarchal family, nor women's roles as wives and mothers therein. Unlike the revivalist discourse of the nineteenth century, women's identities are being reconstituted to explicitly include their roles within the public sphere (Kapur 2005: 43–50; Sarkar 2001). The Hindu Right's discourse on women and equality can be seen as an effort to contain the challenge that this renegotiation presents to the traditional patriarchal family. Within this discourse, women remain the repositories of tradition and culture and the family remains the primary site for performing the role of cultural progenitor. Familial and revivalist discourses have become the terms on which women are permitted to move beyond the confines of the private sphere. It is through these discourses that women's new political and economic roles are being negotiated and articulated.

The issue of trafficking needs to be understood against this backdrop of how women's subjectivity and sexuality is conceived and constructed within the contemporary discourse of the Hindu Right. Migration is indeed seen as advantageous because of the foreign remittances received by the country of origin as discussed in Chapter 2. However, women's conduct should not exceed the normative prescriptions accorded to them. Given this backdrop, it is not difficult to understand the Hindu Right's support for the SAARC Convention and its definition of trafficking, which not only reproduces the conflations between trafficking and prostitution but also addresses women and girls together, and in the process infantilises women (Article 1 [3]; Coomaraswamy 2001: paragraph 39).

The SAARC Convention is consistent with the normative prescriptions regarding women's sexual and moral behaviour. It adopts a position that advances Indian women's distinction from the western woman, preserves the country's national integrity, and reinforces the conflation between trafficking and prostitution. Women's migration is viewed through the lens of coercion and national identity and has been neatly articulated in terms of human rights violations. While this position does little to advance women's choice to move, or complicate the factors that influence female migration, the Hindu Right is able to use the modern, universal discourse of liberal rights, rather than deploy cultural relativist arguments, to restrict her movement, reproduce conservative sexual morality, and also subject her to moral surveillance.[16]

For the Christian Right and the Hindu Right, the most appropriate response to the issue of trafficking in discursive terms is to prevent the violation of the sovereign nation-state as well as women's bodies. In practical terms, this entails strengthening border control, punishing those who engage in trafficking for the purposes of prostitution, criminalising pimps and brothel owners, and increasing moral surveillance over women who seek to cross borders. While the agenda of the religious right-wing forces is rarely concealed, what has become a matter of concern is that the liberal response to trafficking is increasingly difficult to distinguish from that of the right-wing agenda.

The Liberal Response

The Public Broadcast System channel in the USA gave considerable air time to the screening of a film entitled *The Day My God Died*, directed by Andrew Levine, a young independent film maker.[17] It documents the lives of several Nepali women and girls who were trafficked into the sex trade from Kathmandu into Calcutta and Bombay. The director also enters the brothels of Bombay and films the conditions in the brothels and those who work there using a hidden spy camera. The film makes a case for those who seek to rescue and rehabilitate women in the sex trade as well as abolitionists, who want to see the trade abolished. It is replete with images of victimisation, abuse, and subordination of Nepali women and children. The International Justice Mission, a law enforcement and faith-based organisation in Washington, DC, praised for its work by the Bush White House, and local NGOs such as Maiti Nepal in Kathmandu and Sanlaap in Calcutta, are represented as the 'crusaders', the 'real heroes', and saviours of these women. They work with the police to conduct raids on brothels, which eventually lead to the incarceration of women into protective homes, separated from their children who are sent either to shelters, juvenile centres, or inadequate government facilities.

Levine's film constitutes part of a well-intentioned liberal initiative to address the issue of trafficking and goad the international community to respond to the issue. It converges with the efforts of the human rights community, which has been enthusiastically pursuing the anti-trafficking agenda. These efforts are reflected partly in the successful lobbying of anti-trafficking initiatives domestically, regionally, and globally at an extraordinary rate over the past four years. This flurry of activity has promoted a sense that something is being done, that a well-intentioned social justice project is being pursued. Yet, well-intentioned liberal and feminist interventions directed against women's oppression in the non-western or postcolonial world are frequently reminiscent of the imperial moment. Campaigns on violence against women, for example, operate within a similar logic — that the women are victims of a culturally barbaric, monolithically oppressive, and backward context and need to be rescued and rehabilitated (Akram 2000). These interventions invariably involve an appeal to a liberal, secular, and western standpoint as a means for resisting such violence.

Women's bodies remain the terrain for shifting discourses on the victimisation of 'Third World women', especially poor women, contrasted with the agency of western women. It is a discourse that fails to critically examine the ways in which the state and community invoke women's bodies and ultimately reduce women to their bodies. The responses to gender essentialist interventions are equally problematic as they rely on cultural stereotypes (Narayan 2000). As U. Narayan argues, cultural responses are invoked as a way in which to 'void the Scylla of "Sameness"', often resulting in moves that leave one floundering on the 'Charybdis of "Difference"' (ibid.: 83).

Anti-trafficking interventions propelled by well-intentioned human rights advocates also sometimes suffer from similar limitations. They fail to engage with how the colonial encounter together with its assumptions about the sexuality of the Other has shaped the liberal project. When the colonial encounter is placed at the centre of the analysis, the comfort zone of the 'do-good' notions of some well-intentioned human rights campaigners, or of those who believe that they are engaged in a transformative project, lie fully exposed. While the liberal project in its human rights guise seeks to liberate the 'wretched of the earth', it simultaneously results in producing a racist and culturally essentialist construction that is displaced onto a 'First World'/'Third World' divide, here and there, us and them.

In the arena of anti-trafficking laws, Levine's film exemplifies how the colonial past continues to discursively influence the postcolonial present, even in the liberal response. The proliferating discourses on sexuality were not simply present in Europe or the West; they were integral to the sustaining of the imperial project (Stoler 2002: 78–79). The sexual identity of the European self was contingent on the racialised, sexualised Other. As in Mayo's account, sexuality remained a site of contest between the colonial power and the ruled and the central site of struggle over the constitution of national and cultural identity. The legal interventions on issues of trafficking and their focus on prostitution render this history invisible. As a result, the interventions of liberal activists can at times be as problematic or troublesome as those devised by the conservative or religious right.

Some human rights groups are also responsible for reinforcing these divisions and feeding into the moralistic and patronising responses of governments to the issue of sex work. For example, Human Rights Watch recommended that the SAARC should co-operate with Interpol to stem the increase in trafficking in women between India and Nepal (Human Rights Watch 1995: 90). Many of the recommendations in the report were directed towards the curtailment and restriction of rights rather than their facilitation. The report criticised the open border policy, which permitted people to pass freely between the two countries without a passport, visa, or residential permit. Instead of contextualising the strengths and limits of an open border policy in a region closed and isolated from its neighbours, Human Rights Watch stated that the policy 'makes it extremely difficult for border police to check illegal activity. Traffickers and their victims move easily across the border and the onus is on individual police officers to stop and question suspicious-looking travellers' (ibid.: 12). The report recommended that Nepal and India should establish a system for strictly monitoring the border to 'guard against the trafficking in women and girls, including the inspection of vehicles' (ibid.). Despite the fact that 12 years after the publication of this report Human Rights Watch distanced itself from its recommendations, these were subsequently embraced by several governments.[18] For example, the suggestion to tighten borders as a way to control trafficking has been enthusiastically adopted by many governments around the world, especially First World governments that fear the spectre of the immigrant (Munro 2005).[19]

The focus on the victim subject and violence invites remedies and responses from states that have little to do with promoting women's rights. Thus, a related concern is that the victim–subject position has invited protectionist, and even conservative, responses from states. The construction of women exclusively through the lens of violence has triggered a spate of domestic and international reforms focused on the criminal law, which are used to justify state restrictions on women's rights — for the 'protection' of women. The anti-trafficking campaign, with its focus on violence and victimisation, is but one example. It spawned initiatives in the 1990s by states such as Bangladesh and India to impose minimum age limits for women workers going abroad for employment. In 1998, Bangladesh banned women from going abroad as domestic workers. Although Bangladesh is reconsidering the ban, it still remains in effect. Similarly, the government of Burma, reacting to a publication of a report by Human Rights Watch about the trafficking of Burmese women and girls into Thailand's sex industry, imposed rules prohibiting all women between the ages of 16 and 25 from travelling without a legal guardian (Belak 2003).

Such measures conflate women's movement or migration with trafficking, where even women moving (legally or illegally) to seek higher wage work are suspected of being trafficked. There is no mandatory requirement to provide any services or protect the rights of the victim under these documents, as states are reluctant to provide support for non-nationals. Such interventions reinforce women's victim status and resort to a protectionist and conservative discourse that early feminist interventions struggled to move away from through the anti-discrimination discourse. At the same time, the graphic, violent, and often titillating accounts of women's abuse marginalises any understanding of the circumstances that lead women to move or the reasons why they rely on traffickers or smugglers to facilitate their movement. For example, the Levine film completely fails to address the context of poverty, lack of jobs, and education as well as a booming Indian economy that has led adult women and young girls to migrate voluntarily into India to work as domestic workers, sex workers, as well as in the construction and textile industries. The central representation of the women in the film is that they are forced or kidnapped. This corresponds to the image as well as paternalistic responses that some feminists have adopted in relation to the issue of 'sex' trafficking.

Contemporary Feminist Responses to Trafficking

Some of the feminist scholarship on trafficking and sex work that takes place in the postcolonial world evokes the imagery of the abject victim subject, whose sexuality is understood almost exclusively through the lens of violence and coercion. It is an image which also happens to coincide with the position of the religious right. Kathleen Barry, Catharine MacKinnon, and Gloria Steinem have all been involved in the new anti-trafficking crusades that continue to perpetuate the victim image of women especially from the 'Third World'. These feminists regard sex as a primary tool of abuse of women by men and view prostitution per se as the denial of a woman's humanity and the ultimate expression of female objectification by men (MacKinnon 1996). For some scholars, the legalisation of prostitution simply 'normalises domination, torture, cruel, inhuman and degrading treatment' and violates a range of human rights norms and conventions (Marcovich 1999).

Kathleen Barry's work on trafficking, which has been extremely influential in this debate, recreates this colonial imagery (Barry 1979, 1995). She argues that prostitution is violence against women and that it reduces all women to sex and argues in favour of some form of heroic interventions by feminists on behalf of sex workers (and women generally) to save them from violence, and degradation. Barry is a co-founder of CATW, which exerts considerable influence on the strategies being formulated at the international level to combat trafficking. She states that prostitution is per se a violation of women's human rights. Any woman who migrates for prostitution or to work in the sex trade is also regarded as a victim of human rights violations.

This position has been reinforced by Sigma Huda, the former UN Special Rapporteur on Trafficking, and board member of CATW. Huda strongly defended the criminalisation of prostitution and stringent action against clients and others who paid for sex (United Nations Report of the Special Rapporteur on Trafficking 2006). Her report conflates sex work with trafficking and regards prostitution per se as violence against women and hence a criminal act. Her report as well as the position of CATW have been subjected to a considerable amount of critique for being inconsistent with the UN definition on trafficking. The positions adopted by Barry and Huda reinforce colonialist representation of women in the developing world and advocate interventions that are imperialist in nature, especially their recommendations on rescue and rehabilitation (Doezema, 2001; Kempadoo 1998: 11–12, 2001).

These positions reproduce the representation of women in the Third World and non-western world as ignorant, illiterate, tradition-bound, domesticated, and victimised. As feminist scholar Kempadoo states, Barry's representation of the 'Third World woman' leaves her not yet a 'whole or developed' person; instead, she resembles a minor needing guidance, assistance, and help (1998: 11). The image that is produced is that of a truncated 'Third World' woman who is sexually constrained, tradition-bound, incarcerated in the home, illiterate, and poor. It is an image that is strikingly reminiscent of the colonial construction of the eastern woman. Similar assumptions justified incursions into the lives of the native and the colony. Empire would assist in the development of the civilisation until it reached a point at which it was capable of self-determination (Mehta 1999). Civilisational achievement was a necessary precondition for realising progress, and the stage of civilisation was the marker for determining if progressive possibilities would be within the reach of a community at any given point of time. Infantilising women in the postcolonial world reproduces the colonialist rationale for intervening in the lives of the native subject (to save those incapable of self-determination) in order to justify the rescue operations advocated by Huda and others. In striking contrast to this emaciated image stands the image of the emancipated western woman — she has control over her income, her body, and her sexuality. The analysis is structured along the contours of colonial thought, the assumption being that women in the Third World are infantile, civilisationally backward, and incapable of self-determination or autonomy.

Contemporary international feminist legal politics has reproduced the subject of colonial discourse in its articulation of the exploited sex worker in the postcolonial world.

The woman's subjectivity is erased and she is produced in legal discourse as an object — a body that is vulnerable, coerced, and easily accessible to traffickers. She is immobilised in terms of her agency and decision-making ability in the course of crossing borders. Legal interventions have produced a victimised subject, based on assumptions of the female 'Other' as incapable of self-determination, justifying rescue and rehabilitation operations. The image of the victimised subject completely ignores the lived reality of the lives of sex workers in these other parts of the world. As Kempadoo points out, African and Caribbean countries 'where one can speak of a continuum of sexual relations from monogamy to multiple sexual partners, and where sex may be considered as a valuable asset for a woman to trade' are completely ignored in this analysis 'in favour of specific western ideologies and moralities regarding sexual relations' (1998: 12). The image of the victimised subject has influenced the legal strategies being formulated in the international arena and 'First World' countries that have little to do with the rights of the 'victims'.

The understanding of trafficking as linked to organised crime encourages a punitive approach to human trafficking for sexual exploitation. The emphasis is on the purpose of the movement, rather than on the violence experienced by women in the course of being transported, migrating, or moving (Chuang 1998). While women are increasingly encouraged to avail themselves of opportunities outside the confining domestic familial arrangement, these new approaches send a strong message. The representation of the migrant women as victims combined with the conflation of migration (legal or clandestine) with trafficking encourages the notion that the solution partly lies in directing governments to draft legislation to keep their people at home. In the name of protecting women's rights, these initiatives are invariably based on assumptions about women's sexuality, especially about women from the postcolonial world, as victims, infantile, and incapable of decision-making. These assumptions have invited highly protectionist legislation and at times even justified protective detention and intervention strategies that further reinforce gender and cultural stereotypes.

The interventions of Indian feminists, like their western counterparts, also at times collude with nineteenth-century Orientalism, cultural orthodoxies, and a 'neo-Orientalist' human rights discourse. While many Indian feminists might challenge the persecutory and violent representations of Indian culture by western feminists and western human rights advocates, some of them are deeply implicated in reproducing the same gaze when intervening in the lives of women from minority religious communities and even sexual minorities. The language of some Indian feminists engaged in anti-trafficking interventions speaks of sex workers in the language of the 'Other' as fallen women or helpless, victimised subjects. The victim status conferred on the sex worker remains essential to the survival and the purity of the nation and the preservation of Indian womanhood.

THE 'OTHER' WOMAN RESPONDS

> … there are no relations of power without resistances; the latter are all the more real and effective because they are formed right at the point where relations of power are exercised.
>
> — Foucault (1980;142)

Anti-trafficking intervention strategies have intensified mobilisation among sex workers to lobby for their basic human rights as well as to articulate their concerns in related areas, such as the rights of their children, support in their old age, and better working conditions. They have contested the underlying assumption that economic necessity drives women into sex work and revealed that the sex worker is a 'speaking' and 'animated' subject who can and does make choices for economic empowerment, which includes migration. She is an unbounded subject who exists outside the supervision of the family. Her resistance intensifies concerns about the threat to the normative family as well as to the purity of the nation. The sex worker challenges the anti-trafficking regime being advocated as the international regulatory mechanism for ostensibly protecting the human rights of women. She has exposed how this new regime curtails mobility and economic opportunities for women and other migrants, and intensifies the moral surveillance of women's sexual conduct. It is a regime that does not necessarily restrict the number of women who are moving or migrating, but simply makes it more dangerous for women to cross borders. It is not directed towards protecting the rights of women who are in the sex industry or who migrate, albeit clandestinely, for purposes other than sex work.

Sex workers and migrants, amongst others, have questioned the focus on trafficking and the laws enacted in many countries ostensibly to curb the problem (GAATW 2007). The US Act, 2000 has come in for specific criticism as being designed to curb migration of a certain class of people, namely 'nannies, maids, dancers, factory workers, restaurant workers, sales clerks, [and] models', rather than to stop the abuse and violence that takes place in the course of trafficking. They have challenged feminist and orthodox groups which have opposed sex work, and supported this legislation regardless of the fact that it targets migrants and is not directed at the problems of abuse and harm that women may experience in the course of transportation or movement. Indeed, there is now ample evidence that anti-trafficking interventions are producing human rights violations and doing very little to effectively address the problem of trafficking (ibid.).

The sex worker brings about several disruptions. Her claims to rights as a parent, entertainer, worker, and sexual subject disrupt dominant sexual and familial norms. Her repeated encounters with law as well as mobilisation challenge and alter prevailing cultural norms. She brings about a normative challenge by negotiating her disclaimed or marginalised identity within more stable and dominant discourses. By renegotiating and occupying the register of sexual, familial, and cultural norms, she brings out the makeshift and ambivalent character of these norms. She simultaneously creates the potential for a more inclusive politics, opening up a space for subjects who have remained unaddressed in women's human rights politics, such as single parents, other sexual minorities, and religious and cultural minorities.

The idea that the female migrant, in a postcolonial context, can -consent to sex work, and that she may consent to move or enter into a consensual arrangement with someone who arranges her transport from one port to another, free from coercion or violence, is also challenging at a normative level. In crossing borders, to engage in sex work as well as other forms of labour, such as domestic work, the female migrant challenges the dominant assumptions that inform both the contemporary international legal regime as well as feminist legal politics which assume that she is dragged, beaten, forced, kidnapped, or abducted into this work. The female migrant is a market actor who understands the economic and lifestyle opportunities available to her in other parts of the world. As a market actor, she challenges the over simplistic and patronising assumption that women in the postcolonial world enter the sex trade because of conditions of poverty, which begets the question why all poor women do not opt for sex work (Chuang 1998: 84–85). She chooses to cross borders in search of better economic opportunities as do, for example, educated middle-class graduates from emerging economies or developing countries.

The complex subjectivity of the sex worker in the postcolonial context is captured in *Tales of the Night Fairies* (2002), directed by Shohini Ghosh, a reader in media studies in New Delhi, India. A documentary about the lives of sex workers in the Sonagachi red-light area in Calcutta, the film stands in stark contrast to the representations projected by Briski and Levine. It depicts how these women have organised themselves into a movement of over 60,000 members. With help from activists, social workers, and medical practitioners, the Sonagachi women have organised to not only increase condom use from 5 per cent to 90 per cent, but also to reduce the rate of HIV and sexually transmitted infections among sex workers to below 5 per cent, as compared to 80 per cent in Bombay where the sex workers remain unorganised (Pardasani 2005; Swaminathan et al. 2007; UNAIDS 2008: 80). This significant dimension of their lives is afforded no recognition in Briski's film nor is acknowledged in Levine's documentary and is in fact disparaged by some progressive thinkers (Kristof and WuDunn 2009).

The sex workers in Sonagachi have also set up financial institutions to organise loans to assist sex workers and the local community as well as for setting up health clinics, schools, and blood banks and providing sex education throughout the Sonagachi area. Their anti-trafficking initiatives rely on the active participation of residents in red-light areas to monitor the entry of minors into the area and assist in the return of any who try to enter (Durbar Mahila Samanwaya Committee 1997). Over the past several years, sex workers' groups have been organising annual conferences to highlight the situation of sex workers around the country, drawing attention to the issue of trafficking as well as the impact of anti-trafficking measures on their rights and lobbying for more rights protection from the state for sex workers (Ditmore 2006: 302–303).

The work of DMSC and the representation of the sex workers in the film stand in stark contrast to assumptions about their victimisation or their portrayal by others almost exclusively as trafficked and exploited victims. *Tales of the Night Fairies* is a film shot with the informed consent and active participation of all those who feature in the documentary. The women are the real heroes in this representation. The story of these women and their families speaks to their choices, struggle, agency, and also opposition to the anti-trafficking strategies that have become such a significant component of the women's human rights agenda over the past decade.

The fact that women cross borders, and ought to be able to cross borders, has been conflated with the purpose of their journey, rather than with the conditions under which they cross borders. Some of the emerging literature in the area of international human rights continues to invoke the trope of the poor, 'Third World' woman exclusively as a victim, reinforcing arguments, here and there, against sex work per se as inherently exploitative, rather than supporting the rights of these women to move or envisioning the possibility of a more complex subjectivity as opposed to the flattened cardboard cut-outs to which their subjectivity has been reduced. Little attention is given to the coercive and abusive practices that women may be subjected to in the course of movement, including a lack of interrogation of the impact of some of the racist, sexist, and 'neo-colonial' anti-trafficking laws being advocated by 'First World' governments (and supported in some feminist literature an advocacy). These initiatives harm women more than they help and reinforce stereotypes of the poor woman, especially in the postcolonial world, as a victim of barbaric treatment.

CONCLUSION

The legal responses to trafficking and trafficked women are mediated through the nexus of gender, racialised innocence, and criminality. The trafficked woman is usually a young, innocent victim invariably trapped into prostitution. The victim subject and the focus on violence invite remedies and responses from states, supported by some progressive scholars and activists, which have little to do with promoting women's rights. Instead they have triggered a spate of domestic and international reforms focused on the criminal law, which are used to justify state restrictions on women's rights — ostensibly in the interests of protecting women — as well as reinforcing sexual, cultural, and racial stereotypes. The legal regulation of trafficking is largely focused on the point of crossing borders. It is at this point that the female subject's identity is rendered unstable. While women cross as mothers, wives, tourists, professionals, or migrants, the law intervenes to potentially disrupt, if not derail, these subjectivities in order to render her victimised as well as illicit and immoral by the reassignment of her subjectivity through trafficking discourse. All agency is retained by the trafficker, and the focus on criminality enables states to strengthen laws to curb trafficking as well as increase the punishment for trafficking.

The three documentaries discussed in this chapter reflect the different sides of an ever increasing divide over the way in which women in the postcolonial world, and in particular, the female 'Other', have come to be both constructed as well as represented. These constructions and representations epitomise the different ways in which women's subjectivity, especially of the poor, 'Third World' subject, is conceived and understood. In Briski's narrative, the children are victims and her missionary-based interventions are presented as an effort to rescue them from the misery and desperation of their lives. The children are happiest with their cameras and this moment stands in stark contrast to the emptiness of their daily lives. They are imagined as disposable, deficient victim subjects, an image that is starkly familiar given its presence in media and celluloid in the global north (and even within India). At the same time it is Briski's struggle that is centred in the film, giving the impression that no one in India is concerned with or wants to improve the squalid situation of the children, and that the mothers are either violent or just do not care. In the second image, Levine is the well-intentioned liberal, who intends his film to represent the human rights violations occurring in a place he 'deeply cares about'. Once again, the young women are represented as utterly victimised, where the local human rights organisation ally with the (Christian) International Justice Mission to rescue and rehabilitate the girls to live 'more productive' and fulfilling lives, one option being marriage. In the third representation, Ghosh attempts to foreground the subjectivity of the sex workers and represent the complex layering of their lives. They are constantly exercising choices, claiming their identities as sex workers, while also resisting the abuse, sexual exploitation, and violence that they may experience by demanding rights. While the filmmaker remains largely on the margins, the struggle of the women is central to the narrative. There are moments when they are infantilised, prancing around chairs at a carnival, in a version of musical chairs. Yet they are largely depicted as resistive subjects who are not seeking rescue and rehabilitation, but respect and a space from which to assert their rights and subjectivity.

The images inspired by *Born into Brothels: Calcutta's Red Light Kids* and *The Day My God Died* are echoed in the work of evangelicals, liberals, and some feminists (both here and there). The patronising and protectionist responses of liberals through human rights discourse co-joins with the 'crusading' zeal of orthodox groups and evangelicals, revealing at times a lack of sensitivity to the ways in which women live in the postcolonial world despite their situations of disadvantage. While the legal interventions have continued to reproduce and reinforce the well-meaning stereotypes of the female migrant as coerced or duped into movement, this stereotype is shattered by the 'night fairies' and the sexual humour, songs and dances of the Sonagachi women. They explode the neatly sculpted image of the postcolonial subject and the representation of women as existing always and exclusively as poor, unhappy, and unfortunate victims, devoid of sexual agency. This challenge creates the possibility for more genuine alliances that are forged on the basis of respect, regardless of the material and social conditions in which women may exist. It also produces space for complicating the agency and choices of these women and decentres the law's focus on their victimisation. In transcending her victim status, she expands the aperture through which to understand female migration and the conditions and available choices under which she moves.

NOTES

1. See International Agreement for the Suppression of the White Slave Traffic, U.N. Sales No. 1950.IV.1 (1904) (hereinafter IASWST); International Convention for the Suppression of the White Slave Traffic at Final Protocol, United Nations Sales No. 1450.IV.2 (1910) (hereinafter ICSWST, Final Protocol). See also International Convention to Suppress the Slave Trade and Slavery, Sept. 25, 1926, 46 Stat. 2183, 60 L.N.T.S. 253, available at http://www1.umn.edu/humanrts/instree/f1sc.htm. Accessed 28 October 2009; International Labour Organization Convention Concerning Forced or Compulsory Labour (No. 29), 28 June 1930, 39 U.N.T.S. 55 (hereinafter ILO Forced Labour Convention [No. 29]).
2. Article 2 provides 'effective protection' to women and girls against the white slave traffic and calls on governments to monitor ports for persons in charge of

'women and girls destined for an immoral life'; see also Article 7, International Convention for the Suppression of the Traffic in Women and Children, Sept. 30, 1921, 53 U.N.T.S. 39, (hereinafter ICST), requiring member states to draw up regulations 'for the protection of women and children traveling on emigrant ships'.

3. United Nations Protocol on Trafficking Protocol to Prevent, Suppress, and Punish Trafficking in Persons, Especially in Women and Children, G.A. Res. 55/25, U.N. GAOR, Annex II, Supp. No. 49, at 60, UN Doc. A/45/49 (2001), 2000 (hereinafter UN Trafficking Protocol).
4. There are no reliable statistics that substantiate this claim, which is invariably based on figures on that are outdated and anecdotal. The UNESCO Trafficking Statistics project summarises the problem:

   > When it comes to statistics, trafficking of girls and women is one of several highly emotive issues which seem to overwhelm critical faculties. Numbers take on a life of their own, gaining acceptance through repetition, often with little inquiry into their derivations. Journalists, bowing to the pressures of editors, demand numbers, any number. Organizations feel compelled to supply them, lending false precisions and spurious authority to many reports (UNESCO Trafficking Statistics Project, www.unescobkk.org/index.php?id=1022[accessed 28 October 2009]).

   See also Data Comparison Sheet #1 (www.unescobkk.org/fileadmin/user_upload/culture/Trafficking/project/Graph_Worldwide_Sept_2004.pdf [accessed 28 October 2009]). The US State Department in 2002 estimated that 700,000 to 4 million persons who were trafficked were 'mostly women and children'. It subsequently revised its estimates to between 600,000– 800,000 people — mostly women and children — being trafficked annually across national borders. The Department has not published its methodology for collecting these statistics or explained why these figures were so substantially revised.
5. Other relevant provisions are found in the Indian Penal Code, 1908 that outlaws a number of trafficking-related activities. Among the prohibited activities are kidnapping or abducting women and girls in order to force them to have illicit intercourse or to marry against their will (section 366); kidnapping or abducting persons in order to subject them to slavery (section 367); buying or selling, or otherwise giving or receiving, people for the purpose of slavery (section 370); and buying or selling, or otherwise obtaining, a child for the purpose of prostitution or any unlawful or immoral purpose (sections 372 and 373). The penal code also has separate provisions dealing with the procurement of children (section 366A) and the importation of a girl below the age of 21 years of age (section 366B). Section 374 provides punishment for compelling any person to labour against the will of that person. In addition, several laws address the issue of child trafficking including The Juvenile Justice (Care and Protection of Children) Act 2000 (Juvenile Justice Act) was passed in consonance with the Convention on the Rights of the Child, which India has ratified. The Act recognises that a child who is vulnerable and likely to be inducted into trafficking is a child in need of care and protection, and includes elaborate provisions for the rescue and rehabilitation of such a child. The Act empowers state governments to constitute child welfare committees and gives the committees the ultimate authority to dispose of cases

for the care, protection, treatment, development, and rehabilitation of children, as well as to provide for their basic needs and the protection of their human rights (section 31). At the state level the Goa Children's Act, 2003 is relevant as it is the first act to provide a definition for child trafficking. See Nair and Sen (2004) regarding implementation of these laws.

6. Elizabeth Bumiller, for example, dismisses the Indian critique of Mayo and also applauds to some extent the work of Mary Daly, whose arguments were reminiscent of those made by Mayo. Bumiller states that 'Indians still revile Katherine Mayo, although, interestingly, there has been an American radical feminist interpretation of her work. Mary Daly, in her 1978 book *Gyn/Ecology*, wrote that Mayo 'shows an understanding of the situation which more famous scholars entirely lack. Her work is, in the precise sense of the word, exceptional. Mayo, in her own way was a feminist ... Katherine Mayo, egregious as her views were, held a certain fascination for me. She had done, after all, what I was trying to do"' (1990: 20–22).
7. While Indian historiography was meant as a corrective to Orientalism, it continued to rely on certain practices of Orientalism such as mapping or fixing boundaries and identities (Prakash 2000: 60).
8. The term 'Christian Right' has been used by some scholars to include a broad range of American organizations (Buss and Herman 2003: xviii–xxi). I use the term to refer quite specifically to evangelical Protestantism, which is a biblically literalist Protestantism that is more widespread in the USA than anywhere else, and US Catholicism, which is closer to Irish Catholicism in its doctrinal strictness than to less stringent western and southern European Catholicism.

   The Hindu Right refers to a religious right-wing and nationalist movement in India, informed by the ideology of *Hindutva* (not Hinduism) that is dedicated to the establishment of a Hindu state. It has effectively pursued issues of sexuality in and through a liberal rights discourse and been remarkably successful in advancing its agenda. I use the term 'Hindu Right' to refer to the main organisations and movements of the current phase of Hindu communalism in India — the triumvirate of the Bharatiya Janata Party (BJP — The Indian Peoples Party), the political wing of the Hindu Right, the Rashtra Sevika Sangh (RSS — Association of Nationalists Volunteers) — which is the main ideological component of the movement and promotes the religious ideology of the Hindu Right and Vishwa Hindu Parishad (VHP — World Hindu Council), collectively known as the Sangh Parivar (the bonded family) (Cossman and Kapur 2001: 6–15).

   The Christian evangelicals and the Hindu Right recognise women's rights, but within the confines of dominant sexual norms and familial ideology. The difference between them for the purposes of this chapter is that the evangelicals usually have a conservative and scripturally-oriented position on women's roles and rights and the family, while the Hindu Right's is a nationalist movement which may have a less conservative position on women, though they are still shaped by dominant familial ideology. Their enemies are Muslims, and their primary concern is to highlight the gender egalitarianism of Hindus in contrast to the Muslims (Keddie 1999).
9. On 12 March 2004, International Women's Day, George Bush spoke about 'sex slavery'. He extolled the work of Sharon Cohn, director of Anti-Trafficking Operations for the International Justice Mission (IJM), a Christian organisation. Bush went on to state that the IJM was 'working to end sex slavery' and that the

US government would stand with them. 'We abhor — we abhor — the practice of sex slavery, and we will do all we can to help you. Support for human rights is the cornerstone of American foreign policy' (Block 2004; Nathan 2005). See the recommendations for the conference on Pathbreaking Strategies in the Global Fight Against Sex-Trafficking from 23–26 February 2003, organised by the State Department in alliance with the non-governmental War Against Trafficking Alliance (http://www.state.gov/g/tip/rls/rpt/20834.htm, [accessed 18 September 2009]).

10. *New York Times* columnist N. Kristof epitomises this liberal/human rights voice, arguing that such groups can work with the orthodox right on the issue of trafficking, never addressing the serious consequences for the women who are ostensibly the recipients of such well-intentioned interventions (Kristof and Wudunn 2009; Kristof, 2005, 2006a, 2006b, 2006c, 2007).
11. I use the term 'Third World' when it is the preferred term invoked by particular groups or political ideologies. Otherwise, I use the term 'postcolonial context' or 'postcolonial world' to refer to a theoretical position, which analyses the ways in which the historical processes produced during the period of the colonial encounter continue to discursively inform the postcolonial present (Marks 2003: 451; Said 1979, 1995).
12. Laura Lederer was editor of the feminist anti-pornography anthology *Take Back the Night*, New York: Harper Perennial, 1980.
13. President Signs H.R. 972, Trafficking Victims Protection Reauthorization Act January 2006. Online. http://www.humantrafficking.org/updates/213. Accessed 27 July 2009.
14. The sex workers of Sonagachi protested against this film partly on the grounds that Briski refused to submit her work and idea to the Sex Workers Ethics Committee (*The Telegraph*, 15 March 2005). Swapna Gayen, secretary of Durbar Mahila Samanwaya Committee (The Unstoppable Movement of Women) Calcutta (the committee which represents the membership of 60,000 sex workers of West Bengal, in eastern India), states: 'In this age, when it is the norm to respect ethical considerations while making documentaries, the film used hidden cameras to shoot intimate moments in the lives of sex-workers and their work zones' (Gayen 2005).
15. The amendment ensures that no taxpayer funds designated for HIV/AIDS prevention may be used to promote or advocate the legalisation of prostitution or sex trafficking, and that no funds may be given to any group or organisation that does not have a policy explicitly opposing prostitution and sex trafficking: see Public Law 108–25, the United States Leadership Against HIV/AIDS, Tuberculosis, and Malaria Act of 2003, section 301 (e) and (f) ASSISTANCE TO COMBAT HIV/AIDS.http://thomas.loc.gov/cgi-bin/query/C?c108:./temp/~c108tyosT9. Accessed 19 September 2009. Two US district courts have struck down the provisions as unconstitutional and violative of the free speech clause: Alliance for Open Society Inc. *et al.*, v. United States Agency for International Development *et al.*, United States District Court Southern District of New York, 9 May. http://brennancenter.org/programs/pov/AOSI%20v%20USAID%20Decision.pdf. Accessed 18 September 2009 and DKT International Inc. v. United States Agency for International Development et al., United States District Court for the District of Colombia, order, 18 May 2006. http://www.dcd.uscourts.gov/

Opinions/2006/Sullivan/2005-CV-1604~9:33:28~5-18-2006-a.pdf. Accessed 19 September 2009.

16. While the Hindu Rights political wing, the BJP, lost power at the centre in the 2004 general elections, and again in 2009, there was no radical shift from the position of the BJP by the Congress-led government. Armed with well-intentioned liberal credentials and claiming to be devoid of the ideological baggage of the Hindu nationalists, the government nevertheless continues to pursue a paternalistic attitude in the area of women's rights.
17. Screened 1 January 2004 on the Public Broadcasting System.
18. Human Rights Watch has subsequently published quite different recommendations relating to immigration and border control, suggesting that the organisation no longer stands by the measures recommended in its 1995 report. In 2007, the organisation recommended that 'Governments should tackle the links between poverty, unsafe migration, and inadequate labour standards by reforming immigration policies that drive migrants underground to unlicensed recruiters and smugglers. Anti-trafficking programs monitoring borders and women's mobility also threaten to compound the problem. Rather than restricting women's and girls' right to migrate and seek work, the real challenge lies in creating the guarantees for them to do so safely and with dignity' (emphasis added) (Varia 2007: 60).
19. The detrimental stand adopted by Human Rights Watch was also stated in an earlier report on cross-border trafficking between Burma and Thailand, where it requested donors to ensure that loans for the construction of roads and other infrastructure projects near the border take into consideration the effect of such a project on the trafficking in women (Thomas and Jones 1993: 159). The extraordinary assumption implicit in this recommendation is that withholding assistance for the construction of basic infrastructure will help stop cross-border traffic. Indeed, it will curtail, if not entirely stop, border crossings, both legal and illegal.

5

The Citizen and the Migrant Subject: Postcolonial Anxieties, Law, and the Politics of Exclusion/Inclusion

> [M]ost migrants learn, and become disguises.
>
> Rushdie (1991: 49)

> Production of national identity is . . . a contested process and the struggle to produce and reproduce 'pure' citizens out of recalcitrant people accounts for much of what happens at the borderlands of a state.
>
> Samaddar (1999: 108–109)

> [T]he subjectivity of a given social agent is always precariously and provisionally fixed or . . . sutured at the intersection of various discourses.
>
> Mouffe (1988: 90)

In this chapter I focus on the normative criteria on which citizenship laws are based in postcolonial India, which reinscribe citizenship within dominant racial, religious, sexual, and cultural norms. I argue that the migrant subject not only exposes these norms, but also how the 'excess', that which does not fall within the dominant norms and boundaries of citizenship, is regarded as transgressive and justifiably subject to restraint, persecution, censorship, social stigma, incarceration, and even annihilation.

Citizenship, in the postcolonial experience, has not been conceived exclusively within the confines of the modern nation-state.[1] While there have been extensive critiques of citizenship, this chapter builds on scholarship that brings to crisis the very normative content of citizenship by viewing it as serving a normalising function. I illustrate how this normalising function is deployed to regulate subjectivity and access to rights and benefits (Singha 2009). The technologies of citizenship, informed by assumptions about race, caste, religion, sexuality, gender, and civilisational superiority operate to regulate as well as to depoliticise the subject (Cruikshank 1999).

The critique offered in the chapter foregrounds the role of the migrant subject in exposing the more complex and contradictory narrative of citizenship. The analysis is not intended to reject or render defunct the entire project of citizenship, but rather to build on existing scholarship and offer a reading of citizenship that serves as 'an act of reclamation' that takes over 'the object for a different project than that to which it is currently tethered' (Brown 2005: 16). Citizenship is not discussed exclusively in terms of a bundle of formal legal rights belonging to those who are residing within the territorial boundaries of a nation-state. Citizenship performs a regulatory function, where acquisition is not equated with freedom or denial with unfreedom (Cruikshank 1999). The chapter shows how citizenship is not always empowering or emancipatory complicating the liberal argument on citizenship. I discuss how the Other of the citizen, the migrant, plays an important role in the construction of citizenship, and how citizenship laws regulate and exteriorise the migrant. At the same time, the migrant's selective appropriation of the citizenship discourse to her benefit sets her up as a knowing willing subject, contrary to accounts that position the subaltern as victims or less than full subjects or autonomous of dominant discourses. Not only does this challenge disrupt and reconfigure the normative content of citizenship, it also adds a further layer to the arguments about subjectivity developed in subaltern studies, complicating the hypostatisation of the autonomy of subaltern consciousness.

I focus on the migrant in the context of postcolonial India who is semi-skilled or unskilled, semi-literate, working class or lower middle class and unemployed. This migrant occupies a subaltern position, which is not simply a descriptive term but, as discussed in Chapter 1, also has a normative dimension. The subaltern is neither merely a marginalised subject nor a minority member, as understood within the terms of classical liberal thinking. This subject constitutes the excess which is produced in and through the normalising function of law, excluded or marginalised as it cannot be accommodated within the register of norms on which the law is based. Citizenship is one site on which the constitution of the legitimate and illegitimate subject takes place. This promise of citizenship in the post-independent nation and its normalising function sits in tension with those who challenge the homogenising potential of citizenship and reveal the exclusions against which it operates. The insights provided by the colonial past enable us to understand how the technologies of citizenship operate as mechanisms of power and governance to both include and exclude subjects from juridical entitlements in the postcolonial present, though this understanding is not confined to postcolonial states (Thompson 2000).

My aim is not to provide a comprehensive account of citizenship within a postcolonial context, given its complexity and the impossibility of arriving at an exhaustive definition. I provide, instead, an episodic account of the treatment of migrants in law when they come up against the normative boundaries that inform citizenship, exposing the deep and lasting impact of the colonial encounter and the imperial imagination on understandings and constructions of citizenship. The analysis challenges a narrative that views citizenship as a primarily progressive concept that is ever expanding and inclusive (Bosniak 2002). I discuss two recent cases decided in the Indian courts dealing with migrants to exemplify how juridical entitlements are tied to normative assumptions that inform citizenship, regardless of formal legal membership. The first case involves a constitutional challenge to a ban imposed on bar dancers from dancing in certain prohibited establishments throughout Maharashtra, a western state in India, partly on the grounds that they were migrants from outside of the state and country and perceived as corrupting the local men and contaminating Indian culture (*Indian Hotel and Restaurants Association (AHAR) v. State of Maharashtra* (MANU/MH/0088/2006) (hereinafter the *Bar Dancer's case*). The second case, decided by the Indian Supreme Court, addresses the problem of illegal migration of Muslims from Bangladesh into the north-eastern state of Assam, recasting the migrant as an 'aggressor' and a threat to the security of both the state and the country (*Sarbananda Sonowal v. Union of India and Another* (2005) 5 Supreme Court Cases 665 (hereinafter *Sonowal's case*).

The analysis compels us to ask several questions: What is the role of citizenship once its exclusionary and regulatory potential are exposed? How and to what extent does citizenship remain relevant or useful and at what point does it becomes meaningless in the life of the migrant subject?

COLONIAL CITIZENRY

Modernity posits a set of universal truth claims about equality, citizenship, and representation in law. In the context of Empire, modernity was coterminous with colonialism and it also bought into sharp relief how exclusions were built into these supposedly universal concepts (Chakrabarty 2000; Chatterjee 1993: 2). Promises of universality could be reconciled with exclusions in practice through a clear and persuasive logic. The denial of rights normally associated with citizenship was justified through the discourse of difference, whereby the eligibility and capacity for freedom and progress was based on biological determinism, racial and religious superiority, and civilisational maturity. Through this logic, colonial subjugation was legitimised as the natural subordination of lesser races to higher ones. The purportedly universal rights of man could be denied to those not considered to be men or humans.

Liberal discourses of rights, inclusion, and equality could be reconciled with the colonial policies of exclusion and discrimination only by presuming differences between different types of individuals. A similar logic justified the continued subordination of women, where women were understood as different from men, more specifically, as weaker, subordinate, and in need of protection. In the colonial relationship, gender difference was also conflated with cultural or civilisational backwardness, where the treatment of women was used in part as a justification for colonial intervention and the civilising mission (Sinha 2000).[2] Claims to self-determination were contingent on attaining a degree of civilisational maturity, which included the shedding of religious practices that were deemed primitive and acceptable treatment by the colonial subject of its women. The Empire was able to position itself as the infinitely more mature 'Great White (Christian) Saviour' and as the defender of women's rights in the colony, without, however, fundamentally altering its position on gender difference and the representation of women as essentially weak and subordinate. Thus, the colonial project continued to take the existence of gender difference as natural and inevitable. These assumptions constituted part of the technologies of governance and informed the ways in which the postcolonial nation subsequently came to constitute the legitimate citizen. Exclusion based on differences that are either inherent and immutable, or threatening and dangerous, remains integral to understandings of citizenship in postcolonial India.

Re-reading citizenship through a postcolonial lens foregrounds its fractured history and reveals how it served a regulatory and disciplining function, rather than a liberatory one. Challenges to the liberatory promise of citizenship have come from women, Dalits, tribes, environmentalists, and new social movements. The specific role of postcolonial scholarship is to deconstruct how the project of citizenship is itself imbricated in power and in normalising subjects. Its normative content remains tethered to economic expansion, imperial ambition, and the cultural, gendered, racial, and religious identity of the subject (Brodie 2004). By disrupting the dominant narratives of modernity, an analysis of citizenship from a postcolonial perspective denaturalises the relationships of dominance and subordination that underlie such narratives. This perspective captures the complex relationships of domination and subordination and demonstrates how the discourse of citizenship continues to operate as a tool of power and governance in the postcolonial present. Its vagaries are exposed in the contemporary period in and through the challenges posed by the migrant subject.

CITIZENSHIP IN POSTCOLONIAL INDIA

Within postcolonial India, citizenship has been marked by the very feature of exclusion that characterised its colonial incarnations. It was defined primarily against the historical backdrop of the violent and bloody partition of India and its content determined in the context of the fracturing of the subcontinent.[3] Cultural identity, increasingly conflated with religious identity, and the principle of descent and blood ties are central to the constitution of Indian citizenship.

The issue of religious identity featured prominently in the Constituent Assembly debates on the definition of citizenship.[4] The establishment of the state of Pakistan provided a tangible focus for anti-Muslim sentiments and the demonisation of Muslims in the country in the grizzly aftermath of partition (Jaffrelot 1996: 81). Loyalty and love for the Indian nation-state were the paramount values expected from the Indian citizen. Citizenship rights were equated with the possession of these values, and invariably it was the Muslim subject who fell short. What is evident from these debates is the view that Muslims who supported the creation of Pakistan and left India did not deserve Indian citizenship. They could be allowed Indian citizenship only after expressly proving their loyalty for the country and their desire to stay on permanently in India.

The issue of religious identity and citizenship also featured in concerns over Muslim women who were abducted during the period of partition. According to Urvashi Butalia, in demonstrating a concern for Muslim women who were abducted, forcibly converted, or forcibly married, the Indian state intended to exhibit its credentials as civilised, modern, and secular. This modern image was, however, tempered by traditional images of the Hindu man as chivalrous and honourable, who was enjoined by tradition to protect women. The gallantry of the Hindu man was demonstrated in his act of providing shelter to Muslim women found abandoned in Hindu majority areas (Butalia 1995: 68). However, as Veena Das has argued, the regulation of sexuality of abducted women was connected to the fears produced by the presence of illegitimate children. Thus, while the Indian state sought to project its modern, secular image, these images were simultaneously entwined with a concern for national honour (Das 1995).

In contrast, the Other, namely the Muslim and the state of Pakistan, were represented as non-secular and without any exclusive ancient traditions upon which to draw (Butalia 1995: 73). This argument was shored up by the Hindu nationalists who pursued an anti-Pakistan, anti-Muslim rhetoric and argued that while the rape and abduction of Hindu women was shameful, such behaviour was to be expected from Pakistan, 'a nation built on the predatory desire for Hindu property and Hindu women (which) took practically no steps to checkmate the lust and avarice of its champions' (quoted in ibid.: 67). There was a highly selective and manipulative process by which myths and stereotypes were deployed to represent the Muslim male as a marauding and libidinous creature who preyed on the 'the innocent and mother-like Hindu woman', in contrast to the representation of the tolerant, and heroic Hindu male (ibid.: 79). These representations in turn were incorporated into arguments about who should be a citizen and who should be denied Indian citizenship rights. The image of the raped and abducted woman continued to serve as a metaphor of the violated body of a nation, and the responsibility of this violation was placed squarely on the Muslim.

The issue of religion was legally resolved by the Constituent Assembly in favour of inclusive citizenship and was backed by a non-denominational nationalism (Rodrigues 2005: 212, 213). The specific concerns of religious minorities were to be accommodated in an approach to secularism that was based on equal treatment of all religions and a system of quotas and affirmative action measures. It was a vision of citizenship premised on the liberal promise of emancipation for all, regardless of difference. Nevertheless, the discourse on religious identity of the (Hindu) nation continues to infuse contemporary citizenship discourse. Violence against the minority community comes to be justified as an act of self-defence, of the Hindu nation and its women. The process in the Constituent Assembly debates opened up a deep fissure over the role of religion in the construction of Indian citizenship and its Others; this divide continues to rankle and lingers in the debates on citizenship in the contemporary moment.

The debate over the normative content of citizenship has been further complicated in the context of gender, and discussions over electoral representation for women as well as reform of the personal law. Beginning in 1917, the issue of women's suffrage and political representation came to occupy the centre stage of many women's organisations. The issue was initially conceptualised as a means of achieving further social reform, where women leaders were of the view that the enfranchisement of women would mean additional support for reform legislation. The question of women's suffrage was first raised by the Women's Indian Association in 1917. In 1919, the Government of India Act allowed the vote for only 3 per cent of Indian adults in the Provincial Assembly, and less than 1 per cent in the Central Assembly, based on property requirements. While women were not included, the provincial assemblies were empowered to eliminate the exclusion clause, and although many of the assemblies did so, the property qualifications continued to operate to effectively disqualify the vast majority of women who had no independent access to property. As the political movement for self-rule continued, women's organisations continued to push for women's suffrage.

As the campaigns for political representation and legislative reform developed, a contest emerged over the discursive terrain of the movement, that is, whether the demands were to be articulated in the discourse of upliftment or the discourse of equality. The early women's movement, based primarily in the middle and upper classes, drew heavily on revivalist ideals of gender difference and Indian womanhood in support of their efforts to improve women's position. The turn of the century was a time of resurgent Hinduism, where 'Indian womanhood' became the very embodiment of nationalism, as the nation came to be constructed as divine mother, as mother India, and as women became 'the mothers of the realm'.

The early women's movement drew on this reconstructed identity of women as mothers of the nation. More specifically, the discourse of women's upliftment was used to support demands for the reform of social practices. According to this discourse, women's roles as wives and mothers, and their distinctively feminine values such as sacrifice and loyalty, should be strengthened. The elimination of debilitating social practices, alongside education for women would allow women to 'perform their roles in a more enlightened manner', as well as allow for a greater influence of feminine values on society (Chaudhuri 1993: 83). Women's upliftment was linked with national development, and a discourse emerged of Indian women as mothers of the nation (Kumar 1993: 50). In so doing, they relied heavily on revivalist and nationalist discourse insisting, for example, that 'India's greatest will not return until Indian womanhood obtains a larger, freer, fuller life, for largely in the hands of Indian women must be the redemption of India' (Besant 1915: 157). The leaders of the women's movement deployed this discourse of women's upliftment to argue not only for the elimination of debilitating social practices, but also to support a greater public role for women. It was argued that a woman's distinctive roles and values as self-sacrificing mothers and dutiful wives could make an important contribution to the public sphere.

The discourse of upliftment developed alongside the discourse of equality over the course of the twentieth century. Ultimately, the discourse of equal rights, with its emphasis on achieving equality for women within economic, political, and familial spheres, resulted in the passage of laws guaranteeing sex equality and special provisions for women in the areas of employment, politics, education, and some aspects of the family law. This period was marked by a distinct liberal faith in state institutions and the rule of law (Sunder Rajan 2003: 31). Yet, the normative tension whereby the Indian woman as invested in an essentialist and conservative notion of Indian culture and Indian womanhood while simultaneously pursuing a revolutionary enterprise of achieving equality between men and women persisted and remains unresolved in the contemporary moment.

This tension was evident in the context of the debates over reform of the personal law. In the 1930s, demands for the legislative reform in inheritance and marriage were pressed by women's groups, amongst others. These demands for the reform of personal laws, with specific attention being given to Hindu law, and the elimination of legal disabilities was increasingly cast within the equal rights discourse which displaced the earlier women's upliftment discourse.

By 1940, the campaign to reform Hindu personal laws began to receive support from the main national party, the Congress. At the same time, the demand for a Uniform Civil Code was introduced into national debate. The Report of the Sub-Committee for 'Women's Role in a Planned Economy' called for the enactment of a Uniform Civil Code which would gradually replace all personal laws and ensure that a common civil code would be applicable to all communities. In 1941 and 1944, a government committee was established to consider the question of codification of Hindu law. In 1943, the issue of the Hindu Code came before the Legislative Assembly, which commissioned a draft code.

The efforts to reform personal laws proved to be rather more controversial than the demands for women's suffrage and political representation. Conservative and orthodox voices within the Congress, as well as those in the Hindu Mahasabha, a communal organisation established in 1914 for social reform and reconversion of Hindus from Islam, strenuously opposed the Hindu Code Bill. The proposed reforms to Hindu laws were seen as leading to the destruction of the family. No less than 'the purity of family life, the great ideal of chastity and the great ideal of Indian womanhood' was considered to be at stake (Som 1992).[5] Inheritance rights for daughters, equal divorce rights, and the monogamy clause were among the most controversial and intense debates of the proposed returns. Property rights for women were, in the words of a member of parliament, 'equality run mad' (ibid. citing Constituent Assembly Debates 1949: 23). Granting equal property to women would lead to a breakdown of the joint Hindu family, which was seen as the most fundamental unit of society. Opponents feared litigation, fragmentation, and increasing violence among family members. The Bill was seen by many as the 'demolition of the entire structure and fabric of Hindu society' (Chaudhuri 1993: 188). Women's roles and identity was very much at issue in these debates. Supporters of the Bill argued within the discourse of equal rights, insisting that equality within the public sphere be extended to the family. They argued against women's economic dependency and in favour of independence and equality. Opponents of the Bill held very different views about women's roles and identities. The basic argument against the Bill was that men and women had different obligations in the family and it would be unfair for them to have the same property rights. Others claimed that women had the same rights as men under Hindu law, but that the notion of equality was based on difference and harmony and not sameness. The more conservative voices used a more convoluted argument that women had always occupied a revered place in Indian society and its past, and hence to give them equal property rights would indicate a decline in that status. In all instances the denial of certain rights to women, such as property rights in ancestral property, was justified as Hindu women were upholders of family integrity and unity and thus not entitled to a share in property for this would disintegrate the family — the microcosm of the nation.

The opponents of the Hindu Code Bill drew on many of the assumptions about gender and gender difference (discussed in Chapter 2) that were used to shape understandings of the subject in law as well as to determine the content of citizenship along gendered lines. The idea of women as naturally different from men, with distinctive roles and values, was very much a part of the discourse of those opposing the Bill. This understanding of gender difference, which had informed both the social reformers and the political nationalists in the nineteenth century, remained dominant. In contrast, the women's movement, which had gradually begun to argue in favour of equality rights and abandon the discourse of upliftment, found itself in a position of challenging and attempting to displace this prevailing discourse.

When the Hindu Code was put to the Indian Legislative Assembly in 1945, it was defeated. After Independence, the Code was brought to the provisional Parliament, and it again produced a storm of opposition. The Hindu Code Bill was defeated, resulting in the resignation of the Law Minister, Ambedkar. Further efforts at reforming Hindu personal law were delayed until 1955, when four separate pieces of legislation were enacted that significantly improved the legal status of women under Hindu personal law. The Hindu Marriage Act, the Hindu Succession Act, the Hindu Minority and Guardianship Act, and the Hindu Adoption and Maintenance Act were all enacted in 1956.

The legal regulation of the family and of women's roles therein was a site of intensive discursive struggle, as the women's movement sought to extend the promise of equality rights to the private sphere. The outcome was integral to understandings of whom and what constituted the Indian citizen and on what terms rights were conferred. The very same political actors, who had agreed to those equality rights within the public sphere but a few years earlier, fiercely resisted the effort to renegotiate the boundaries between the public and private. The idea of women as full and equal citizens in the political and economic sphere carried the day. But the idea of women as full and equal citizens in the domestic sphere was simply too radical. Despite the fact that the reforms were ultimately passed into law, there was no decisive discursive victory. The discourse of equality was not able to successfully challenge and displace the ideological construction of women as wives and mothers within the family.

These struggles and debates on women's status and subjectivity in the newly emerging nation-state produced mixed results. The discursive struggle to construct a legitimate political subjectivity for women in the public sphere was successful to the extent that political representation and constitutional equality rights were achieved. This political subjectivity was initially constructed within the discourse of Hindu revivalism, of women as mothers of the nation. However, in the post-Independence period and during the formulation of the legal edifice of the new Indian state, the discourse through which this position was constructed shifted to one of equality. The discourse of equality was successful in the public sphere: political representation and constitutional equality rights were achieved. But the discourse of equality proved to be considerably less well suited to the discursive struggles within the private sphere of the family. The discourse of equality — of women as the same as men and entitled to the same treatment — ran head on into the dominant ideological construction of women as wives and mothers, as fundamentally different from men. The inability of the discourse of equality to challenge and displace this ideological construction within the private sphere further cast a shadow back on the discursive struggles within the public sphere. While women were ultimately granted full citizenship on equal terms with men, its normative content continued to be tied to an essentialist and conservative notion of Indian culture and Indian womanhood. The outcome in the private sphere suggests that those achievements did not entirely displace the construction of women as wives and mothers. Women could be 'equal' in the public sphere, without being the same as men in the private sphere. Women could be equal in the public sphere at the same time as they were wives and mothers in the private sphere. The discourse of equality could gain hold in the public sphere, without fundamentally challenging or displacing the hold of familial ideology in the private sphere. The normative content of citizenship emerged as deeply gendered, according women formal equal rights with men, without disrupting the register of sexual, familial, and cultural norms that define Indian womanhood and on which laws addressing women's rights continue to be based.

CITIZENSHIP LAW AND THE MIGRANT SUBJECT

At one level, citizenship seems somewhat removed from migration and the migrant subject, and in particular, the illegal migrant subject. However, the migrant shadows the development of citizenship law and is deeply implicated in the constitution of legitimate and illegitimate, as well as less legitimate subjects (Chimni, 2005). Citizenship was initially defined in an inclusive fashion at the time of the adoption of the Indian Constitution, and it was even conferred on a vast majority of people who were refugees, indentured labourers and poor emigrants.[6] Legal formal citizenship came into being with the enactment of the *Citizenship Act* of 1955 and the *Citizenship Rules* of 1956. Both enactments refer to the migrant while addressing the situation of displaced persons, evacuees and Pakistan returnees. The migrant was introduced more conspicuously in the amendment to the *Citizenship Act* in 1986, which addressed the issue of large scale migration from Bangladesh into the northeastern state of Assam, and again in 2005, which recognised the role of the 'overseas Indian' and their potential relevance to India's status as an emerging economic power (Roy 2006). In each context the migrant becomes a relevant spectre and integral to the resulting demarcations of citizenship. Unlike the period after partition, where the migrant entered into citizenship upon crossing the territorially demarcated border, in the later instances, the migrant, quite specifically the subaltern migrant, is associated with illegality. Under the 1986 Act, provisions are set out for identifying 'foreigners' and 'illegal migrants', deferring citizenship in some cases and attributing illegality in others (Roy 2005: 223). In the 2005 Citizenship Amendment Act (CAA 2005), the introduction of the overseas Indian citizen acknowledges the delinking of citizenship from territory, at the same time reaffirming the link of Indian citizenship to descent. It also denies citizenship to the nation's Other by explicitly closing off the category of overseas Indian to those who are or have been citizens of Pakistan and

Bangladesh, as neither can claim the status of an overseas Indian citizen or a person of Indian origin. The nation thus solidifies its boundaries against its 'Others' even as it tries to attract the wealthy non-resident Indians who can be assimilated culturally. The category of the 'illegal migrant' also makes its appearance in the amendment where any person born of a parent who is an illegal migrant at the time of her birth, will not be considered a citizen of India. This appearance occurs precisely at the moment the overseas Indian citizen, the one who is wealthy and reclaimed through the gravitational pull of culture and allegiance to 'Mother India' is recognised (section 7A, CAA 2005) .

In recent times, there has been a growing emphasis on the majoritarian ascriptions of citizenship where Indian descent has become an overriding consideration, as has Hindu identity (Rodrigues 2005: 221–22). What has emerged during the course of the past 40 years is an increasing emphasis on cultural and religious bonds and Indian origin in relationship to citizenship, rather than territorial boundary. The concept has been increasingly confined to people born to Indian citizens or whose parents were of Indian origin and did not forego their citizenship.[7] With the re-emergence of Hindu majoritarianism throughout the 1990s in the form of the Hindu Right, the entrenchment of citizenship in blood ties and cultural ascriptions reached a crescendo and citizenship became more exclusive. The Hindu Right has continuously regarded citizenship as an exclusively cultural and religious enterprise, prioritising religious identity in its definitions of citizenship in the hope of establishing a Hindu state in India where religious minorities, especially Muslims and Christians, would have to conform. The Hindu Right has pursued a narrow conception of citizenship, privileging religious identity from its very inception in the early 1920s.

The issue of religious identity has become particularly significant in the debate over the migration of thousands of Bangladeshis into Assam since 1971. While a number of families have established firm roots in the state, their presence has produced tensions with the local indigenous communities who are claiming erosion of their cultural and political identity. There are also competing claims between different groups of migrants, namely the Hindi-speaking migrants, who have entered the state from different parts of India, in particular Bihar and Rajasthan, and the Bangladeshi migrants, who have ostensibly entered the state from Bangladesh (Misra 2007:

273–75; Prabhakara 2007: 271). While the story of migration into the north-east is a complex one, the Hindu Right has polarised the issue by viewing it almost exclusively through the lens of religion — as a tension between the Hindu insider and the Muslim outsider. The equation of Muslim identity with alterity and danger was overtly manifested in the decision of the Indian Supreme Court in the *Sonowal* case which cast the Bangladeshi Muslim migrant as an 'aggressor' and a security threat, and in the process further entrenched the issue of religion into the normative definitions of Indian citizenship, of who belongs and who does not. Those who do not belong are expelled from the realm of juridical entitlements conferred through citizenship, and are subject to policing under migration, anti-terror, and national security laws.

Un-Becoming Citizens

In the *Sonowal* case, the Supreme Court reinforced the relationship of citizenship with cultural status or religious identity. The case involved the treatment of Bangladeshi Muslim migrants crossing the border into Assam. The Court's harsh response to this influx into India foregrounds religion as integral to the formation of Indian citizenship, rendering the situation of the Indian Muslim, who is a citizen, increasingly suspect and unstable.

The case has to be set against the backdrop of the secession of Bangladesh from Pakistan in 1971. Hundreds of thousands of Muslim migrants fled into Assam in the early 1970s when East Pakistan was liberated and the new country of Bangladesh was formed. The migrants continued to pour into Assam throughout the 1980s in search of a better life. However, the influx created resentment amongst the local population, leading to a popular uprising and the slaughter of thousands of migrants in 1983. In response to the massacre, the Indian government signed the Assam Accord in 1985 with the representatives of the student-led agitation. Pursuant to the Accord, the government granted citizenship to all settlers from the former East Pakistan who had come to Assam before 1971. In one stroke, thousands of migrants became Indian citizens. But thousands of others, who had arrived after 1971, remained illegal. In the 1990s, the Bhartiya Janata Party (BJP — Indian People's Party), the political wing of the Hindu Right, launched an aggressive national campaign against the so-called Bangladeshi migrants (Gillian 2001; Ramachandran 2003). This campaign needs to be located within the broader ideological framework of the Hindu Right, which casts all Muslims as outsiders.

The influx of migrants, many of whom are women, continues largely unacknowledged by Bangladesh (Siddiqui 2003: 171). India however regards the issue of mass migrations across the shared border as a matter of national security (Samaddar 1999: 44). The security rhetoric has led to demands for the border to be sealed, a call that would transform the Bangladeshi migrant, who is predominantly a peasant or trader, into a potential infiltrator and terrorist (Baruah 1999; Samaddar 1999: 38, 66). Against this background, the Illegal Migrants (Determination by Tribunal) Act (IMDT Act) of 1983 was enacted by the Indian government, partly to prevent a witch hunt against illegal migrants, but also with the professed aim of making the detection and deportation of illegal migrants easier. As stated in its preamble, the Act was adopted in light of

> [t]he influx of foreigners who illegally migrated into India across the borders of the sensitive eastern and north eastern regions of the country and remained in the country [and] posed a threat to the integrity and security of the said regions . . . . After taking into account the need for their speedy detection the need for protection of genuine citizens of India and the interests of the general public.

The IMDT Act resulted in the establishment of tribunals to determine whether or not a person was an illegal migrant and was specifically and exclusively applicable to foreigners in Assam, with foreigners in the rest of India covered under the provisions of the Foreigners Act, 1946 (FA, 1946).[8] The FA, 1946 specifically provides that the onus of proving citizenship status rests on the person accused of being a non-citizen.[9] However, the IMDT Act contained no such provision, and, in effect, its provisions accorded greater protection to anyone accused of being a foreigner by placing the burden of proof on the prosecution to establish that he or she was not a citizen of India.

In the *Sonowal* case, the petitioner, a former president of the Assamese Students Union, alleged that the IMDT Act was unconstitutional as it discriminated against a class of citizens of India, making it impossible for citizens resident in Assam to secure the detection and deportation of foreigners from India. The petitioner claimed that the Act had actually ended up protecting illegal migrants. The Court declared the Act unconstitutional on the ground that it violated Article 355 of the Indian Constitution, which places a duty on the central government 'to protect every State against external aggression and internal disturbance and to ensure that the Government of every State is carried on in accordance with the provisions of this Constitution'. According to the Court, the word 'aggression' should be broadly defined and not limited to a threat or act of war. On the broad meaning of aggression, the court referred to the US Supreme Court decision in *Chae Chan Ping*:

> To preserve its independence, and give security against foreign aggression and encroachment, is the highest duty of every nation, and to attain these ends nearly all other considerations are to be subordinated. It matters not in what form such aggression and encroachment come, whether from the foreign nation acting in its national character or from vast hordes of its people crowding in upon us (*Sonowal's Case:* paragraph 57 citing *Chae Chan Ping v. United States,* 130 U.S. 581 [1930]).

The Court also quoted Lord Denning, former Justice of the UK Court of Appeals:

> In recent times England has been invaded not by enemies nor by friends, but by those who seek England as a haven. In their own countries there is poverty, disease and no homes. In England there is social security, a national health service and guaranteed housing all to be had for the asking without payment and without working for it. Once here, each seeks to bring his relatives to join him. So they multiply exceedingly (*Sonowal's Case:* paragraph 36, citing Lord Denning, *The Due Process of Law*, p. 155).

The Court relied heavily on an Indian army report of 1998, which stated that the influx of illegal migrants was a major contributory factor in the outbreak of insurgency in the state (*Sonowal's Case*: paragraph 17). The report alleged that Muslim militant organisations had mushroomed across Assam and that large-scale illegal migration was tantamount to external aggression and causing internal disturbance. The report claimed that 'dangerous consequences' would result from large-scale illegal migration from Bangladesh, 'both for the people of Assam and more for the Nation as a whole . . . . No misconceived and mistaken notions of secularism should be allowed to come in the way of recognising this reality' (*Sonowal's*

Case: paragraph 17 [22]). The report warned that the Assamese would soon become a minority in their own state and that their very cultural survival was in jeopardy. Moreover, the cultural threat was specifically identified as a Muslim threat:

> The influx of these illegal migrants is turning these districts into a Muslim majority region. It will then only be a matter of time when a demand for their merger with Bangladesh may be made. The rapid growth of international Islamic fundamentalism may provide a driving force for this demand. In this context, it is pertinent that Bangladesh has long discarded secularism and has chosen to become an Islamic State. Loss of lower Assam will sever the entire land mass of the North East, from the rest of India and the rich natural resources of that region will be lost to the Nation (*Sonowal's Case*, paragraph 17 [24]).

The report identified the IMDT Act and Rules as the main barrier in the identification and deportation of illegal migrants. On the basis of this logic, the Court held that

> the presence of such a large number of illegal migrants from Bangladesh, which runs into millions, is in fact an "aggression" and had resulted in seriously hampering the growth of the State of Assam although it has vast natural resources as people from [the] rest of the country have a general perception that it is a disturbed area and this factor has resulted in not generating any employment opportunity, which has contributed to a large measure in giving rise to [the] insurgency (*Sonowal's Case*: paragraph 64).

In striking down the Act, the Supreme Court produced a bloated definition of aggression by incorporating economic aggression into the ambit of Article 355. The Court's heavy reliance on the army's report is telling of its approach to the issue of citizenship. By equating illegal immigrants with infiltrators and Muslims, the report highlights the state's anxiety over the loss of the north-east from the Indian landmass. The Indian nation continues to be defined with reference to Pakistan and Bangladesh. The nation-state has never achieved completeness and the line between the migrant and citizen, self and the 'Other' remains blurred and fluid. The Indian state remains suspended in the space between a 'former colony' and 'not yet nation' (Samaddar 1999: 15). The report manifests the continuing anxiety over the yet to be formed nation-state and the yet to be formed nation, and the desire of the Indian state for territorial and cultural assimilation of the north-east (Hazarika 2000).

A major consequence of the decision was to bring these migrants into the scope of the FA, 1946, which places the burden of proving citizenship on the person accused of being a non-citizen. Cultural and religious identity was integral to the definition of citizenship in the *Sonowal Case*, to the exclusion of the rights of migrants. The question of migrants' rights is entirely absent from the decision as is their voice in the dispute. Those accused of being illegal migrants were invariably referred to as Muslims, though Muslims also constitute 12 per cent of the national population and a significant minority. The decision blurred the distinction between citizenship and migrants by foregrounding religious identity.

The *Sonowal* decision as well as the foreigners' issue as a whole needs to be further understood within the context of the re-emergence of the Hindu Right. As discussed in several chapters in this book, the movement had its origins in the revivalist and nationalist movements of the nineteenth century, which sought to revitalise Hindu culture as a strategy for resisting colonialism.[10] Central to the ideology to the Hindu Right is the installation of religion and culture as primary attributes of nationalism and citizenship identity. In early discussions about citizenship in the Constituent Assembly debates, the threat of being overwhelmed by the Muslim presence was expressed as an 'air-born baby boom' (Rodrigues 2005: 225). A similar fear was echoed 50 years after independence, in the statements of India's then Home Minister Lal Krishna Advani of the nationalist BJP, calling the 20 million 'illegal' Bangladeshis in India a security risk (Das 2005; Gillian 2001; Ramachandran 1999). The BJP has consistently tried to challenge the legitimacy of 'illegal' migrants or non-citizens who are often conflated with Muslims, who may or may not be legal or migrants.[11]

The Hindu nationalists have been vociferous in their calls to scrap the IMDT Act on the grounds that it protected 'Bangladeshi illegal immigrants at the cost of the country's security' (*The Hindu*, 30 October 2004). They declared that the Supreme Court decision of striking down the Act had constituted a 'clear and total vindication of the BJP's stand'.[12] The case demonstrates how Indian citizenship is deeply anchored in assumptions about cultural and religious identity and not confined to formal legal status. The current cultural paroxysms around illegal migrants in India, especially from neighbouring countries, and their relationship to citizenship identity must be seen in the wider context of how culture has been central to the legitimacy of the Indian subject since the nineteenth century. This story of the constitution of the Indian subject and its integral relationship to culture remains as germane in the current moment as it was in the nineteenth century. The suturing of culture into the fantasy of the nation continues to set the discursive stage on which the emerging debates on who is and who is not a legitimate citizen subject are being played out. The role and meaning of Hindu culture and how it emerged as integral to the formation of the Indian citizen at the point of independence have remained significant into the twenty-first century.

The Bangladeshi migrant is addressed almost exclusively within the discourse of surveillance and security that constitute part of the technologies of citizenship. Their rights remain in suspended animation, as they are cast as threats, 'infiltrators', and potential terrorists (Kumara 2006). This enables bright lines to be drawn between legitimate and illegitimate subjects. The legitimate subject is a Hindu subject, who requires protection through stringent deportation laws and anti-terror legislation. Religious identity is foregrounded as a central category in determining who is loyal and who is suspect. Citizenship becomes wobbly as its borders, terms, and processes are constantly re-negotiated. The more the line is drawn in an insular and inwardly direction the more some subjects are pushed outward, like dark energy, in the direction of alien space. The Muslims, who are Indian citizens, are at risk of being pushed into the realm of illegitimacy and becoming a complete 'outsider'. They come to be increasingly policed through migration, security, and anti-terror laws.

The division of the nation along the lines of religion as evidenced in the response to the crossing of Bangladeshi migrants into India is producing an inside/outside distinction, where even insiders are rendered as outsiders. This division is born of a history where the postcolonial nation has been unable to achieve a complete symmetry between its territorial boundaries and its inhabitants and thus complete the formation of its identity as a nation. The migrant is rendered an alien subject, increasingly demonised as a threat to the *real* nation, to be either fully assimilated or incarcerated or possibly even eliminated if he or she refuses to conform.

Identity was pivotal to the emergence of the postcolonial nation, a nation-state that was not born from the spirit of the Enlightenment nor addressed within the dominant narrative of the emergence of the modern nation-state. It was a nation that was conceived of in terms of cultural identity and its distinction from the West. Culture remains an overriding influence in constituting the identity of the Indian sovereign state and sovereign subject. Under the aggressive emergence of Hindu nationalism, central to this project has been the construction of the Indian citizen as a Hindu citizen. The politics of inclusion and exclusion manifested in the colonial encounter and the treatment of the colonial subject as the 'Other' remain integral to the constitution of the citizen subject in postcolonial India.

The Muslim continues to be placed on the peripheral boundaries of citizenship, where cultural assimilation becomes a criterion for legitimacy and proof of loyalty to the nation. While the Bangladeshi migrants are not formal legal citizens, their presence destabilises the claims and constitution of the Indian Muslims, who are citizens. Muslims who are citizens within India are nevertheless rendered suspect should they fail to conform, or claim special or preferential treatment. Muslims, citizen and non-citizen, must prove their legitimacy by establishing loyalty as well as continued subordination to Indian citizens who are Hindu. In the process, the technologies of citizenship — law, surveillance, security, and social, sexual, cultural, and religious norms — set up a hierarchy of citizens who are 'real' or 'authentic' and those who are suspect or regarded as threats. The projection of the Bangladeshi migrant as a threat foregrounds religion as a relevant criterion in determining belonging and the shaping of citizenship along the lines of intolerance and disapproval of difference. The migrant needs to be contained and even deported to counter the threat of aggression.

The case illustrates how citizenship, while it sets out the terms for political inclusion, has been and continues to be based on political exclusions in practice. While the exclusion of the 'Other' has also occurred outside of the postcolonial context and on historical terms that may have little to do with the colonial encounter, a postcolonial reading unmasks how such treatment is integral to the operations of citizenship. A postcolonial reading of citizenship through the analysis of the *Sonowal Case* exposes how citizenship more generally, while it bestows formal legal status on the subject, also has a dark side. Citizenship incorporates a relationship of domination and subordination that discursively infuse the postcolonial present, albeit in different ways. It lends itself to an analysis and critique that can account for the complex relationships between law and the liberal subject that are not adequately explained through older and increasingly dubious narratives. The case illustrates the terms on which citizenship is established. While formal legal status is important, this can be easily compromised or nullified through cultural affiliation, religious identity, or national origin. Within the contemporary period, Muslims are particularly vulnerable to being cast outside the comfort zone of citizenship simply by virtue of their religious identity and the association of Islam in the public domain, both within India and at the broader global level, with 'terror', 'injustice', and 'illiberal' values.

STRATEGIC ENGAGEMENTS WITH THE TECHNOLOGIES OF CITIZENSHIP

I want to broaden this analysis further and expand on how the technologies of citizenship operate by highlighting the tactical use of these technologies by the migrant subject, quite specifically, by the female migrant. Anti-colonial nationalism was formative in the moulding of Indian women's citizenship after Independence. While citizenship served as a marker of modernity, the grounding of Indian women's citizenship in normative assumptions about sexual conduct, cultural compliance, familial roles, and religious identity served to distinguish the nation from the 'West' and also set the terms of the Indian woman's identity in modern India. The constitution of citizenship for women came to be embedded in both an anti-colonial patriotism as well as prevailing sexual, cultural, and familial norms. The construction of women as wives and mothers as partially constitutive of women's citizenship status continues to be delineated within the confines of a Hindu nationalist identity as well as marks their distinctness from the 'loose' or 'fallen' woman. At the same time, the legal regulation of women in and through these dominant sexual, familial, and cultural prescriptions sustains their marginalisation, subordination, or even exclusion from the juridical entitlements conferred on legitimate subjects. When women have been good wives and mothers, when they have lived up to the expectations that these norms impose on them, they are more likely to be the recipients of rights and benefits associated with citizenship. But, by the same token, a woman whose life has deviated from the roles allocated to her by these norms may often be denied such rights and benefits. The role of cultural and sexual normativity in the production of the Indian woman's citizenship is subtle and complex and cannot be understood within a framework that limits the understanding of citizenship to a territorial boundary or formal legal status. It requires nothing less than an interrogation of the normative content of citizenship and its normalizing function in the technologies of governance.

This content becomes explicit in the *Bar Dancers* case, which involved a challenge to a legislative ban enacted by the state legislature of Maharashtra, a western province in India, on dance performances in certain specific establishments, namely, eating halls, permit rooms, and beer bars (section 33A (1)(a)).[13] The law exempted dance performances in theatres, cinemas, auditoriums, sports clubs, and luxury hotels (section 33B). The state's justifications for issuing the ban were based on concerns over preventing obscenity and protecting the dignity of women as well as assertions that many of the bar dancers were victims of trafficking and forced to work in exploitative conditions. The government relied primarily on a field action project conducted by a local NGO funded by the USAID (Prayas 2005) as well as the 1949 International Convention on Immoral Trafficking in Women and Girls, ratified by India. The ban was supported by the US State Department in its June 2005 Trafficking in Persons Report, which spoke in favour of the decision to close down the dance bars stating that the ban 'may check a new trend of traffickers favouring this more sophisticated and concealed format for selling victims trafficked for the purpose of sexual exploitation over more blatant brothel-based trafficking' (US TIPS 2005: 123).

The ban was also justified as a means for stopping the inflow of women from outside the state as well as the country, especially from Bangladesh, as they were introducing a 'dance bar culture into the state that was against Maharashtrian tradition, derogatory to the dignity of the women', and 'likely to deprave, corrupt or injure the public morality or morals'.[14] The dancers were alleged to be damaging families, destroying Indian culture, corrupting and spreading vice in the 'lives of the young in the rural areas due to the impact of the bar culture' (*Bar Dancers Case*: paragraph 76; *The Times of India*, 22 July 2005).

The ban was challenged by the Bharatiya (Indian) Bargirls Union, together with several women's NGOs, HIV/AIDS organisations, sex workers' groups, and hotel associations. The dancers argued that the ban violated their fundamental rights to equality,[15] freedom of speech and expression,[16] livelihood, and life.[17] They denied the allegation of being trafficked, stating that they had migrated voluntarily due to economic exigencies and the breakdown of traditional support structures in their home villages (*Bar Dancers Case*: paragraph 2). The petitioners relied on a study conducted by SNDT Women's University, which found that the bar dancer was conscious of the implications of her choice and agreed to the specific working conditions in the job for which she was hired (SNDT Report 2005: 12).

The dancers asserted that their skills were based on traditional dance forms embedded in the local culture (*Bar Dancers Case*: paragraph 54.). They were careful to distinguish their work from sex work, arguing that while there was scope to perceive their work as of a sexual nature, they could not be labelled sex workers (*Bar Dancers Case*: paragraph 38). Indeed, they merely imitated the dance styles and gestures seen in Indian commercial cinema, advertisements, and music videos. By forcing the women out of the bars, the ban would make them more vulnerable to being forced into sex work and subject to highly exploitative working conditions and violence (*Bar Dancers Case*: paragraph 5(iv)).

In April 2006, the Bombay High Court struck down the ban, holding that it violated articles 14 and 19(1)(g) of the Constitution. While the order constituted a victory for the bar dancers, the court's central concern revolved around compliance with Indian cultural and sexual norms rather than the fundamental rights of the dancers. The court focused on the fact that the ban made a distinction between these different types of establishments. Since the primary objective of the ban was to prevent dances that were 'obscene, vulgar or immoral and hence derogatory to the dignity of women and to prevent exploitation of women', the court held that the banning of such dances only in the prohibited establishments was not a reasonable measure. The ban should apply to all such dances regardless of where they were performed, even in the exempted establishments. The court also observed that the second objective of the ban was to prevent exploitation, in which case even work such as waitressing should have been covered by the ban in the prohibited establishments (*Bar Dancers Case*: paragraph 93).

The decision did not disrupt the central premise of the government's justification for the ban — that the dances were obscene, immoral, vulgar, and contrary to Maharashtrian culture. At stake was not a woman's right to equality or livelihood, but rather the moral turpitude of the state and the nation. Women must be protected from this cultural and sexual contamination, and the state must further protect citizens who are exposed to this contamination. This contamination is invariably displaced onto the 'outsider'. While the court does not address the claim that this contaminant was a foreign national, namely, Bangladeshi, its remarks demarcate and identify attributes that can not and do not belong to Indian culture and are implicitly alien imports.

The court upheld the state's competence to legislate on matters dealing with women's 'dignity' and issues of morality and public decency and did not dispute the central premise of the ban — the need to protect women from derogatory treatment as well as to protect society from immoral, indecent, and vulgar activity (*Bar Dancers Case*: paragraph 17). The decision assumes that female citizens or even occasionally legal non-citizens can be granted these rights if they conform in a normative sense. The transgression of prevailing sexual and familial norms is not compatible with the Indian citizen's cultural status and identity as established during the course of the colonial encounter and the anti-colonial nationalist struggle.

The issues raised by this case — anxiety about culture, gender roles, sexual conduct — all of which are implicated in the construction of normative womanhood, have been discussed in Chapter 4. And the legal issues raised by the case do not directly deal with citizenship laws. If the women were illegal immigrants they could have been denied their right to dance as Article 19 freedoms are available only to citizens. Yet what is of significance is the fact that normative evaluations of the women's conduct and behaviour took precedence over any serious interrogation of their formal citizenship status. This case highlights how citizenship and the rights associated with it — including the right to carry on one's trade — serve a wider discursive purpose. Citizenship performs a normalising function, where the dancers are required to demonstrate that they are 'good women'. They are required to counter assertions that bar dancing is a foreign import and not compatible with Indian culture, through claims that the dances are a part of Indian culture in order to claim citizenship rights. Their responses foreground the tactical use of the technologies of citizenship by the migrant. While she may not be a citizen in the formal sense, she uses the normative content of citizenship, including cultural and sexual conformity or legitimacy, to claim the rights of a citizen. The case exemplifies how the normative content of citizenship is at times determinative of citizenship.

The argument moves beyond positions that focus on securing justice for migrants or non-citizens by redefining the substance of citizenship, either by extending it to include more robust considerations of social and economic rights or to incorporate more sites, including the home and workplace, where citizenship needs to be more fully articulated. L. Bosniak argues that focussing exclusively on political citizenship deflects attention from the practical protections that non-citizens may require and which exist independent of political citizenship (2009: 143–45). My position argues in favour of the need to identify both the formal and normative mechanisms of subordination and exclusion, and to direct political advocacy to specific protections for those who do not have citizenship.

The *Bar Dancers Case* illustrates how the migrant can deploy the normative content of citizenship in and through the basic claim that the dancers' fundamental rights had been violated. They sought to establish that their sexual and cultural identities were perfectly consistent with Indian cultural values and sexual mores by arguing that the performance of 'erotic' dance sequences from Bollywood cinematic sequences was compatible with Maharashtrian culture and also distinct from sex work. The women were able to deflect attention from an inquiry into their formal citizenship status and instead concentrate on the state's central concern, that is, their compliance with cultural and sexual norms. While the bar dancers demanded their fundamental rights to equality and livelihood, they did so fully conscious of the need to comply with the normative demands. The dancers continuously embedded their arguments in cultural practices and cultural belonging, and also by distinguishing themselves from sex workers. The legal challenge brought by the bar dancers cannot be read simply as a desire to acquire liberty and freedom through their rights claims, but also as an engagement with the technologies of citizenship and a challenge to the homogenous and essentialist approach to Indian cultural values and the location of women in that culture. Such a reading exposes the fluidity of sexual and cultural norms that operate within the technologies of citizenship and make it available to the migrant subject.

The *Bar Dancers Case* is evidence of the fact that normative sexuality and cultural conformity remain the important markers of citizenship in relation to women in postcolonial India. While the migrant status of the dancers remained largely unaddressed in the case, implicit was the fact that their 'foreignness' or 'otherness' could be muted only through compliance with strict normative criteria that could render them 'insiders'. In the case, the migrant women demonstrated their alignment with specific gender-based and culturally normative criteria in order to 'belong' and secure protections regardless of whether they were in fact citizens. In the process they exposed the disciplining and normalising functions of citizenship. It can of course be argued that the victory was momentary, for the court struck down the ban on the grounds that the ban needed to focus on *all* women in *all* establishments. Should the state adopt a broader, more inclusive, non-discriminatory ban, then presumably it would be upheld. While the dancers were able to deploy the normalising content of citizenship to acquire some legitimacy and protections, they remained vulnerable to exclusion and marginalisation. Despite the successful challenge to the ban, the grounds on which it was upheld and the subsequent stay of the High Court decision by the Indian Supreme Court rendered thousands of dancers unemployed and destitute. The loss of rights or entitlements ultimately reinstated the normalising discourse that the dancers sought to simultaneously challenge as well as deploy to secure their own protections. While their claims were disruptive and transgressive, ultimately, the decision reinstated the normative boundaries of citizenship based on the understanding of the Indian woman as pure, chaste, familial, and heterosexual.

CONCLUSION

In the postcolonial imagination, citizenship emerged from the colonial encounter, where gender, culture, race, and civilisational maturity determined who was entitled to benefits and recognition and who was not. While formal legal status associated with citizenship was never conferred on the native subject, access to benefits and rights was contingent on this subject's ability to conform to or mimic the colonial power. The technologies of citizenship operated against normative boundaries that determined the line between inclusion and exclusion. In the contemporary moment, these technologies of citizenship continue to inform the way in which citizenship plays out in the legal arena. Even when formal legal status is conferred, the starting point of citizenship remains always and already exclusive.

Read in this way, citizenship can be understood to have an appeal not because of a strong identification with it by citizens within the nation-states in which they are living. Citizenship provides very conditionally an 'in' to the migrant subject who recognises her exclusion, her 'otherness', and the fact that her disadvantage can only be offset by establishing her legitimacy and seeking some benefits, as in the bar dancers' case. Citizenship becomes a makeshift strategy in the hands of the migrant to use when it serves a purpose or to change and cast off when it does not. In this sense, citizenship is a very useful tool for survival as well as for gaining access to advantages or benefits. Migrants, who flowed into Assam over the past three decades, consciously acquired ration cards, proof of residence and other 'official' documentation, through a system of clandestine operations, in order to establish their belongingness. Without these, the migrant is condemned to remain the 'Other', as illustrated by the *Sonowal Case*. But citizenship is also expendable. The historical narrative presented here and the discussion of the cases reflects how this tool is not an enduringly positive one. It can cease to be of service and turn on its bearer. The migrant subject is acutely aware of these side effects, as well as the functionality and limitedness of citizenship, of how it disciplines and regulates.

While migrants may engage with citizenship strategically, this strategy is not divorced from the normative consequences of invoking and using citizenship. It is a strategy that appeals to dominant assumptions about gender, religion, culture, and civilisational evolution. By participating in the technologies of citizenship, the migrant subject is not insulated from the normative content of this concept. Her sexual and cultural conduct and religious identity can all serve to exclude her from being regarded as the 'real thing'. As the normative content of citizenship is being increasingly strengthened against more rigid, frozen conceptions of the 'Other', the 'Other' is condemned to continue to contest or challenge these conceptions and secure protections, through challenging and reconfiguring this normative content.

NOTES

1. The classic account of citizenship by Marshall examines the emergence of citizenship in the last 250 years in Britain and defines citizens as 'a status bestowed on those who are full members of a community. All who possess the status are equal with respect to the rights and duties with which the status is endowed' 1950: 14).

As discussed in Chapter 1, there has been a proliferation of scholarship that complicates this account of citizenship, including its embeddedness in claims to territoriality (Kymlicka and Wayne 1994) as well those that take into consideration the phenomenon of imperialism in accounts of citizenship (Chimni 1998).

2. See also Sunder Rajan, who argues that the British imperial project was partly justified as a measure to improve the conditions of Indian women and, at the same time, to ensure that the interventions left indigenous patriarchy untouched (2003: 3).
3. The colonial presence in South Asia determined identity partly through the demarcation of national borders. The very notion of national borders was alien to the Asian subcontinent and came into being during the British period of colonisation as a method of dividing the 'locals' and 'migrants' and was the precursor to contemporary contests over citizenship and identity (Murayama 2006).
4. Constituent Assembly Debates (CAD), Lok Sabha Secretariat, Delhi 2003, Vol. IX, pp. 353–45, 364–70, 11 August 1949.
5. N. C. Chatterjee, '26 April 1955 *Lok Sabha Debates*', 1955 Vol. IV Part II (as cited in Som 1992).
6. Citizenship is defined in Part II of the Constitution, which addresses the central question — 'Who is a citizen of India?' (*Constitution of India*, Articles 5–11). See also Roy (2005: 1421). Under the Constitution, persons who reside outside of India can register as Indian citizens if they or either of their parents or grandparents was born in India (Article 8). However, no person is entitled to become a citizen of India if he or she has voluntarily acquired the citizenship of a foreign state (Article 9). The courts have also held that a person who migrated to Pakistan after 1 March 1947 and acquired Pakistani nationality could not subsequently claim Indian citizenship. See *Kulathil Mammu v. State of Kerala* All India Reports 1966 Supreme Court 1614; *State of Madhya Pradesh v. Peer Mohammed* All India Reports. 1963 Supreme Court 1645; *State of Andhra Pradesh v. Abdul Khader*, All India Reports 1961 Supreme Court 1467; *Mubarak Ali v. State of Bombay*, All India Reports 1957 Supreme Court 1857.
7. The Citizenship Act of 1955 made elaborate provisions specifying how citizenship could be acquired by birth, descent, registration, or naturalisation or through incorporation of territory: *The Citizenship Act, No. 57 of 1955, India Code (1993), Volume 2*. Subsequent amendments reinforced the emphasis on ethnicity as well as birth and descent — *The Citizenship (Amendment) Act, 1986, No. 51, Acts of Parliament, 1986*. While the Citizenship Act of 1955 provided that every person born in India on or after 26 January 1950 was to be a citizen of India by birth, from 1 July 1987, every person born in India on or after 26 January 1950 would be a citizen of India if either of 'his' parents was a citizen of India at the time of his birth. Similarly, the Citizenship (Amendment) Act, 1992 provides that a person born outside of India on or after 26 January 1950 and before the commencement of the Act would be a citizen of India if either of his parents was a citizen of India at the time of his birth (*The Citizenship (Amendment) Act, 1992, No. 39, Acts of Parliament, 1992*).
8. The Foreigners Act confers wide-ranging powers to deal with all foreigners, prohibiting, regulating, or restricting their entry into India or continued presence in the country including through arrest, detention, and confinement. It has been

used to evict those assumed to be illegal migrants from Bangladesh who have no proof of citizenship. In a public interest litigation filed in the Delhi High Court, the petitioner alleged that nearly three million illegal Bangladeshi migrants resided in Delhi (*Chetan Dutt v. Municipal Corporation of Delhi*, Civil Writ Petition No. 3170 of 2001). The Delhi High Court accepted that the presence of a large number of 'illegal migrants' in Delhi placed undue pressure on the cities civic amenities and deprived the 'rightful citizens of India' of those facilities (*Chetan Dutt*, Order of the Delhi High Court, 24 September 2003). On several occasions, the court lamented the Delhi government's failure to implement its plan to deport 100 illegal migrants a day (*Chetan Dutt*, Order of the Delhi High Court, 24 September 2003 and 25 February 2006).

9. Section 9 of this Act is important and reads as follows:

> *Burden of proof*—If in any case not falling under section 8 any question arises with reference to this Act or any order made or direction given thereunder, whether any person is or is not a foreigner or is or is not a foreigner of a particular class or description the onus of proving that such person is not a foreigner or is not a foreigner of such particular class or description, as the case may be, shall, notwithstanding anything contained in the Indian Evidence Act, 1872 (1 of 1872), lie upon such person.

10. The attack on the legitimacy of religious minorities to be full-fledged citizens plays out in a number of sites, including the call of the Hindu Right to enact a Uniform Civil Code to govern the personal affairs of all communities. Currently, each religious community is governed by its own personal laws. The rise of the Hindu Right has produced a fear within religious minority communities that such a Code could be used to impose 'Hindu' norms and values on all other communities. But any resistance to such a Code is being cast by the Hindu Right as anti-secular, as well as a way for Muslim men to continue their subordination and discrimination of Muslim women (Menon 1998: 244).
11. See, for example, *Dr. Ved Vyas Mahajan, Secretary Bharatiya Janata Party, Delhi v. The Election Commission of India*, Civil Writ Petition of 2003, High Court of Delhi (challenging the inclusion of alleged illegal migrants on voter registration list in violation of the Representation of People's Act, 1950).
12. Statement Issued by L. K. Advani, leader of the opposition, and Rajnath Singh, leader of the BJP. 4 April, 2006. http://www.bjp.org/content/view/2740/394/. Accessed 22 September 2009).
13. *Bombay Police (Amendment) Act, Maharashtra Act No. 35 of 2005, Maharashtra Government Gazette, 2005.*
14. *Bombay Police (Amendment) Act*, Preamble.
15. Article 14 of the *Indian Constitution* states, 'The State shall not deny to any person equality before the law or the equal protection of the laws within the territory of India.' Article 15 (3) prohibits discrimination on the grounds of religion, race, caste, sex, or place of birth and states that '[n]othing in this article shall prevent the State from making any special provision for women and children'.
16. *India Constitution*, Article 19(1)(g) states that all citizens shall have the right 'to practice any profession, to carry on any occupation, trade or business'.
17. *India Constitution*, Article 21 provides that '[n]o person shall be deprived of his life or personal liberty except according to procedure established by law'.

6

The Fear Factor: Muslims, the Gujarat Riots, and the Purge from Within

How does it feel to be Indian Muslim? To be constantly told by rabid elements that your real home is across the border?

— From *Dev* (Applause Entertainment, Udbhav Dreamzone 2004)

In Sonowal's case, Bangladeshi Muslim migrants are addressed in and through the discourse of security, given the threat they ostensibly pose to law and order, as well as the fear factor their presence produces. Fear is reiterated and reproduced ideologically through the discourse of the religious right, as well as the global war on terror that has targeted Muslims in the contemporary period. The construction of the Muslim as a subject to be feared and who poses a threat from which the sovereign subject requires protection erodes the legitimacy of the Indian Muslim, who is increasingly cast as a foreigner, alien, and outsider. This claim is used to recast the insider as an outsider, regardless of her formal legal status. Normative boundaries solidify to place this subject squarely outside the realm of juridical entitlements, legibility, and belongingness. And the Hindu Right, through its ideology of *Hindutva*, aggressively pursues this normative purging of the Muslim, even after the waning of their political power subsequent to the 2009 national elections. While law can offer redress at the level of reparations and recognition of the harms inflicted on legitimate subjects, such redress does not address the normative processes that have rendered these subjects illegitimate.

In this chapter I specifically address the role of law and rights discourse in producing the insider as an outsider. I address how the migrant subject enjoys a contingent position in law, whose inclusion or exclusion is partly determined by normative and ideological contests within the legal arena. I specifically examine the context of the Gujarat riots that took place in 2002, which resulted in the death of over 1,000 Muslims. While innumerable mechanisms were set up to provide justice to victims and their families, most paid insufficient attention to the critical role of law and rights discourse in both producing and justifying such violence. The riots were carefully calibrated with legal discourse to relegate all Muslims as outsiders, foreigners, and aliens, whose refusal to assimilate threatened the very existence and identity of the nation-state. The riots were justified as an expression of self-defence, and the Muslim insider transformed as a migrant presence, malignant, and, much like the Bangladeshi migrant in Sonowal's case, portrayed as a threat to the (Hindu) identity of the Indian state.

In February and March 2001, the Vishwa Hindu Parishad (VHP — World Hindu Council), a religion-based organisation set up to mobilise 'the Hindu masses', sounded the drum roll of the Ram Mandir (Ram Temple) movement. The primary objective of the movement has been to construct a temple on the very spot in Ayodhya where the mobs of the Hindu Right tore apart a sixteenth-century mosque with their bare hands in December 1992. The VHP declared that the mosque stood precisely on the spot where *God* was born and remained determined to carry out its objective of constructing the temple in pursuit of its broader mission — to establish a Hindu state for a nation consisting primarily of Hindus.[1] In preparation for the event, their foot-soldiers visited the site of the now cordoned off area to pay respects and prepare for the *bhumipuja* (grand prayer). While some of these participants were returning from the site by train, allegedly shouting god chants ('*hail ram rajya*' — Hail to the Rule of Lord Ram) and anti-Muslim slogans ('*Muslims Bharat chodo!*' — Muslims leave India!), their coach was purportedly set alight by mobs of Muslims as the train moved through Godhra station in Gujarat (Lakshmi 2002: A13). The carnage that followed left 58 Hindus dead. This event ignited the second catastrophic event — the slaughter of over 1,000 Muslims throughout the state of Gujarat both within sight of the state's law enforcement officers, who simply stood by as witnesses to the massacre and, in some cases, with the active support of state officials (Communalism Combat 2002: 2; PUCL Interim Report, 2002).[2]

Dev (2004), a Bollywood film directed by reputed filmmaker Govind Nihalani, depicts the isolation of the Indian Muslim as an alien, foreigner, and unwelcome migrant in the post-Gujarat riots scenario where even secularists turned partisan, rendering the country's law and order machinery into a force capable of the most horrifying violence. At the centre of the power game are two police officers — Dev Pratap Singh (Amitabh Bachchan) and Tejinder Khosla (Om Puri). Although the film is located in Bombay, it serves as a metaphor for what happened during the Gujarat riots in 2002. Dev, the Joint Commissioner of Police, is a proud and seasoned police officer representing the liberal subject with complete faith in the supremacy of law. Dev is the conscience of the film, and has a tough time comprehending the real politics behind the riots. He is initially simply disgusted with the violence and refuses to see how the majoritarianism of the Hindus has turned into a process of gradual disentitlement and marginalisation of the Muslims. His neutral stance and fence-sitting political ideology persists throughout the film, until he is attacked by a young Muslim, Farhan (Fardeen Khan), an unemployed law graduate who holds Dev responsible for his father's death. Farhan's father, Ali Saheb, was accidentally shot and killed by the police during a march protesting police injustices against the Muslim community. Ali Saheb infused Farhan with ideas of patriotism, non-violence, and faith in the democratic process and rule of law, which are the very same liberal values to which Dev subscribes, but the violent death of his father leaves Farhan emotionally orphaned and disillusioned. He chooses the path of violence and joins forces with a corrupt and ambitious politician, Lati, with the intent to kill Dev.

Unlike Dev, who goes through a process of gradual realisation of the enormity of the politics behind the isolation of minorities in India, Tejinder represents a one-dimensional, almost villainous communalisation. He is a boorish communal cop who throws shocking lines into the film's narrative. 'They're all terrorists and foreigners,' claims Tejinder, who lives by his communal convictions until the very end, including at the moment of his suicide.

The untangling of the complex ideological tension between the film's main protagonists is set against a subtext — Bollywood's mandatory romantic interlude. A rather infantile love story unfolds during the time of the communal riots, where Farhan's attachment to the young Muslim woman next door, Aaliya (Kareena Kapoor), is celebrated through furtive glances thrown at one another from a terrace. Aaliya's role is modelled on Zaheera Sheikh, a key eyewitness in the real life Vadodara's *Best Bakery Case* that became emblematic of the destruction and killings that took place in the Gujarat riots and is discussed below. In what constitutes perhaps a climactic moment in the film, Aaliya, at the behest of Dev, comes forward before the police commission to expose the powerful rioters. She steps forward to reveal the names of the politicians and police officers who encouraged the rapes and murders of hundreds of Muslims, including members of her own family and friends. Aaliya's testimony represents a moment of complex subjectivity. It is not expressed exclusively through the lens of victimisation nor as a free agent exercising her freedom to complain about the violation of her individual rights. She is aware that her act is condemned by members of her own community who are convinced that no justice can be secured from a Hindu-dominated structure, process, and state, and that justice can only be attained through violent revenge. At the same time, members of the Hindu Right, including the chief minister of the state (mimicking the real life staunch Hindu nationalist Chief Minister of Gujarat, Narendra Singh Modi), seek to characterise her accusations, as well as Dev's efforts to bring the truth before a commission of inquiry, as further examples of the appeasement of minorities and a failure to recognise that the riots were simply an expression of anger on the part of Hindus against decades of oppression by the Muslim minority, who have refused to assimilate and are suspect because of their 'otherness'. Aaliya's complex subjectivity is constituted in and through the discourses of Hindu majoritarianism and Muslim religious identity. She epitomises the precarious location of the Indian Muslim and how 'otherness' is produced in and through the legal process.

The film ends with Farhan assuming his lawyerly robes to complete Dev's task of securing justice for the battered Muslim community. Dev himself is killed by his lifelong friend Tejinder, who is unable to comprehend Dev's defence of these 'traitors' and 'foreigners' whose holy land lies outside of India and whose loyalties are always suspect. Dev's murder exposes how justice does not find a neat and tidy resolution in and through the establishment of a commission of inquiry and an emphasis on prosecutions. The legal, political, and religious discourses of the Hindu Right that constitute the space, location, and subjectivity of Aaliya and the entire Muslim community remain unaddressed, and continue to proliferate even after such inquiries are brought to a close.

Dev becomes the point of departure for my discussion of the large-scale riots that took place in Gujarat in 2002. My discussion of the riots focuses on how they were cast as a justifiable act of self-defence by the Hindu majority against those who 'refused' to assimilate and were rendered suspect in terms of their fealty to the nation. The insider — the Indian Muslim — is portrayed an outsider, migrant, and foreigner, because of her refusal to abandon her cultural specificity. The remedy for the victims of these riots cannot be framed within a narrow understanding of justice, limited to a focus on the victim subject and repair through the criminal law process. The discussion reveals how the past informs the present and the future, and discursive practices that can transform the 'insider' into an 'outsider', the victim into a threat, which can themselves produce the large-scale traumas of the sort that took place in Gujarat.

Obtaining justice in the context of such large-scale trauma usually takes the form of prosecuting perpetrators for gross human rights violations and obtaining redress for the victims of horrific crimes (Crocker 1999; Orentlicher 1991: 2544). While the focus on 'gross human rights violations' in the form of killings, disappearances, custodial torture, and abductions/illegal imprisonment is important, the remedies remain legalistic and state-focused. What this focus leaves out is how the institutional arrangements and structures may be deeply implicated not only in the production of the violation of the harm in the first place, but also justify it. Legal solutions draw clear and straight lines between guilt and innocence, leaving a sense that the very state responsible for the violent ruptures is able to reincarnate and bring about reconciliation and repair.

This chapter focuses on how the harms experienced by the Muslim in the Gujarat riots cannot be remedied within the formal frameworks of law. Instead, there is a need to critically examine how injustices are normalised and the violence against the Muslim community, and Muslim women in particular, are partly produced in and through the legal, political, and religious discursive practices of the Hindu Right. The story of the Gujarat riots and subsequent efforts to address the harms and injuries through criminal law prosecutions do not pay attention to the institutional and discursive mechanisms within a democratic polity that can produce moments of extreme violence, moments that cannot be written off as aberrational and deviant. This chapter exposes how the riots were a logical product or outcome of a discursive strategy pursued partly in and through liberal rights discourse that represents the Muslim as an outsider or foreigner and a threat to the security of the state, and not in opposition to such rights.

The Hindu Right has deployed at least two discursive shifts to render Muslims as outsiders. The first is to pursue its majoritarian agenda in and through equality rights to argue in favour of 'sameness in treatment' and against special treatment for any community, in particular the Muslims (Kapur and Cossman 2001). This strategy is both logical and persuasive, and has come to constitute part of general common sense. It is also based on the Hindu Right's historical argument that the partition of the subcontinent and the formation of the separate states of India and Pakistan was the 'final solution' for Muslims. The second is to persist in complaints against Muslims as being constantly appeased through special treatment, including rights to their own personal law, educational institutions, and autonomy in Muslim majority states such as Kashmir, fomenting the ire of Hindus within the nation. Such special treatment is being conferred on a community who has not demonstrated its loyalties to the motherland. The Muslim is depicted as dangerous and foreign — a migrant and an alien from whom the honour and integrity of the Hindu nation and Hindu women must be protected. Gujarat symbolises the culmination of a strategy that justifies retribution for the oppression and violence inflicted by the (alien) Muslim minority on the Hindu majority, including its women, as an act of self-defence on behalf of Hindu women as well as the Hindu nation. I focus on this second strategy in the remainder of this chapter.

The ability to use rights discourse to pursue a deeply ideological agenda exposes how a project conceived in terms of progress and emancipation has a dark side. The so-called 'extraordinary violence' that took place within the context of Gujarat, resulting in the large-scale massacre of Muslims and rape of Muslim women, comes to be situated within the enabling conditions of normalised violence that is justified when articulated as self-defence against an external threat and foreigner. These conditions include the ideologies of Hindu majoritarianism built into dominant ideas of the nation-state and the historical predicament of Muslim minorities in India. Individual prosecutions and accountability, while important, do not address the broader discursive practices that produce the 'interiorised' outsider, that relegate Muslims to the margins, and justify their marginalisation. My concern is with the broader discursive framework that normalises extraordinary violence and its common sense appeal, and the way in which religious identity comes to determine 'otherness' — who belongs and who does not within the Indian state.

THE CONTEXT — HINDU MAJORITARIANISM

The Hindu Right is a contemporary right-wing religious and nationalist movement that is dedicated to the ideology of *Hindutva* — the establishment of India as a Hindu state. The Bharatiya Janata Party (BJP), the political wing of the Hindu Right, led the national coalition government between 1999 and 2004. The Rashtriya Swayamsevak Sangh (RSS), the main ideological component of the movement, was founded in 1925 (Embree 1994; Goyal 1979; Kanungo 2002). It has small training units (*shakha*s) operating throughout the country. These units hold ideological and combat training sessions on a daily basis. The training is a blend of physical exercises, martial arts, speeches and tales, songs and theatre, games, and organised sports. Each activity replicates the same message and sense of purpose in a different medium. They also run schools, leisure centres, cultural organisations, welfare societies, tribal and slum-level educational projects, and audio and video stations. They control temple networks, associations of priests, and *sadhu*s (holy men), and, as in the case of Gujarat, they sometimes rule over states. The Vishwa Hindu Parishad (VHP), the promoter of the religious ideology of the party (Chandra 1984; Pandey 1990), was founded in 1964 at the behest of the RSS, with the intention of infusing the politics of *Hindutva* with a specifically religious vision. Unlike the RSS, which functioned as an elite organisation, the VHP was intended to popularise *Hindutva* identity among 'the masses'. This phase of populism has been characterised by an increasingly extreme and violent anti-Muslim rhetoric which, in the contemporary period, has been repeatedly (and successfully) defended in the courts as an exercise of the right to free speech. The VHP's top leaders are all members of the RSS, and many are also members of the BJP. Other smaller bodies under the umbrella of the Hindu Right include the militant and virulently anti-Muslim Shiv Sena (SS — 'foot-soldiers of Lord Shiva') and the Bajrang Dal (BD — Hanuman Squad). The BD, the official youth wing of the VHP, was established in the mid-1980s. The BD is deployed primarily for vendettas and in what one scholar describes as 'tit-for-tat situations' (Sarkar 2002: 2874).

As discussed in Chapter 1, the basic precepts of the ideology of the Hindu Right are that Muslims and Christians are to be considered suspect because, unlike Hindus, their holy lands lie outside of India (Pandey 1990: 210). The Hindu Right has its basis in revivalist and nationalist movements of the nineteenth century, which sought to revitalise Hindu culture as a strategy for resisting colonialism. As it developed through the twentieth century, it began to take on its distinctively right-wing, anti-minority stance, particularly in the 1920s with the publication of Vinayak Damodar Savarkar's *Who is A Hindu?* ([1923] 1989) and the founding of the RSS. Savarkar developed the idea of *Hindutva*, a communal discourse, which seeks to constitute Hindu subjects to understand the fractured society in a particular way. A central paradoxical strategy of the Hindu Right is to install religion and culture as primary attributes of nationalism and national identity and, at the same time, deploy the discourse of secularism, free speech, and equality to pursue what is in fact an anti-secular agenda — that is, the establishment of a Hindu state. *Hindutva* is a call to unite against religious minorities; at best, it is a call to assimilate these minorities into the ostensibly more tolerant fabric of Hinduism and, in its more radical form, it is a call to simply destroy, purge, or incarcerate, as in the case of the response to the Bangladeshi Muslim migrant.

The Hindu Right works in and through the discourse of rights, including secularism, equality, and free speech, to pursue its religious and cultural vision. This vision is consistent with and corresponds to the ideology of *Hindutva* — the positing of the Muslim Other as a migrant and hence as suspect in terms of this subject's loyalty to the nation as well as constituting a threat to the security of the Hindu majority and the Indian nation. This strategy reflects how the Hindu Right is engaged in a discursive struggle in which they are attempting to establish *Hindutva* as ideologically dominant and consistent with liberal values. Through their collective efforts, they are seeking to naturalise the ideas of *Hindutva* by making these ideas a part of the 'common sense' of an increasingly large segment of Hindu society.

THE GUJARAT RIOTS: EXTREME POLITICAL VIOLENCE OR JUST COMMON SENSE?

In light of the ideological context and discussion of the politics of *Hindutva*, the riots in Gujarat cannot be understood simply as a law and order issue to be handled within the confines of the criminal justice process. Nor are alternative mechanisms designed to deal with gross human rights violations up to the task of addressing the ideological seepage that has occurred. The relationship of the riots with the prevailing notions of Muslims as outsiders, an understanding constructed in and through political as well as legal discourse, has simply become a part of common sense.

A central tool in producing such narratives includes the revising of educational texts in the state-run schools (Ramakrishnan 2002). The willingness to perpetrate such extreme violence against Muslim neighbours in Gujarat was partly nurtured through a conscious campaign to rewrite the educational curriculum through the standpoint of *Hindutva*. At the state level, textbooks in Gujarat encouraged students to view minority religious groups as foreigners, intent on colonising India, and who needed to be resisted.[3] The former Minister for Human Resource Development, Murli Manohar Joshi, a member of the RSS, sought to incorporate Vedic mathematics and astrology into the national educational curriculum during his tenure from 1999–2004. As discussed in Chapter 2, it is precisely those aspects of the elite Indian intellectual tradition, such as mathematics, highlighted by Amartya Sen to argue in favour of a 'genuine liberalism', which are being advocated by the Hindu Right to advance its *Hindutva* agenda.

The prevailing narrative of Hindus as victims who were expressing their suppressed anger persists in the statements of the Hindu Right in the post-Gujarat riots scenario. Narendra Singh Modi, a hardcore member of the RSS, framed the riots as an understandable expression of the anger of Hindus in response to the Godhra killings. The Godhra incident was narrated as the murder of Hindu martyrs by Muslim rioters and terrorists.[4] Modi stated that the killings in Gujarat were nothing more than a Newtonian law in action, a view that is founded on the belief that Muslims do not belong to India, in much the same way as Hitler thought the Jews did not belong in Germany and as white supremacists believe that non-whites do not have a right to live in countries ruled by whites (Narula 2003b; Tafadar and Khadijah 2002).[5] Similarly, a top leader of the BD in Gujarat expressed his belief that '[t]here was no rioting. This was just an expression of the way the majority community has felt . . . Most of the shops and establishment burned down do not belong to Hindus. People wanted their revenge for Godhra and they got it' (*The Hindu*, 3 May 2002; Noorani 2002: 12). Modi added that '[i]t wasn't merely a communal riot, but something like a mass agitation. There was already great anger against terrorism and anti-national activity. The Godhra episode symbolized that' (Aiyar and Mahurkar 2002; Noorani 2005: 50). While condemning the massacre, the RSS stated that the violent aftermath of Godhra was a 'natural reaction' (CCT 2002: 60). The RSS further pointed out in its all-Indian general council resolution that the real safety of Muslims lay 'in the goodwill of the majority' (ibid.: 60). Even the then Prime Minister endorsed this position, stating that the massacres in Gujarat were a direct fall-out of the Godhra killings. He asked: 'Who lit the fire? How did the fire spread?' (Vajpayee 2002). Thus, the killing of the Hindus in the train at Godhra was projected as a calculated and premeditated action on the part of the Muslim community in Gujarat and served as a reminder of the insecurity of Hindus within their own country.

The representation of the Hindus who were killed in Godhra as martyrs, and the Muslims as terrorists and rioters, was played out in several responses to the riots by both the state and the central government. Modi ordered that the victims of Godhra, who were Hindus, be awarded twice the amount of compensation than the Muslims who had been slaughtered in the subsequent rioting (CCT 2002: 77; Coalition Against Genocide 2005). Second, although over 1,000 Muslims were killed in the state, over 60 Muslims were arrested under the Prevention of Terrorism Act, 2002 (Human Rights Watch 2002: 50–51, 2004: 4–5).[6] Not a single Hindu was arrested or detained under these provisions (*The Hindu*, 26 October 2003). They were primarily detained under provisions of the Indian Penal Code (IPC) and innocuous sections such as violating curfew timings, where their rights to due process and a fair trial were assured (PUCL Interim Report 2002: Chapter 4). Indeed, the Godhra killings were used as an opportunity for the government to rush through the renewal of the Prevention of Terrorism Ordinance, which was due to expire in April 2002. The fact that only Muslims were arrested under its provisions in the context of the Gujarat riots spoke to the concerns that many human rights and civil liberties groups expressed during the debates on introducing such legislation — that it would be used against minorities and other groups that the government did not like or wanted to eliminate (Narula 2003a: 58). In the prevailing climate of the elusive and ill-defined 'war on terror', the Hindu Right had at hand the rhetoric and justification for enacting such legislation in the name of the security of the nation and protection of the citizens (Hindus) from the dangerous Others (Muslims).

THE BLIND PROLIFERATION OF JUSTICE

There has been intensive documentation of the violence and abuse that took place during the Gujarat carnage (Human Rights Watch 2002; PUCL Interim Report 2002). Reports suggest that the death toll resulting from the riots was as high as 2,000. In addition, the Indian government estimates that 98,000 more became refugees living in relief camps run by NGOs (Human Rights Watch 2002: 6), although NGO reports put the refugee numbers at 150,000. These refugees feared returning to their homes, knowing that they were regarded as members of a despised minority group (Human Rights Watch 2002: 59; McGivering 2002).

Several mechanisms have been set up to try and secure justice for the Muslims and specifically the women who experienced horrific violence during the Gujarat riots. The primary mechanism established to inquire into the Godhra incident and Gujarat riots was the 'fast track' court. The clear emphasis is on prosecution and conviction of those involved in the violence in order to demonstrate in the most visible way that action is being taken by the state to redress the harm experienced by a significant section of its citizenry. However, in one of the first cases to be decided by the court, *The Best Bakery Case*, which arose out of the killing of 14 people on the nights of the main riots in 2002, in a building named Best Bakery, the court acquitted all of the 21 accused (*State v. Baria*, (*Best Bakery Case*) No. 248/2002, Gujarat Fast Track Ct. June 27, 2003). Many of the key eyewitnesses turned hostile, refusing to repeat testimony that they had previously given to the police for fear that they would be subjected to reprisal. Subsequently, the National Human Rights Commission (NHRC) successfully petitioned the Supreme Court to set aside the High Court's orders of acquittal and secure a retrial of the case outside of Gujarat (*Human Rights Commission v. State of Gujarat*, Special Leave Petition (Criminal) of 2003 (India 2003)).

A commission of inquiry, the Nanavati Commission, was set up by the state government to investigate both the Godhra incident, as well as the subsequent riots, and place its recommendations before Parliament.[7] The establishment of commissions of inquiry is a part of a long tradition in India of investigating events that are catastrophic and demand redress.[8] Such commissions have not tended to provide justice in a substantive sense but rather, a short-term rule of law-oriented state action that does not provide long term redress to the victims. In September 2008 the commission delivered the first part of its findings specifically on the Godhra train carnage, concluding that it was a 'pre-planned conspiracy' and that the coaches were attacked by mobs of Muslims (Nanavati Commission of Inquiry 2008). The report contradicted the findings of the UC Bannerjee panel set up by the Railway Ministry, which had said that the fire was accidental. In its preliminary findings, the Commission exonerated Narendra Modi, as well as the state's law enforcement officials from any lapse in their handling of the riots.

Several non-government initiatives were also set up to investigate into the riots. These included two specific initiatives to investigate the gendered nature of the violence inflicted during the course of the Gujarat riots. One initiative consisted of an investigation undertaken by a six-member fact-finding team of women, which recorded the testimonies of minority women affected by the massacre (Citizen's Initiative 2002). The team recorded tales of brutal and horrific sexual violence and a specific targeting of the Muslim community, their homes and businesses; this constituted nothing short of genocide. Its recommendations focused primarily on ensuring that all those involved in the perpetration of acts of genocide and large-scale sexual violence be prosecuted regardless of their level of seniority in the political or police hierarchy. The second panel report of the International Initiative for Justice (IIJ) was prepared with the objective of securing justice for women harmed during the riots, guaranteeing their basic rights to citizenship as well as ensuring that democracy provided security to all (IIJ 2003).[9] The report mirrored the findings of the Citizen's Initiative, with the panelists drawing attention to the fact that the sexual violence and killings of Muslim women constituted genocide as increasingly recognised and defined in international law and jurisprudence (ibid.: 87–88).[10] The report also declared that *Hindutva* was a genocidal project and that sexual violence against Muslims was integral to this project (ibid.: 11). At the same time, the report acknowledged that reparation and justice in such a complex context would be difficult to secure, though recognition of the state's failure to prevent the massacres was nevertheless important. As the report pointed out, the Gujarat government has been careful not to use the word 'reparation', but rather 'assistance', 'aid', and 'relief', thus absolving it of any sense of entitlement or accountability to the affected citizen (ibid.: 72). The recommendations focused primarily on the international and legal mechanisms that needed to be applied to establish that the Gujarat riots constituted genocide and crimes against humanity and that the harms experienced by women had to be specifically addressed (ibid.: 117–20). The panelists also emphasised that justice for Muslim women had to be addressed separately from the justice to be secured for the community as a whole.

Another major independent non-governmental mechanism set up was the Concerned Citizen's Tribunal, consisting of eight eminent members from the country and constituted in consultation with a large number of groups within Gujarat and across the country (CCT 2002: 7).[11] The Tribunal's report acknowledged the particularly horrific nature of the sexual violence perpetrated against the Muslim community during the Gujarat riots (ibid.: 38–43). It stated that rape was used in the riots as an instrument for the 'subjugation and humiliation' of a community (ibid.: 38; Singh 2002). The Tribunal documented many of these cases in graphic detail, asserting that such violence in post-independent, democratic and secular India' is shocking and demands justice as well as reparations (CCT 2002: 43).

The Tribunal found that the state-sponsored crimes committed in Gujarat amounted to genocide and crimes against humanity (CCT 2002: 53).[12] It recommended that the central government enact legislation to 'implement the Genocide Convention, which India has signed and ratified', and 'use these measures to prosecute and punish all those who participated in the planning and the execution of murder, sexual violence, theft, and destruction in the state of Gujarat during the communal carnage' (ibid.: 169). It recommended that the Chief Minister and his ministerial colleagues be prosecuted under the relevant provisions of the IPC, POTA of 2002, and the Unlawful Activities Act, 2001 (ibid.: 162).[13] It further recommended that the activities of the VHP and the BD be curtailed and possibly banned for disturbing the law and order of a democratic country such as India (ibid.: 54). It also proposed that a reparations tribunal for victims be established to provide compensation for the loss every individual suffered during the violence, including the impact of sexual assault on women and their families (ibid.: 171).

On the issue of gender, the Tribunal recommended some long-term measures, including expanding the definition of rape. In situations of mass rapes and gang rapes, as occurred in Gujarat, it would be impossible to collect evidence and apprehend the rapists. In such situations, the Tribunal recommended that the onus of proof in all such cases of mass and gang rape rested on the accused and not the victims (CCT 2002: 177). The testimony of witnesses in cases where women were burnt or killed would be given considerable weight and the concept of justice in such cases would be widened (ibid.). According to the Tribunal, justice meant not simply 'punishment of those found guilty of the crime, but also . . . reparation for the women who suffered physical and mental injuries, since such assaults further curtail women's rights to be a part of mainstream social life, besides inflicting a damning long term impact on the coming generation' (ibid.: 178). The failure to protect the basic human rights of these citizens placed an obligation on the state to provide them with reparation. In addition, since all individual women were not in a position to register their complaints, the Tribunal recommended that reparation be provided to all women of the affected community (ibid.).

The trouble with each of the initiatives generated to provide justice to the victims, especially women, is that they have tended to focus on the victimisation of women and the community. These initiatives have focused almost exclusively on providing redress through the mechanisms of international legal instruments dealing with genocide as well as prosecutions under the criminal law at the domestic level. While these mechanisms have provided important forums for victims to give voice to the harms inflicted on them and form the basis for a historical record of the violence, it is not evident that they have addressed the broader discursive context in which the violence took place. This context constituted the Muslim as the outside perpetrator and the Hindu as an internal victim.

The nature of the violence inflicted on women in Gujarat seemed to be particularly brutal and sadistic.[14] As Flavia Agnes, a leading feminist activist who testified before the Nanavati Commission in June 2002, stated, the 'scale and extent of atrocities perpetrated upon innocent Muslim women during the recent violence ... far exceeds any reported sexual crime during any previous riots in the country in the post-independence period' (Agnes 2002: 71). Martha Nussbaum argues that the complete incineration even of the body can be explained in terms of the feminist conception of 'objectification' (Dworkin 1987; Nussbaum 2004a: 33). Nussbaum borrows from the account of misogynistic disgust sketched by Andrea Dworkin in her book, *Intercourse*, as well as in Nussbaum's own book, *Hiding from Humanity*, elaborating on this thesis of the presence of disgust and shame in law and its impact on women (Nussbaum 2004b). She argues:

> Objectification is treating as a mere thing what is really not a thing. It has multiple aspects, including the denial of autonomy and subjectivity and the ideas of ownership, fungibility (one is just like the others), and violability (it's all right to break the thing up or abuse it) . . . In the domain of human relations . . . sinister connections begin to be woven among these different aspects. At the heart of all of them, I would argue, is the idea of *instrumentality*: a thing, unlike a person, is an instrument or means to the ends of persons; it is not an end in itself. The objectification of women is primarily a denial that women are ends in themselves (Nussbaum 2004a: 34–35).

Nussbaum uses this account to present a more universal thesis about the psychological dynamics that are widespread in gender relations. In Gujarat, she explains, they took a 'particularly anxious and aggressive form in this concrete political context' (Nussbaum 2004a: 34). This instrumentalist analysis is used to explain why women are burnt, raped, abused, and killed, in other words, why they are violable. In the Gujarat riots, the Muslim female body represented the recalcitrant part of the nation that was yet to be dominated by Hindu male power. Although one response to domination might have been to abduct women and use them for procreation of the Hindu species, when viewed as instruments, their bodies could also be, and indeed were, used in horrific ways to satisfy the desire for power, honour, and security.

Nussbaum concludes that Muslim women in the Gujarat riots were victims of extreme violence and that the assault on the Muslim community as a whole constituted genocide. As she argues, the centrality of rape in the riots, usually followed by murder, was evidence of the intent to destroy the Muslim minority community in all of the ways specified under Article 2 of the UN Convention on Genocide.[15] She argues that the riots signalled a fundamental breakdown of the rule of law and promoted hate and fear. She relies on the recommendations of the Concerned Citizens' Tribunal for the trial and punishment of the main offenders as a mechanism for reconciliation, democratic consolidation, and restoration of faith in the law. She asserts that the politics of difference and the pluralism of Indian society must be restored, and can only be grounded in traditional notions of citizenship, equality, and rights (Nussbaum 2003: 15).

Yet, this instrumentalist analysis that seeks resolution in liberal rights once again misses a significant aspect of the Hindu Rights' agenda — its discursive strategy. The treatment of women in *Hindutva* politics is an extremely complex one and cannot be reduced either to simply vicious or barbaric behaviour on the part of men against women, or understood exclusively within the confines of a system of justice focused on individual human rights violations or through an instrumentalist analysis. While the NGO interventions and the participation of feminists in these mechanisms revealed a fairly sophisticated level of understanding about the nature of the violence inflicted on Muslim women, there continued to be a focus on the victimisation of the women, and the provision of redress primarily through the mechanisms of international legal instruments dealing with genocide as well as prosecutions under the criminal law at the domestic level. While important, these efforts failed to address the broader discursive practices of the Hindu Right and the ideology of *Hindutva* in constructing 'alien' subjects as well as producing the violence unleashed in Gujarat. The NGO initiatives accorded the victims of violence with a voice, but they did not fully address the broader discursive context in which the violence took place. This context constituted the Muslim as the outside perpetrator, the Hindu as an internal victim, and the violence inflicted against the Muslim community as a justified act of self-defence. In order to understand the nature of the violence that took place during the riots, it is important to return to the ideology of the Hindu Right and the broader discursive context that produced and normalised such violence through the construction of the Muslim man and woman as alien, and the Muslim man in particular as lustful and rapacious.[16]

Tanika Sarkar, a leading Indian historian, and one of the several feminists on the Concerned Citizen's Tribunal which investigated the events that took place in Gujarat, has drawn particular attention to the harm inflicted upon women. She argues that the preoccupation with destroying women's sexual organs revealed 'a dark sexual obsession about allegedly ultra-virile Muslim male bodies and over-fertile Muslim female ones, that inspire[s] and sustain[s] the figures of paranoia and revenge' (Sarkar 2002: 2874). The incitement to violence, which was in evidence in some of the literature discovered in the riot-torn areas, represented an anxiety about (Hindu) male sexuality, and the treatment of women resulting in acts of sadism that seemed to go beyond mere revenge (ibid.: 2875). Sarkar argues that the violence cannot be explained merely in terms of a collapse of state machinery, but rather as an example of the effective penetration of the ideology of the Hindu Right into state and grassroots institutions, including the police and hospitals. She counters arguments that blame the riots on the ineptness of the state government or the limitations of the BJP-led coalition at the centre. Instead, she insists that the Modi government and the Hindu Right have been spectacularly successful in pursuing their agenda. She states, 'What is happening in Gujarat is not a mark of weakness or inadequacy but a sign of the strength of the Sangh Parivar [the Hindu Right family], its firmness of resolve, its ideological consistency' (ibid.: 2872).

Modi's successful run at being elected as the Chief Minister of Gujarat for the fourth time in May 2009 is evidence of this strength. Moreover, according to Sarkar's analysis, the initiatives of the Tribunal, the arguments based on the objectification and victimisation of women, and a focus on reparation all tend to miss the broader ideological agenda and discursive aspects of the Hindu Right's strategy that have constituted the subjectivities of both the majority and minority, including the subjectivity of Muslim women. Sarkar does not simply focus on the incineration of the Muslim women's body. She argues that bodies, houses, shrines, and mosques disappeared overnight. In their place, roads were laid, and Hindu temples were built where Muslim homes used to be. Complete identities were erased. In the relief camps for those rendered homeless by the riots or too scared to return, they had 'neither documents nor identification papers of any sort to prove that they ever had property, jobs, bank balances, land, families, Indian citizenship' (Sarkar 2002: 2873). Muslim men and women were not only rendered homeless and displaced, overnight they were characterised as outsiders, foreigners, and non-citizens, while the identity of the Indian was simultaneously established as Hindu.

Sarkar explains that the riots and the horrific nature of the violence inflicted on Muslim women are ideologically consistent with the goals and concerns of *Hindutva*. Such concerns revolve around the increasing fertility rates of Muslims, the uncontrolled breeding and imminent outnumbering of the Hindu majority (Sarkar 2002: 2875). These concerns in turn stem from the erroneous assumption that the presence of polygamy among Muslims is responsible for higher fertility rates. Such myths and doubts fed the riots and the specific attacks on women and children and have become a part of 'common sense' thinking. The violence, in other words, was not aberrational. It was justified on the basis of a discursive strategy that has come to constitute Muslims as unacceptable, as foreigners, and as oppressors of the majority community. A related justification for the infliction of violence on women in the minority community is connected to the threat that the Muslim man poses to the Hindu woman. As discussed elsewhere, the nation is only secure if the honour of the Hindu woman is secure (Anand 2005: 206). In this process, emphasis is placed on the construction of Hindu masculinity. As Sarkar has argued, '[t]he hindu [sic] woman is given an externalized enemy to focus on that helps obliterate and displace personal and immediate experiences of oppression within the family' (Sarkar 1993: 23).

These layers of meaning are completely lost in a focus on the victim subject, an emphasis on prosecution, and an instrumentalist analysis of the violence inflicted on Muslim women. These also remain unaddressed in the proliferation of justice mechanisms designed to provide relief to women and the Muslim community. A reassertion of the values of liberty, equality, and secularism fails to appreciate how these very values have been used to pursue the ideology of *Hindutva* and assimilative politics that strip the Muslim of their cultural and religious identity or externalise this subject as a threat if they seek to retain their cultural and religious specificity. Even the broader analysis of the IIJ, which addresses the context within which the Gujarat riots took place and the role of women in the ideology of *Hindutva*, ends up describing *Hindutva* as a genocidal force, and thus once again situates the project outside of the very liberal values that actually helped to constitute the project, including the reconstitution of the Muslim subject as Other and outsider.

A response that attends to the injuries inflicted on Muslim women exclusively through the lens of victimisation, objectification, prosecution, and reparation does not address how the attack on Muslim women and men constitutes a central element in the discourse and ideology of the Hindu Right. Its fear of the Other breeding and multiplying its presence in India or raping and impregnating Hindu women finds no space in an instrumental analysis. Nor does it problematise the victimisation rhetoric and the gender and cultural essentialism that such an analysis produces (Kapur 2005: 95–136). The analysis ignores the complex understanding of the ways in which women's lives and experiences are mediated by religion and the history of the colonial encounter and the project of nationalism, amongst many other factors. Nor does it address the ways in which liberal rights discourse has produced and reinforced specific subjectivities in the hands of the Hindu Right, rather than serve emancipatory political goals. The analysis and recommendations do not assist in achieving the stated goal of justice — contributing to an alleviation or elimination of the violence experienced by Muslim women, *together* with Muslim men. Indeed, it may be missing the point altogether.

While the pursuit of justice in Gujarat is directed at pursuing rights in ways that will bring resolution and repair to victims of atrocious violence, it ignores how groups with less progressive agendas have appropriated and deployed the rights discourse in ways that have set the framework and context for the emergence of such violence. The Hindu Right has been quite successful in articulating its political agenda within the language of secularism and equality. At the same time, its vision undermines much of the prevailing understandings of these concepts. With regard to women, while the Hindu Right has articulated women's issues within the language of rights, it has also attempted to reinscribe women's traditional roles within the family. Simultaneously, it frames the Muslim as an alien threat, existing outside the values of liberal democracy — opposed to the principles of equality and secularism. The threat is manifested in terms of the sexual violence and rape of Hindu women perpetrated by Muslim men. Retributive violence against the Muslim community is justified because Muslims do not deserve due process or human rights protections, as they stand in opposition to these very protections. They are positioned along the same axis as the Bangladeshi migrant who is perceived almost exclusively in terms of being 'the enemy'. Further, Hindu men are justified in avenging the honour of their women. Rights discourse combined with familial discourse casts the violence as a normalised and natural outcome. The Hindu Right is pursuing a political agenda diametrically opposed to the agendas of progressive social and political movements, yet it has appropriated their languages and is operating in and through the language of rights.

The Layering of the Subject Position: Muslim Women and The Best Bakery Case

In light of the above analysis, I examine how the judiciary has dealt with the harms committed during the Gujarat riots, focusing on how the tensions between 'otherness' or foreignness and belonging play out for the Muslim woman in law. I specifically identify how this tension is located in the Gujarat riots through a discussion of the *Best Bakery Case* (State v. Baria, (*Best Bakery Case*) No. 248/2002 (Gujarat Fast Track Ct. June 27, 2003)), discussed earlier (*Best Bakery Case*, 2003: 11; Menon 2001). The judgment stated that it was proven beyond doubt that a 'violent mob had attacked the bakery and that the lives of 14 persons were lost . . . but the prosecution has not led any acceptable legal evidence to prove that the accused . . . had committed any such offences' (*Best Bakery Case* 2003: 9). The judgment was critical of the police delay in registering the first information reports of victims, not investigating the incident properly, and harassing innocent people. National and international newspapers reported that key witnesses in the case had lied in court out of fear for their lives as they had been given death threats.

Among the key witnesses who turned hostile was Zaheera Sheikh, the daughter of the bakery owner, who was killed in the attack. According to her original testimony to the police and the NHRC, 500 people armed with petrol bombs had attacked the bakery. She also accused the BJP and other party politicians of threatening and harassing witnesses into withdrawing their statements. Prior to her retraction, she was simultaneously portrayed by the state government as a liar and an unreliable witness while being heralded by NGOs and human rights groups seeking 'justice' in Gujarat as a 'star attraction', an anti-establishment heroine, lionised for 'taking on' the system.

The Supreme Court ordered a retrial of the case, and Sheikh decided to return as a key prosecution witness in the retrial. However, she once again retracted her statement in the retrial process, stating that the original judgment passed by the Gujarat trial court was correct (Bunsha 2004: 40–41). She claimed that all the statements she made were due to pressure exerted by her activist lawyer, Teesta Setalvad, who worked with the NGO Citizens for Peace and Justice. The Gujarat government, which had earlier portrayed Sheikh as a liar, promptly offered her complete state protection and special care and treatment.[17] For Sheikh, the pursuit of justice by the NGO could not bring an end to the communal discourse, majoritarian politics, and constant representation of the Muslim as the 'enemy' and 'traitor'. Her alignment with the Hindu Right ultimately exposes the tension between the assimilative gestures on which justice can be secured, and the exclusive impact of liberal democratic politics and the rule of law.

After she turned hostile, the social justice groups presented Sheikh as a mere victim, a pawn, whose right to justice had to nevertheless be pursued if the Muslim community was ever to find faith in the Indian body politic, the legal process, and as citizens of the country. They sought to rescue and rehabilitate her and restore the faith of the Muslims in the rule of law. Yet this position utterly failed once again to address the broader discursive context within which the real Zaheera Sheikh had to live and survive. It is this discursive context that presented her with the choice either between her identity as a Muslim, that is, as an outsider, peripheral, and foreign, and hence vulnerable as a Muslim woman in a Hindu-dominated state, or to align with the Hindu community in order to ensure her safety and right to life.

The riots were projected as an aberration by the Hindu Right and Sheikh as a victim of vicious anti-Hindu hate propaganda. The Hindu Right had the power to transform her from a liar and enemy of the state into a victim of Muslim-run organisations and anti-Hindu advocates. As long as she remained allied to the Hindu majority, her security was assured. Late in 2004, Sheikh was ousted from the Muslim community on the grounds that she was constantly lying. This decision received the endorsement of the Muslim personal law board.[18] She was regarded as a traitor and ostracised from her religious community, subsequently being sentenced to one year in prison for perjury by the Supreme Court, after being indicted by a Supreme Court-appointed committee 'as a "self-condemned liar" falling to "inducements" by "certain persons" to give "inconsistent" statements during the trial of the case'.[19] While nine people were finally convicted of murder in the retrial of the *Best Bakery* case, Zaheera's fate remained intricately linked with the politics of Hindu majoritarianism.[20]

CONCLUSIONS

It is imperative that the story of the Gujarat riots is not reduced to one of mere victimisation of a minority section of Indian citizens. Such a linear and monochromatic analysis evades the discursive struggle that has been taking place both within as well as outside of the legal arena over who constitutes the authentic Indian subject, the location of women within that struggle, and representation of the Other in liberal rights discourse as invariably different — someone who must either be tamed or assimilated through some form of cultural strip. Refusal to conform is either treated as an immutable condition or, as in the case of the discourse of the Hindu Right, regarded as an 'Other', foreign, and threatening, such that incarceration and even elimination are justifiable in the interests of the security of the nation or to protect liberal democracy and the rule of law from that which has no regard for it and threatens to destroy it.

This is not to suggest that the Hindu Right has been a strong advocate of the democratic process. Indeed, Golwalkar, second chief of the RSS and main ideological exponent of the Hindu Right's politics, had a particular disdain for democracy. However, when India gained independence and adopted a Constitution based on adult universal franchise, regardless of religion, gender, caste, and class, such positions were muted. In the contemporary period, the BJP has formulated a strategy for engaging with rights discourse. Its agenda is not being pursued in opposition to the constitutional principles of secularism and equality, but rather in and through them. The Muslim is thus constructed as utterly Other or an outsider, who must either assimilate or be incarcerated or annihilated if he fails to conform. Both responses are justified; the former in and through liberal rights discourse of equality which emphasises sameness, and the latter by constructing the Muslim as existing outside the norms of liberal democracy and values, and hence needing to be contained or even eliminated (Porras 1995). This general sentiment of Hindus as oppressed is then followed by increasingly brutal rhetoric that calls on Hindus to fight back against these Muslim oppressors and often expressly calls for violent confrontation. This rights approach is pursued together with the promotion of a militant *Hindutva* and a militaristic nationalism by the RSS, as well as a popularisation of *Hindutva* by the VHP amongst exploited social groups.

The various forums set up to examine the bloody riots that took place in Gujarat in 2002 and investigate claims that the police and political machinery played a critical role in permitting the unleashing of horrendous violence against the Muslim minority community functioned with complete fealty to the norms and tenets of the liberal notions of justice and resolution. The ultimate function of initiatives such as the Nanavati Commission is to report on its findings, and for the government to take action, if any, on the commission's recommendations. There is no doubt that the commission and comparable forums are benignly positive in providing an important space where victims can voice their grievances and receive powerful forms of redress for those who have experienced such horrific carnage. They serve as forms of repair to the damage inflicted on the psyche of the minority community in India. However, this chapter has focused on how the layering and complexity of the subjects' position are absent in these initiatives. The pursuit of justice is narrowly defined and does not address the normative aspects of these struggles. It deals only with immediate justice and facts, but does not consider the broader discursive context in which the issues of communalism and majoritarianism have emerged. It is this history that defines the Muslim as an alien (so how can they be victims?), as oppressing the majority (read Hindu) community (so how can they claim to be persecuted?), and as threatening to the security of the nation-state and liberal democracy (hence not entitled to the same protections and notions of justice that apply to the liberal subject).

This brings me back to the story of Zaheera Sheikh and the Gujarat riots. By situating her almost exclusively as a victim, as the social justice groups and NGOs did, merely addressed the immediate, individual harm or injury she suffered or experienced. But they failed to engage with this broader discursive construction of Muslim and Hindu subjectivity in the discourse of the Hindu Right and how these subjectivities have come to be embedded in law. Justice in Gujarat cannot be limited to the violence that erupted during those few days in March 2002. It needs to consider much more: the discursive contest that produced this kind of violence and the subjectivities of the different communities. It must broaden its lens of inquiry to understand how ordinary common sense is linked to the extraordinary infliction of political violence. The riots were not simply a vicious expression of uncivilised hoards. They were an expression produced as a result of the successful discursive battle waged by the Hindu Right, partly in and through law.

Neither the terms of the commission nor the court cases addressed the role of rights discourse in producing this event. The various responses to the victims of the Gujarat riots focused on the gross human rights violations, addressing them within the framework of criminal law or international human rights claims. While this approach draws attention to the horrifying nature of the violence, it also tends to distort and individualise the abuse. It tends to treat the violence as an aberration, as outside the terms of liberalism and liberal rights. It also limits the range of victims and those who are accountable. As discussed in this chapter, this approach masks the deeper ideological and discursive practices that have constructed the insider as outsider, and produced the context within which the so-called gross violations take place. For example, by focusing on the killings, abuses, and disappearances, the various mechanisms set up to inquire into the riots continuously failed to address the structural and ideological factors that have produced the alien, foreigner, and migrant location of Muslim minorities in India, which has been used to justify the violence inflicted on them. A focus on individual acts of human rights abuse cannot capture this broader canvas (Nessiah and Keenan 2004: 272–81). Such mechanisms need to move beyond the simple formula of focusing on the guilt and innocence of the different parties involved and address the broader systemic and ideological context that enables exclusion and justifies such extraordinary violence. The Gujarat riots need to be located in the context of the enabling conditions of *Hindutva* and its anti-Muslim ideology. The ideologies of majoritarianism, as well as the colonial legacies that drove an arbitrary wedge between these communities, have increasingly defined the meanings of equality, secularism, and the right to free speech in India. Justice for victims must move well beyond the narrow reading of rights and justice as well as a legalistic, victim-focused, and state-oriented approach.

Coming back to the discussion of *Dev* with which this chapter began, the film itself was subject to the very discursive practices that this chapter addresses in the context of the Gujarat riots. The film was protested against in Gujarat at the moment of its general release. One resident from a small town in Gujarat filed a case against the director for making a film that threatened to ignite communal clashes between two communities. The complainant requested an injunction against the screening of the film in any part of the country, 'either by himself, through his agents or distributors; or even on television' (Pandya 2004). The fact that the film was challenged in the state that was still under the stewardship of Narendra Modi, the Chief Minister and RSS sympathiser, was not a coincidence.

After the defeat of the Hindu Right wing-led government in May 2004, the suit was dropped before the court heard arguments and the new government granted permission to screen the film on 26 January 2005, India's National Republic Day, on the state-run television channel. It was hailed by human rights and social justice groups as a move to restore the minority community's faith in liberal democracy. And yet, the election of Modi for the fourth consecutive time as Chief Minister of Gujarat in May 2009 and the findings of the Nanavati commission of inquiry in 2008 on the Godhra train incident serve as constant reminders to the entire Muslim community of the injustices of 2002, of its own outsider, alien status, and the fact that the ideological edifice of the Hindu Right remains intact.

NOTES

1. K. C. Sudarshan, the former appointed leader (*sarsanghachalak)* of the Rashtriya Swayamsevak Sangh (RSS) (Association of Nationalist Volunteers), the ideological component of the Hindu Right, stated that every citizen in India is a Hindu, for Hinduism is a way of life and not a religion (PTI 2002).
2. The PUCL report discusses how some residents of Sama appealed to the Councillor of their region for assistance, but the Councillor claimed he could not do anything. The Councillor

   > ranted at length about the unpatriotic and criminal nature of the Muslim community (such as for instance their habit of abducting Hindu girls), and dwelt on the desirability of Muslims going and living in "their own areas." He also produced a list which, he explained, showed the voting patterns . . . in the most recent assembly bye-election, and how Muslim localities had voted against the BJP. On being repeatedly asked whether he could assure that there would be no further violence in the area, he replied that he could not do so, and one of his associates explained that what had happened that day (Feb. 28th) was "only a sample," and that it was best to be prepared for what would follow the next day. (PUCL Interim Report 2002: Annexure 2)

3. The Human Rights Watch report on the Gujarat riots states that the goal of the RSS was to introduce anti-minority propaganda onto the streets and inside the classrooms (Human Rights Watch 2002); S. Narula analyses the implications of the 'communalisation' of India's educational system by the Hindu Right (Narula 2003b).

4. Modi is a *pracharak*, or regional leader, within the RSS hierarchy. This position requires him to be celibate, without any ties of family or job, and immerse himself totally in the work of organising, teaching, and disseminating the values of the Hindu Right. It is a life dedicated to spreading the message of hate (Sarkar 2002: 2875).
5. Modi's claims about the Jews are inspired by Golwalkar's position that 'To keep up the purity of the Race and its culture, Germany shocked the world by her purging the country of the semitic Races—the Jews. Race pride at its highest has been manifested here. Germany has shown how well nigh impossible it is for Races and cultures, having differences going to the root, to be assimilated into one united whole, a good lesson for us in Hindustan to learn and profit by' (Golwalkar 1947: 43).
6. The Prevention of Terrorism Act (POTA) was repealed by the United Progressive Alliance (UPA) coalition in 2004 and replaced by the Unlawful Activities (Prevention) Amendment Act, 2004 (UAPA). The repeal of POTA does away with some of the bail and confessions provisions that had the effect of eroding the personal liberties of the accused as well as violating the rights to due process (Jayanth 2004). However, the provisions dealing with the definition of terrorist acts, banning of terrorist organisations, and interception of electronic communication are all retained under the UAPA of 2004. A specially constituted Review Committee is to sift through the cases filed under the POTA, identify those where trials should continue as if the act existed, and drop charges in all cases where there is evidence of the misuse of the POTA (Mohapatra 2004; PUDR 2004: 4).
7. Commissions of inquiry are set up under the terms of the Commissions of Inquiry Act, No. 60 of 1952. On 6 March 2002, the Commission of Inquiry was constituted by the state government, led at that time by the BJP, to conduct an investigation into the Godhra incident. Subsequently, Nanavati was appointed the Chairman of the Commission, and its terms were expanded to investigate the riots that took place in Gujarat in 2002 as well. The commission has received over 3,000 affidavits from riot victims, which have included allegations that the police and government machinery were involved in provoking the riots (Narula 2003a: 26–27).
8. A recent famous example is the report of the Nanavati Commission on the 1984 anti-Sikh riots submitted to the government in February 2004, concluding its inquiry into the riots that erupted following the assassination of former Prime Minister Indira Gandhi, where hundreds of Sikhs were slaughtered in what was viewed as an act of retaliation for the assassination. The Commission suggested that a number of sitting members of parliament belonging to the Congress Party, led by Sonia Gandhi, were involved in orchestrating the riots and made recommendations regarding compensation to the victim's family (*The Hindu* 2005).
9. The panelists on the International Initiative for Justice (hereafter IIJ), included Sunila Abeysekara, Director of Inform, Colombo, Sri Lanka; Rhonda Copelon, Professor of Law, City University of New York and Director, International Women's Human Rights Law Clinic; Annisa Helie, Women Living Under Muslim Law, UK; Gabriela Mischkowski, historian and co-founder of Medica Mondiale, Germany; Nira Yuval-Davis, Professor of Gender and Ethnic Studies

at the University of Greenwich, UK; Uma Chakravarti, feminist historian, Delhi University; Vahida Nainar, Researcher of International Law, board member, Women's Initiative for Gender Justice, The Netherlands and board member, Women's Research and Action Group, Bombay; Farah Naqvi, co-founder of *Nirantar*, and independent writer and consultant on issues of women, democracy, and development; and Meera Vellayudan, Institute for Environmental and Social Concerns, Coimbatore. The panel was constituted to address the issue of gender violence in Gujarat in the context of the following:

- An understanding of sexual violence against women and how this can be effectively addressed by a legal system not equipped to deal with crimes of this nature and scale.
- The historical context of the Indian subcontinent, where divisions along religious community and caste lines, along with the rise of Hindu fundamentalism, have led to immense violence, intolerance, and divisiveness.
- The globalised representation of the Muslim as a terrorist worldwide and the alliances and attacks that this has fostered over the various Muslim communities all over the world.

10. Elements Annex of the Rome Statute of the International Criminal Court art. 6(b) n.3, PCNICC/2000/I/Add.2 & PCNICC/2000/Add.2 (July 17, 1998); see also Prosecutor v. Kovac et al.; Prosecutor v. Akayesu; Prosecutor v. Delalic; Prosecutor v. Furundzija.
11. The members of the Tribunal included V. R. Krishna Iyer and P. B. Sawant, both retired Justices of the Supreme Court of India; Hosbet Suresh, retired judge of the Bombay High Court; Aruna Roy, Magasaysay Award winner for community leadership; K. G. Kannabiran, senior counsel in the Karnataka High court; K. S. Subramaniam, former Director General of Police; Ghanshyam Shah, Professor of Political Science at Jawaharlal Nehru University, New Delhi; and Tanika Sarkar, Professor of History, Jawaharlal Nehru University.
12. The current Congress-led coalition government has begun work on drafting a comprehensive law against communal violence. The Prevention of Genocide and Crimes Against Humanity Act of 2004 is to include provisions for investigations by a central agency, prosecution by special courts, and uniform compensations to victims.
13. These recommendations were submitted prior to the repeal of the POTA.
14. There were innumerable reports of rapes and mutilations of women (CCT 2002: 39–43, 177–178; CPI(M) and AIDWA 2002; Hameed et al. 2002; IIJ 2003). Many women were gang-raped by public officers and rioters before being burned alive (Hameed et al. 2002; Human Rights Watch 2002: 16, 27–29; IIJ 2003). Even the police physically, verbally, and sexually abused women, paraded them through the streets, and beat them (PUCL Interim Report 2002: 6). Many of the survivors of these abuses have testified before the Nanavati commission set up to investigate into the riots.
15. Article 2 of the Convention defines genocide as 'any of the following acts committed with intent to destroy, in whole or in part, a national, ethnical, racial or religious group, as such: (a) Killing members of the group; (b) Causing serious bodily or mental harm to members of the group; (c) Deliberately inflicting on the group conditions of life calculated to bring about its physical destruction in whole

or in part; (d) Imposing measures intended to prevent births within the group; (e) Forcibly transferring children of the group to another group.' (Convention on the Prevention and Punishment of the Crime of Genocide, Dec. 9, 1948, 78 U.N.T.S. 277, http://www.unhchr.ch/html/menu3/b/p_genoci.htm).

16. I do not address the manner in which the issue of sexual violence is constituted within a communalised discourse that implicates the honour of Hindu women as it is beyond the scope of this chapter. Rape is understood in the ideology of the Hindu Right not as a violation of an individual woman's right to bodily autonomy, but rather, in a more traditional and patriarchal discourse, as a violation of a woman's honour. This honour is in turn closely associated with a family's honour and the honour of the broader community. As Amrita Basu has observed, '[t]he BJP has made the raped Hindu woman symbolic of the victimization of the entire Hindu community' (1993: 25–29). This communal discourse further provides women within the Hindu Right with a legitimate focus for their personal and political anger about sexual violence.
17. 'Zaheera is under Vadodara Police Protection: Commissioner,' Rediff on the Net, 4 November 2004. http://in.rediff.com/news/2004/nov/04best.htm. Accessed 18 September 2009.
18. 'Majlis-e-Shura declares Zaheera an outcast,' Rediff on the Net, 24 December 2004. http://in.rediff.com/news/2004/dec/24best.htm. Accessed 18 September 2009.
19. 'Zaheera Sheikh a "Self Condemned Liar": SC Panel', PTI, 30 August 2005. http://www.expressindia.com/fullstory.php?newsid=53608. Accessed 18 September 2009; 'Supreme Court Panel Calls Zahira a Liar', Rediff on the Net, 29 August 2005. http://www.rediff.com/news/2005/aug/29best.htm. Accessed 5 July 2009.
20. 'Best Bakery Case: 9 Accused Convicted', Rediff on the Net, 24 February 2006. http://in.rediff.com/news/2006/feb/24gujarat.htm. Accessed 18 September 2009.

7

Conclusion: Insurrectional Subjects

In the closing segment of the film *Traffic Signal,* with which this book began, the audience witnesses Silsila being hauled off in a police van, being mobbed by his supporters and claiming that he will find justice for the community in a court of law. While law is hailed as a place of justice and redress, the preceding chapters have illustrated how it is also a discursive space which constitutes, regulates, includes and excludes, and disciplines. Belonging and non-belonging are determined not simply by the formal processes of law, such as citizenship, but by the dominant normative assumptions about the legal subject, in this case, the female migrant subject, that set the terms of inclusion as well as exclusion. While the female migrant is able to expose and disrupt these normative boundaries, her transgressions also tell us a good deal about the role of the law.

The formal as well as normative borders that regulate and constitute the migrant subject in law are exposed as sites of tension and contest. They implicate struggles over the way in which the Indian state is conceived and understood, including the gender and religious ascriptions that inform the state's identity. Legal interventions by the Indian state reveal a level of ambiguity about the migrant subject that is informed by a history where geographical borders were not solely constitutive of the nation. The territorial, material, and normative borders of the postcolonial nation have been constantly challenged by the migrant subject ever since its formation, rendering its identity indistinct and incomplete. This uncertainty is addressed through more rigid assertions of the borders that demarcate or distinguish the citizen from the migrant, where even insiders, such as bar dancers, sex workers, and Muslims are rendered suspect, untrustworthy, and alien through dominant ideological and normative structures. These borders are framed against dominant narratives about women as upholders of the nation's integrity, relegating their roles to within the private sphere, as well as the framing of the Muslim as 'Other' and outsider, who is a potential traitor and terrorist. While these positions are most stridently asserted by the Hindu Right, they have become both naturalised and universalised in legal discourse and inform the politics and advocacy of many progressive scholars and advocates alike. These normative assumptions have come to inform the national common sense though they are constantly contested by the migrant subject inside as well as outside of law. These contests emerge partly through the migrant's claims to belonging and legitimacy, which not only continue to produce anxieties and resistance, but also expose the deep fissures that remain present within the nation.

The non-legal discursive sites in which the makeshift migrant is produced are significant in determining some of the legal responses to this subject. For example, global economic expansion has created a demand for migrants, in particular, female migrants. Yet the sexual division of labour and dominant sexual, familial, and cultural norms filter the legal regulation of such movement. In the current moment of economic globalisation there has been an expansion of the informal sectors of the economy that has fostered an increase in the labour force participation of women especially in the reproductive sphere. This inclusion has challenged the construction and identity of the nation as well as class relations, without necessarily resulting in the reconstitution of gender relations between sexes. Women continue to be relegated into the tasks of reproduction and the domestic arena. When they do participate in non-reproductive arenas, such as sex work, their work is subject to more intense moral and sexual scrutiny, which invariably renders them less entitled to rights and access to justice.

Anti-trafficking discourses also demonstrate how the legal regulation of the female migrants plays out. The discussion reveals how anti-trafficking interventions continue to conflate consensual and non-voluntary movement, as well as sex work, with sexual exploitation or sexual violence. The subjectivity of the female migrant gets dismembered through legal discourse and objectified within the realms of criminality, violence, and containment. The tension between her desire to move and the protective instincts of both state and some non-state actors highlights how her subjectivity remains contested and this tension remains present in legal discourse. While many well-intentioned human rights and social activists continue to foreground the image of the battered sexual subject in the post-colonial world, such images stand in contrast to the fact that women continue to choose to move through clandestine routes when safe legal routes remain unavailable.

The sexual and cultural stereotypes invented during the colonial period continue to be reproduced in the legal regulation of migrant women. The idea that women are victims of a horrific culture that is mechanical, timeless, and immutable persists and continues to inform anti-trafficking laws. These ahistorical narratives about the sexual and cultural 'Other' lie at the centre of the critique of scholarship on 'Third World' women by American and European scholars. In brief, the continuing political and economic domination by 'First World' countries of former colonies informs western feminist discourse on the 'status of women' in other societies and keep it focused on the cultural nature of women's oppression. These cultural discourses generate a static image of an oppressed woman in the postcolonial context, devoid of any economic, political, or historical analysis — a somewhat mindless universalism. My analysis illustrates how it is impossible to address issues of female migration and women's sexuality through such a myopic position. It obscures the complex web of shifting, multiple relations made up of race, ethnicity, and Empire that continue to discursively inform the postcolonial present and the female migrant's subjectivity (Eisenstein 2004; Liddle and Rai 1998: 497–98).

As is evident from the anti-trafficking debates, women's sexuality remains a contested site for fixing competing discourses. Women are fixed with an unproblematic identity that is inscribed in culturally materialist practices and institutionalised structures. The female body enables the discourse of curtailment and containment (Campbell 1992: 79). The production of this stable identity requires the casting of certain elements of the body, such as sexuality, into a 'defiling otherness' (Butler 1990: 133–34). Such a move enables the body to become naturalised and immobilised. Yet, as J. Butler argues, the body is performative and gender 'tenuously constituted in time' and through the process of repetition (ibid.: 140–41). And resistance is produced at the very point where relations of power are exercised (Foucault 1980: 142). Law born of violence and projected as force operates along trajectories of regulations, prohibitions, and penalties, designed to monitor, deter, and punish. In the context of the female migrant these prohibitions operate partly along the fault lines of normative sexuality — marital, non-commercial, and heterosexual. Yet legal prohibitions, as expressions of power, are productive in contradictory ways. These very attempts to contain the female migrant have set the stage for the resistive subject, the insurrectional subject, who has been rendered visible and active partly because of the impact of the mechanisms that are designed to specifically exclude her. For example, while the body of the sex worker remains a site of regulation and discipline, it also produces resistive practices that move beyond the focus of disciplinary surveillance. As a result, legal prohibitions can bring to the fore the very subject they seek to actually curtail, silence, or incarcerate. The migrant subject is brought into the public domain and invested with subjectivity through the very acts of prohibition and punishment.

Much like anti-trafficking laws, citizenship laws have also been deployed to deny protections to the migrant. Such denial is not necessarily premised on whether the migrant has formal legal citizenship status. Nor can the problems encountered by the migrant be resolved primarily within the realm of formal citizenship. As the discussion of the bar dancer's case indicates, citizenship is constructed through a register of sexual, familial, and cultural norms.

As briefly stated in the preceding chapters, there is an abundance of critical scholarship on the limitations of a classical understanding of citizenship as well as on how to move beyond citizenship in a globalised world. One strand of scholarship has put forth an alternative conception of citizenship, one that is denationalised and articulated in more universal terms. Such positions are expressed in terms of 'global', 'world', or 'transnational' citizenship, and argue that the conferment of rights and benefits on human beings, regardless of their citizenship status, constitutes part of our moral obligation (Featherstone 2002; Linklater 1998; Nussbaum, 1996; Young, 1989). One version of this argument, developed in the context of the stateless individuals, proposes a model of formal global citizenship that flows from the concept of dual or multiple nationalities and exists in tandem with national citizenship, based on the idea of the universality of human rights (Hernandez-Truyol and Hawk 2005). Another proposal argues in favour of a 'world citizen', based on the metaphor of expanding concentric circles, the outermost being humanity as a whole, or the notion of a *polis* extending around the globe (Featherstone 2002; Nussbaum 1996). While a comprehensive analysis of these debates is beyond the scope of this book, it is not at all self-evident that appeals to human rights bound to conceptions of a 'global' or 'world' citizen would inevitably rescue or benefit the migrant or unlawful non-citizen and accord her a recognition that transcends the monopoly power of nation-states to determine who counts and who does not. As some scholars have argued, the idea of global citizenship is invariably a call made from within the western academia and 'is inextricably linked to the West's long and torturous history of engaging in overzealous civilising-cum-universalising missions in the non-Western world' (Bowden 2002: 350).

Revisiting the colonial encounter is critical in order to understand the limitations and possibilities of newer projects formulated around conceptions of global or world citizenship. These new universal projects have often denied the reality of those whom they claim to represent and speak for, disclaiming their histories and imposing another's through hegemonic moves. For example, the search for a standard to both explain and justify exclusion of non-European subjects from international law in the nineteenth century was based on the prevailing, and uninterrogated, assumption that European states were civilised. They were similar to the *polis* that constituted the centre of gravity from which all good values emanated. In order to gain entry into the community of international law and family of civilised nations, outside communities had to strive to resemble the European. Yet that standard remained an elusive one (Anghie 2005: 32—114; Kennedy 2004; Koskenniemi 2002: 98–178). It was a standard that was unattainable, for no matter how hard the native struggled to mimic the European at the cost of her own subjectivity, the non-European remained, at most, 'almost white, but not quite' (Bhabha 1994: 15). Similarly, there is now considerable scholarship demonstrating how human rights have emerged from the same liberal tradition that not only incorporates arguments about freedom and equal worth, but also incorporates conceptions of civilisation, cultural backwardness, and racial and religious superiority. Human rights remain structured by this history (Baxi 2002; Douzinas, 2007; Kapur 2006; Nessiah, 2003). This dark side is intrinsic to human rights, rather than something that can be resuscitated and refashioned in terms such as that of a global or world citizen.

Apart from the limitations of human rights discourse as providing a remedy to the migrant, citizenship has already acquired a global guise in the emergence of a neoliberal citizen. Wendy Brown argues that neoliberalism is becoming as dominant as governmentality and may emerge as the dominant ideology where privatisation schemes and a flourishing market economy become the measure of democracy (2005: 37–50). This formation is global though constructed through local manoeuvres such as corporate-owned media or schools (ibid.).

It is also a formation that is established partly through the production of a neoliberal citizenry, where individuals are entrepreneurial actors across all dimensions of their lives.

The neoliberal citizen is generally defined as someone who has earned her rights and for whom duties necessarily precede rights. This stands in contrast to classic liberal notions of citizenship that have focused on rights, and on the idea that every individual enjoys rights regardless of the duties performed or not performed on her part. This tradition places an obligation on the state to ensure the protection of the rights of the citizen, including social and economic rights. But the welfare regimes ostensibly set up to promote the basic social security of citizens have faced continuous erosion in the context of neoliberalism, which discourages the dependency of the individual on the state. This has led to an emphasis on duties, the performance of which is a condition for rights. The role of the state has thus shifted to one of ensuring the freedom necessary for self-reliance and intervening only vis-à-vis those who are incapable of meeting their citizenship obligations through the market (Kabeer 2005: 17).

There is evidence that citizenship in India is being increasingly shaped by the global economic enterprise, where the primary attributes of the citizen are as a consumer or entrepreneur. The emergence of the neoliberal citizen in India is both similar to as well as distinct from its western counterpart. In the context of postcolonial India, the rise of the neoliberal citizen has taken a unique form in relation to the more affluent migrants, or what are more popularly described as non-resident Indians. The Indian government has enabled overseas Indians to acquire dual nationality, a move that is primarily intended to tap into the wealth of the non-resident Indian and provide an incentive to invest in one of the world's most rapidly growing economies (Ministry of External Affairs 2002: 510). They constitute the diaspora of the country, who are usually businessmen, capital-oriented, and defined in terms of their market success. They have also simultaneously performed their duties as the 'sons' and 'daughters' of the motherland, and have demonstrated their loyalty and reliability. The normative criteria of family, loyalty, and devotion are constantly invoked in order to tie these disparate elements and entities to the motherland. These attributes have earned them the right to claim citizenship from the homeland, though this claim also comes with expectations of increased investment in the homeland

and corporate success. Formal legal status is not relevant here. While the overseas Indian citizen does not have the right to vote (as yet), what is of importance is the forging of umbilical ties between this non-resident and the motherland through the mode of financial and economic investment. The overseas Indian represents and is invited to more intimately participate in India's arrival as a significant market player and promoter of neoliberal market ideology. This appeal to the non-resident Indian is also packaged and sold in and through the discourse of culture and religion. 'They live in different countries, speak different languages and are engaged in different pursuits. What gives them their common identity is their Indian origin, their cultural heritage, their deep attachment to India' (ibid.: 2).

This deterritorialising move is consistent with the cultural conception of Indian citizenship. Proof of Indian lineage, that is, evidence that parents or grandparents were born in India, is still an absolute requirement. The new scheme specifically excludes any person who was ever a citizen of Pakistan or Bangladesh from acquiring Indian citizenship, thus retaining the notion of Indian-ness/Hindu-ness that was made explicit in the *Sonowal* case. The new amendments also specifically exclude 'illegal migrants' from rights to citizenship, providing that citizenship by birth can accrue to a person born in India only where both of her parents are citizens of India or one of her parents is a citizen of India and the other is not an illegal migrant at the time of her birth. This new classification explicitly incorporates the fear articulated in both the *Sonawal* and the bar dancers' cases, and is reinforced in the claims of the Hindu Right that the Bangladeshi Muslim migrant is not only a threat to the security of the nation, but is equally threatening to the purity and identity of the Indian (read Hindu) nation. Bangladeshi migrants are treated as law and order problems because of the ostensible threat they pose to the Indian (Hindu) state. Right-wing forces, such as the Hindu Right, have been able to attach their agendas to such logic to render unstable even Muslims who reside within the country, regardless of their citizenship status. Their loyalties are rendered suspect and their failure to surrender their cultural identities make them vulnerable to suspicion and targets of horrific violence. While Indian-ness derives its origins from the colonial encounter and resistance to colonial rule, it remains germane in the contemporary environment in the context of neoliberalism and market ideology.

The neoliberal citizen in India stands in contrast to those who, while formally recognised as citizens, do not have access to the full spectrum of rights to which citizens are presumably entitled, primarily because of their subaltern status. While it is unlikely that neoliberal citizens will displace the rights-seeking subject, what remains evident is that the subaltern migrant's route to the full enjoyment of citizenship is normatively determined. As made explicit in the bar dancer's case as well as the discussion on the economic and moral regulation of the migrant subject, their rights are contingent on a register of sexual, cultural, and familial norms. Their roles as market actors, workers, and sexed subjects come into collision with the normative criteria. While the market demand for cheap exploitable labour in part produces the movement of people, the trespassing of normative boundaries renders their subjectivity and claims to citizenship less stable.

My argument draws attention to how the technologies of citizenship play a critical part in revealing the way in which subjects are legitimised and regulated. The mechanisms of law, security, surveillance coupled with dominant social, sexual, and cultural norms are constitutive of the legitimate subject, sometimes regardless of whether she has formal citizenship. These norms are central to her eligibility to rights and state entitlements. Sexual and cultural conformity more than law come to patrol the borders of legitimacy and belonging within the nation-state. Thus, migrant subjects cannot be understood through a linear and monochromatic lens of citizenship. Their subjectivity is also constituted through multiple and intersecting identities and forms of difference, including gender and religion. The border between belonging and non-belonging, entitlement or disentitlement are constantly contested and refashioned as illustrated in a number of legal cases analysed in the preceding chapters.

The critique offered in this book on the legal regulation of the migrant, focusing on the female migrant, illuminates how this subject has injected herself into a host of debates on law, human rights, citizenship, and the market. While the female migrant's engagements with law can be empowering in so far as it can offer some benefits, these benefits are shaped according to dominant assumptions about race, religion, gender, culture, and civilisational evolution on which legal provisions are based. Invoking legal rights is not divorced from the normative consequences that inform the legal regime. By engaging with law, the migrant subject is not insulated from the normative content of law and her sexual and cultural conduct and religious identity can all serve to exclude her from being regarded as a legitimate subject. This normative content of law is being increasingly informed by the fear factor and strengthened against more rigid, frozen conceptions of the Other, while the Other continues to contest or challenge these conceptions, as made explicit in the discussion on citizenship as well as the Gujarat riots.

The female migrant is thus a complex subject. She is not exclusively defined and shaped by power, but is produced both through the exercise of power, in particular the process of exclusion, as well as by insurrection and insistent visibility. When the migrant woman asserts her rights to mobility and participates as a market actor, she stakes her claim to subjectivity, including her decision-making abilities and also her transgressive potential. She defines herself as a worker, an economic actor, a public woman, as well as a mother and parent, and, in the case of sex workers, a solicitor of sex. In the process, she transgresses established normative boundaries. She challenges the definition of productive labour, the borders of dominant familial ideology, and renders visible the intersection of consent and compulsion. By insisting on making visible her marginalisation from the register of sexual, familial, and cultural norms, she exposes their translucency and fluidity, as well as their vulnerability.

It is not possible to provide a precise mapping of the directions in which to move once the legal regulation of the migrant subject is exposed as riddled with contradictions and at the same time used to consolidate the identity of the nation state as well as the sovereign subject. While there is an increasing need to foreground the migrant subject in our politics and theoretical work, there is always the risk of losing the radical edge this subject brings to both. What is clear however, it that the empowerment of the migrant subject cannot simply be produced through access to rights. Rights themselves are neither self-consistent nor always liberating. The discussion illustrates the need to understand the political deployment of rights based on culturally and historically specific discourses of power. Unmasking the innocence of rights and exposing their relation to power enables us to ground rights. They cease to occupy a transcendent, neutral status. Instead, rights are revealed as historically embedded and constitutive of the liberal project of organising and producing subjects — those who count, those who count less, and those who do not count at all. Each subject is regulated through separate legal regimes, entitled to rights when they demonstrate their fealty to the nation, or restrained and confined if they threaten to disrupt sexual and cultural norms, or incarcerated and expelled if they are perceived as a law and order problem or security threat.

The analysis provokes the need to think about future policy formulations and legal reforms to deal with this complex subject as well as theoretical possibilities of legal theory and postcolonial feminism. At the international level, there have been a vast array of reports and policy recommendations on the issue of migration and the treatment of migrant workers (UNESA 1998, 2002). At the domestic level, a preliminary step should involve the ratification and implementation of the UN Convention on the Protection of the Rights of All Migrant Workers and their Families (hereafter Migrant Rights Convention), which entered into force in July 2003. The stated purpose of the Migrant Rights Convention is to assist in preventing and eliminating the exploitation of migrant workers throughout the entire migration process. In particular, as stated in the preamble, the Migrant Rights Convention is intended to 'prevent and eliminate clandestine movements and trafficking of migrant workers, while at the same time assuring the protection of their fundamental human rights'. The Convention sets out binding international standards to address the treatment, welfare, and human rights of both documented and undocumented migrants, imposes specific obligations on the part of sending and receiving states. However, the reluctance of states to commit to these standards is evident from the fact that very few countries of origin, not a single country from the industrialised world, and only one from South Asia — Sri Lanka — have ratified it. This response serves as continuous evidence of the fragmented and selected approach being developed by nations including India towards the issue of migration. Ratification of the Migrant Workers Convention, while limited in terms of gender and problematic in the extensive deference given to the state's provision of expansive rights to law enforcement officials, has significance at the symbolic level and reflects a reorientation towards the issue.

At the policy level, the Indian state as well as countries within the South Asian region need to develop a well articulated and gender sensitive migration policy. In the context of female migration, this is a critical need if the Indian state seriously wants to tackle the problem of trafficking and guidelines are already available to enable the preparation and drafting of such a policy (Chammartin 2005). At the moment, policy formulations rest with the Ministry of Overseas Indian Affairs, which is increasingly concerned with affluent non-resident Indians, remittances, and cultivating cultural loyalties. Migrants crossing borders from within the South Asian region are invariably addressed through the lens of criminality and security rather than as economic subjects. Within the domestic context, the emergence of schemes such as NREGA as well as the newly enacted social security bill for the unorganised sector promise some protection and entitlements for migrant labour. However, these interventions are rarely gender-specific nor do they disrupt the register of sexual, cultural, and familial norms that inform legal discourse.

Most importantly, rights and justice for migrants need to be understood from the perspective of the migrant or 'Other'. This does not necessarily translate into the need for more law. As is evident from the analysis in the preceding chapters, more law does not equal more freedom or equality for migrants nor does it address how law itself produces inclusion and exclusion. My critique of law is not intended to create more uncertainty, nervousness, or anxiety about the project of rights and justice. It is to ensure that complacency or surrender to the lofty claims of rights and justice as always rooted in virtue do not become the substitute for a transformative politics and an alternative political vision. The starting point of developing an empowering politics for migrants has to commence from an analytical position. This involves turning a critical postcolonial gaze onto the legal regulation of the migrant, and how she is produced as either a legible or illegible subject, depending on her familiarity and conformity to dominant norms. Such an inquiry provides insights into understanding the historical features of this regulatory edifice and its distinct operations in the postcolonial world.

The response to the migrant subject needs to be detached from an insular vision of the modern nation-state while, at the same time, not reinscribed in new universal projects, which are also being exposed as built along a similar axis of exclusion and inclusion. We must not lose sight of the fact that law is but one of the many discursive strategies available, however, it is an important one with which the migrant subject must engage. Law can neither be a solution to the problems encountered by the migrant subject, in particular the female migrant, nor should it be viewed as the exclusive site of the problem. The dilemmas and obstacles encountered by the migrant are constituted through both legal and non-legal discourses, including popular culture, right-wing ideologies, the market, and even the interventions of progressive, social justice groups. It is therefore important for the migrant subject to engage legal as well as non-legal sites. She needs to engage with law in a manner that does not end up simply reifying gender and cultural stereotypes or the axis of inclusion and exclusion. She can stage her insurrection through such critical engagements, which destabilise the dominant norms that have justified the curtailment or punishment of her movement.

The analysis of the legal regulation of the migrant directs attention to the questions of gender, belonging, and borders. Belonging is not determined exclusively through the legal process, but also through the register of cultural, sexual, and social norms. There is a need for further interrogation into contemporary responses to the migrant and how the register of norms can be more productively negotiated. The migrant is not a subject simply to be managed. She is an insurrectional subject who challenges her denial and erasure and, in the process, opens up spaces for recognition of her subjectivity on terms that remain resistant to total assimilation.

Bibliography

Agnes, F. (ed.). 2002. *Of Lofty Claims and Muffled Voices: A Perspective of* the *Gujarat Carnage*. Bombay: Majlis.

Agustin, L. 2007. *Sex at the Borders: Migration, Labour Markets, and the Rescue Industry*. London: Zed Books.

AIDS Bhedbhav Virodhi Andolan. 1993. 'Homosexuality in India: Culture and Heritage', in R. Ratti (ed.), *A Lotus of Another Colour*, pp. 48–57. Boston: Alyson Publications Inc.

Aiyar, V. S. and U. Mahurkar. 2002. 'It Wasn't Merely a Communal Riot, it was Like a Mass Agitation: Interview with Narendra Modi', *India Today*. 18 March. http://www.bjpguj.org/interviews/itwas.htm. Accessed 28 October 2009.

Akram, S. M. 2000, 'Orientalism Revisited in Asylum and Refugee Claims', *International Journal of Refugee Law*, 12 (1): 7–40.

Albinia, A. 2005. 'Womanhood Laid Bare: How Katherine Mayo and Manoda Devi Challenged Indian Public Morality', in M. Narula, S. Sengupta, J. Bagchi, and G. Lovink (eds), *Sarai Reader*, pp. 428–35. New Delhi: Sarai.

Anand, D. 2005. 'The Violence of Security: Hindu Nationalism and the Politics of Representing "the Muslim" as a Danger', *Round Table*, 94 (379): 203–15.

Anghie, A. 2005. 'Finding the Peripheries: Sovereignty and Colonialism in Nineteeth-Century International Law', in idem (ed.), *Imperialism, Sovereignty and the Making of International Law*, pp. 32–114. Cambridge: Cambridge University Press.

Arya, S. and A. Roy (eds). 2006. 'When Poor Women Migrate: Unravelling Issues and Concerns', in idem (eds), *Poverty, Gender and Migration* (*Women and Migration in Asia*, vol. 2), pp. 18–48. New Delhi, Thousand Oaks, and London: Sage Publications.

Asia Foundation and Horizons Project Population Council. 2001. *Prevention of Trafficking and the Care and Support of Trafficked Persons*. Nepal and India: The Asia Foundation and Horizons Project Population Council.

Bacchetta, P. 2004. *Gender in the Hindu Nation: RSS Women as Ideologues*. New Delhi: Women Unlimited.

Bagchi, J. and S. Dasgupta. 2003. *The Trauma and the Triumph: Gender and Partition in Eastern India*. Calcutta: Stree.

Bailancho Saad. 1997. 'Evictions in Goa: Case Study of Baina', A Fact-finding Team's Report. Goa: Bailancho Saad.

Balagangadhara, S. N. 1994. *The Heathen in His Blindness: Asia, the West and the Dynamic of Religion*. Leiden and Boston: E. J. Brill.

Balibar, E. 2003. *We the People of Europe: Reflections on Transnational Citizenship*. Trans. J. Swenson. Princeton: Princeton University Press.

Bannerjee, H. 1998. 'Age of Consent and Hegemonic Social Reform', in C. Midgley (ed.), *Gender and Imperialism*, pp. 21–44. Manchester: Manchester University Press.

Bannerji, H., S. Mojab, and J. Whitehead. 2001. *Of Property and Propriety: The Role of Gender and Class in Imperialism and Nationalism*. Toronto: University of Toronto Press.

Banerjee, N. 1999. 'Can Markets Alter Gender Relations?', *Gender Technology and Development*, 3 (1): 103–22.

Banerjee, P. 2002. 'Frontiers and Borders: Spaces of Sharing, Spaces of Conflict,' in R. Samaddar (ed.), *Space, Territory and the State: New Readings in International Politics*, pp. 27–42. Hyderabad: Orient Longman.

Banerjee, S. 1998. *Dangerous Outcast: The Prostitute in Nineteenth Century Bengal*. Calcutta: Seagull Books.

Barry, Kathleen. 1979. *Female Sexual Slavery*. New York: Avon.

———. 1995. *The Prostitution of Sexuality: The Global Exploitation of Women*. New York: New York University Press.

Baruah, S. 1999. *India against Itself: Assam and the Politics of Nationality*. Philadelphia: University of Pennsylvania Press.

Basu, A. 1993. 'Feminism Inverted: The Real Women and Gendered Imagery of Hindu Nationalism', *Bulletin of Concerned Asian Scholars*, 25 (4): 25–29.

Basu, T., P. Datta, S. Sarkar, T. Sarkar, and S. Sen. 1993. *Khaki Shorts, Saffron Flags: A Critique of the Hindu Right*. New Delhi: Orient Longman.

Baxi, U. 2002. 'The (Im)Possibility of Constitutional Justice: Seismographic Notes on Indian Constitutionalism', in Z. Hasan, E. Sridharan, and R. Sudarshan (eds), *India's Living Constitution*, pp. 31–63. Delhi: Permanent Black.

———. 2002. *The Future of Human Rights*. New Delhi: Oxford University Press.

BBC News. 2007. 'Gere Kiss Sparks India Protests'. 14 April. http://news.bbc.co.uk/2/hi/entertainment/6560371.stm. Accessed 28 October 2009.

Belak, B. 2003. 'Migration and Trafficking of Women and Girls', in B. Belak (ed.), *Gathering Strength: Women from Burma and Their Rights*, pp. 194–225. Thailand: Images Asia. http://www.ibiblio.org/obl/docs/GS12.migration-and-trafficking.pdf. Accessed 28 October 2009.

Beneria, L. and S. Bisnath (eds). 2004. *Global Tensions: Challenges and Opportunities in the World Economy*. London and New York: Routledge.

Berman, J. 2003. '(Un)Popular Strangers and Crisis (Un)Bounded: Discourses of Sex-Trafficking, the European Political Community and the Panicked State of the Modern State', *European Journal of International Relations*, 9 (1): 37–86.

Besant A. 1915. 'India: Essays and Addresses'. http://www.archive.org/stream/india00besarich/india00besarich_djvu.txt. Accessed 21 July 2009.

Bezanson, K. and M. Luxton. 2006. 'Introduction: Social Reproduction and Feminist Political Economy', in idem (eds), *Social Reproduction: Feminist Political Economy Challenges Neo-Liberalism*, pp. 3–10, Montreal: McGill-Queen's University Press.

Bhabha, H. 1994. *The Location of Culture*. London: Routledge.

Bhalotra, S. 2002. *The Impact of Economic Liberalization on Employment and Wages in India*. Geneva: International Policy Group, International Labour Organization.

Bharat, S. and P. D'Cruz. 2001. 'Beyond Joint and Nuclear: The Indian Family Revisited', *Journal of Comparative Family Studies*, 32 (2): 167–94.

Bharti, B. n.d. *Implementation of SAARC Convention: The Way Forward*. http://www.csrindia.org/Reports&Documents/Articles/Implementation%20of%20SAARC%20Convention%20Bharti.pdf. Accessed 28 October 2009.

Bhatt, C. (ed.). 2001. *Hindu Nationalism: Origins, Ideologies and Modern Myths*. Oxford: Berg Publishers.

Bhatt, E. 1988. 'Shram Shakti Report of the National Commission on Self-Employed Women and Women in the Informal Sector'. New Delhi: National Commission on Self-Employed Women and Women in the Informal Sector.

Bhattacharya, N. 2005. 'Notes towards a Conception of the Colonial Public', in R. Bhargava and H. Reifeld (eds), *Civil Society, Public Sphere and Citizenship: Dialogues and Perceptions*, pp. 130–58. New Delhi, Thousand Oaks, and London: Sage Publications.

Block, J. 2004. 'Sex Trafficking: Why Faith is interested in the Sex Trade', *Conscience*, 25 (2): 32–35. http://new.vawnet.org/category/Documents.php?docid=993&category_id=683. Accessed 28 October 2009.

Bose, B. and S. Bhattacharya (eds). 2007. *The Phobic and the Erotic: The Politics of Sexualities in Contemporary India*. Calcutta and London: Seagull.

Bosniak, L. 2000. 'Citizenship Denationalized', *Indiana Journal of Global Legal Studies*, 7: 447–509.

———. 2002. 'Critical Reflections on "Citizenship" as a Progressive Aspiration', in J. Conaghan, R. M. Fischl, and K. Klare (eds), *Labour Law in an Era of Globalization: Transformative Practices and Possibilities*, pp. 339–51. Oxford: Oxford University Press.

———. 2006. *The Citizen and the Alien: Dilemmas of Contemporary Membership*. Princeton, New Jersey: Princeton University Press.

———. 2009. 'Citizenship, Noncitizenship, and the Transnationalization of Domestic Work', in S. Benahabib and J. Resnik (eds), *Migration and Mobilities: Citizenship, Borders, and Gender*, pp. 127–56. New York and London: New York University Press.

Botti, A. 2000. 'The Trade in Human Beings is a Worldwide Scourge', *International Herald Tribune*. 1 June.

Bowden, B. 2002. 'The Perils of Global Citizenship', *Citizenship Studies*, 7: 349–62.

Boyd, M. and E. Grieco. 2003. 'Women and Migration: Incorporating Gender into International Migration Theory', *Migration Information Source*. March. http://www.migrationinformation.org/Feature/display.cfm?id=106. Accessed 28 October 2009.

Breckenridge, C. and P. van der Veer (eds). 1993. *Orientalism and the Postcolonial Predicament: Perspectives on South Asia*. Philadelphia: University of Pennsylvania Press.

Brettell, C. B. and R. J. Simon. 1986. 'Immigrant Women: An Introduction', in idem (eds), *International Migration: The Female Experience*, pp. 3–20. New Jersey: Rowman and Allanheld.

Brodie, J. 1994. 'Shifting the Boundaries: Gender and the Politics of Restructuring', in I. Bakker (ed.), *The Strategic Silence: Gender and Economic Policy*, pp. 46–60. London: Zed Books.

———. 1995. *Politics on the Margins: Restructuring and the Canadian Women's Movement*. Halifax: Fernwood Publishing.

———. 2004. 'Introduction: Globalization and Citizenship Beyond the National States', *Citizenship Studies*, 8 (4): 323–33.

Broude, T. 2007. 'The WTO/GATS Mode 4, International Labour Migration Regimes, and Global Justice', *International Law Forum*, Research Paper 7–07. Hebrew University of Jerusalem. http:www.srsn.com/sbstractid=987655. Accessed 28 October 2009.

Brown, W. 2001. *Politics Out of History*. New Jersey: Princeton University Press.

———. 2005. *Edgeworks: Critical Essays on Knowledge and Politics*. New Jersey: Princeton University Press.

Buch, C. M., A. Kucklenz, and Marie-Helene Le Manchec. 2002. 'Worker Remittances and Capital Flows', Working Paper No. 113. Germany: Kiel Institute for World Economics.

Bumiller, Elizabeth. 1990. *May You be the Mother of a Hundred Sons: A Journey Among the Women of India*. New York: Random House.

Bunsha, D. 2004, 'Zahira's Somersault', *Frontline*. 20 November–3 December. http://www.frontlineonnet.com/fl2124/stories/20041203003304000.htm. Accessed 28 October 2009.

Burton, A. 1994. *Burdens of History: British Feminists, Indian Women and Imperial Culture, 1865–1915*. Chapel Hill: University of North Carolina Press.

Burton, D. 1999. *Emptiness Appraised: A Critical Appraisal of Nagarjuna's Philosophy*. Richmond: Curzon Press.

Buss, D. and D. Herman. 2003. *Globalizing Family Values: The Christian Right in International Politics*. Minneapolis, London: University of Minnesota Press.

Butalia, U. 1995. 'Muslims and Hindus, Men and Women: Communal Stereotypes and the Partition of India ', in T. Sarkar and U. Butalia (eds), *Women and the Hindu Right: A Collection of Essays*, pp. 58–81. New Delhi: Kali for Women.

———. 1998. *The Other Side of Silence: The Voices from Partition*. New Delhi: Penguin Books.

Butler J. 1990. *Gender Trouble: Feminism and the Subversion of Identity*. New York: Routledge.

Butler, J. and G. Spivak. 2007. *Who Sings the Nation-State?: Language, Politics, Belonging*. London, New York, and Calcutta: Seagull.

Cagatay, N., D. Elson, and C. Grown. 1995. 'Introduction', *Gender, Adjustment and Macroeconomics*, special issue of *World Development*, 23 (11): 1827–1936.

Campbell, D. 1992. *Writing Security: United States Foreign Policy and the Politics of Identity*. Minneapolis: University of Minnesota.

Carling, J. 2005. *Migrant Remittances and Development Cooperation*. Oslo: International Peace Research Institute.

Census of India. 2001. Office of the Registrar General. New Delhi. www.censusindia.net. Accessed 18 November 2009.

———. 2001. Data Highlights, Migration Tables (D1, D1 [Appendix], D2 and D3 Tables). www.censusindia.net/results/dseries/data_hightlights_D1D2D3.pdf. Accessed 28 October 2009.

Centre for Feminist Legal Research (CFLR). 2006. 'Trafficking Reform: An Analysis of the Protection of the Rights of Positive People, Children, and Sex Workers'. New Delhi: CFLR.

Chakrabarty, D. 2000. *Provincialising Europe: Postcolonial Thought and Historical Difference*. New Jersey: Princeton University Press.

———. 2002. 'A Small History of Subaltern Studies', in idem (ed.), *Habitations of Modernity: Essays in the Wake of Subaltern Studies*, pp. 3–19. Chicago: University of Chicago Press.

Chakravarti, U. 1989. 'Whatever Happened to the Vedic *Dasi*? Orientalism, Nationalism, and a Script for the Past', in K. K. Sangari and S. Vaid (eds), *Recasting Women:Essays in Colonial History*, pp. 27–87. New Delhi: Kali for Women.

Chammartin, G. M. 2005. *Guidelines for Countries of Origin on how to Prevent and Reduce Trafficking of Women through Migration Policy Measures*. Geneva: International Migration Programme, International Labour Organization.

Chandra, B. 1984. *Communalism in Modern India*. New Delhi: Vikas Publications.

Chandra, S. 1998. *Enslaved Daughters: Colonialism, Law and Women's Rights*. New Delhi: Oxford University Press.

———. 2005. 'Subjects' Citizenship Dream: Notes on the Nineteenth Century', in R. Bhargava and H. Reifeld (eds), *Civil Society, Public Sphere and Citizenship: Dialogues and Perceptions*, pp. 106–29. New Delhi, Thousand Oaks, and London: Sage Publications.

Chandrasekhar, C. P. and J. Ghosh. 2004. *The Market that Failed:A Decade of Neoliberal Economic Reforms in India* (2nd edn). New Delhi: Leftword Books.

Chang, G. 2000. *Disposable Domestics: Immigrant Women Workers in the Global Economy*. Cambridge, Massachusetts: South End Press.

Chant, S. (ed.). 1992. *Gender and Migration in Developing Countries*. London and New York: Bellhaven Press.

Chatterjee, M. 1993. 'Saffron Extremism', *Frontline*. 16–29 January.

Chatterjee, Partha. 1989. 'The Nationalist Resolution of the Women's Question', in K. K. Sangari and S. Vaid (eds), *Recasting Women: Essays in Colonial History*, pp. 233–53. New Delhi: Kali for Women.

———. 1993. *The Nation and Its Fragments: Colonial and Postcolonial Histories*. New Jersey: Princeton University Press.

———. 2003. 'Beyond the Nation? Or Within', in C. M. Elliot (ed.), *Civil Society and Democracy: A Reader*. New Delhi: Oxford University Press.

———. 2004. *The Politics of the Governed*. New York: Columbia University Press.

Chaturvedi, S. 2001. 'The Mental Borders in South Asia', in R. Samaddar and H. Reifeld (eds), *Peace as Process: Reconciliation and Conflict Resolution in South Asia*, pp. 61–80. New Delhi: Manohar.

Chaudhuri, M. 1993. *Indian Women's Movement: Reform and Revival*. New Delhi: Radiant.

———. (ed.). 2004. *Feminism in India: Issues in Contemporary Indian Feminism*. New Delhi: Kali for Women and Women Unlimited.

———. 2005. 'Betwixt the State and Everyday Life: Identity Formation among Bengali Migrants in a Delhi Slum', in M. Thapan (ed.), *Transnational Migration and the Politics of Identity (Women and Migration in Asia, Volume 1)*, pp. 284–311. New Delhi, Thousand Oaks, and London: Sage Publications.

Chaudhuri, R. 2000. 'Young India: A Bengal Eclogue- or Meat-eating, Race and Reform in a Colonial Poem', *Interventions: International Journal of Postcolonial Studies*, 2 (3): 424–41.

Cheng, Shu-Ju A. 1999. 'Labor Migration and International Sexual Division of Labor: A Feminist Perspective', in G. A. Kelson and D. L. DeLaet (eds), *Gender and Immigration*, pp. 38–58. New York: New York University Press.

Chimni, B. S. 1998. 'The Geopolitics of Refugee Studies: A View from the South', *Journal of Refugee Studies*, 11 (4): 350–74.

———. 2005. 'Outside the Bounds of Citizenship: The Status of Aliens, Illegal Migrants and Refugees in India', in R. Bhargarva and H. Reifeld (eds), *Civil Society, Public Sphere and Citizenship*, pp. 277–313. New Delhi: Sage Publications.

Chishti, M. 2007. *The Phenomenal Rise in Remittances to India: A Closer Look*. Washington, D. C.: Migration Policy Institute.

Chuang, J. 1998. 'Redirecting the Debate Over Trafficking in Women: Definitions, Paradigms, and Context', *Harvard Human Rights Journal*, 11: 65–107.

———. 2006. 'The United States as Global Sheriff: Using Unilateral Sanctions to Combat Human Trafficking', *Michigan Journal of International Law*, 27 (2): 437–94.

Citizen's Initiative. 2002. *How has the Gujarat Massacre Affected Minority Women? The Survivors Speak*. Ahmedabad: Citizen's Initiative. infochangeindia.org/200109076001/Human-Rights/Books-Reports/Gujarat-riots-The-impact-on-women.html. Accessed 28 October 2009.

Coalition Against Genocide. 2005. 'Genocide in Gujarat: The Sangh Parivar, Narendra Modi, and the Gujarat Government'. 2 March. http://www.coalitionagainstgenocide.org/reports/2005/cag.02mar2005.modi.pdf. Accessed 28 October 2009.

Communalism Combat. 2002. 'Police: Criminals in Uniform'. March–April. http://www.sabrang.com/cc/archive/2002/marapril/police.htm. Accessed 28 October 2009.

Concerned Citizen's Tribunal (CCT). 2002. 'Annexure 9: Police Dereliction of Duty', *Crime Against Humanity: An Inquiry into the Violence in Gujarat*, vol. 1, pp. 255–57. http://www.sabrang.com/tribunal/tribunal1.pdf. Accessed 28 October 2009.

Conklin, G. 1976. 'The Household in Urban India', *Journal of Marriage and the Family*, 38 (4): 771–79.

Coomaraswamy, R. 2001. *Report of the Special Rapporteur on Violence Against Women, its Causes and Consequences: Mission to Bangladesh, Nepal and India on the Issue of Trafficking of Women and Girls*. E/CN.4/2001/73/Add.2. 28 October–15 November 2000. New York: United Nations Office of the High Commissioner for Human Rights.

Coombe, R. 1998. 'Contingent Articulations: A Critical Cultural Studies of Law', in A. Sarat and T. Kearns (eds), *Law and the Domains of Culture*, pp. 21–64. Ann Arbor: University of Michigan Press.

Coombe, Rosemary J. 1998. 'Contingent Articulations: A Critical Cultural Studies of Law', in Austin Sarat and Thomas R. Kearns (eds), *Law in the Domains of Culture*, pp. 21–64. Ann Arbor: The University of Michigan Press.

Cossman, B. 2007. *Sexual Citizens: The Legal and Cultural Regulation of Sex and Belonging*. Stanford, California: Stanford University Press.

CPI (M) and AIDWA. 2002. 'Violence in Gujarat', *PUCL Bulletin*. April. http://www.pucl.org/Topics/Religion-communalism/2002/gujarat-cpm.htm. Accessed 18 November 2009.

Crago, Anna-Louise. 2003. 'Unholy Collaboration: Feminists and the Christian Right are in bed together'. 15 May. http://www.rabble.ca/news_full_story.shtml?x=21681. Accessed 27 July 2009.

Crocker, D. A. 1999. 'Reckoning with Past Wrongs: A Normative Framework', *Ethics and International Affairs*, 13: 43–64.

Cruikshank, B. 1999. *The Will to Empower: Democratic Citizens and Other Subjects*. Ithaca, New York: Cornell University Press.

Darian-Smith, E. and P. Fitzpatrick. 1999. 'Laws of the Postcolonial: An Insistent Introduction', in idem (eds), *Laws of The Postcolonial: Law, Meaning and Violence*, pp. 1–14. Ann Arbor: University of Michigan Press.

Darian-Smith, E. and P. Fitzpatrick. (eds). 1999. *Laws of the Postcolonial*. Ann Arbor: University of Michigan Press.

Darwin, C. (1871) 1971. *The Descent of Man and Selection in Relation to Sex (1871)* (Limited Editions Club edn). Adelaide: The Griffins Press.

Das, B. 2005. 'Muslim Setters Fear Persecution in Assam', *Daily Times*. 30 July. www.dailytimes.com.pk/default.asp?page=story_30-7-2005_pg4_10. Accessed 18 November 2009.

Das, V. 1995. *Critical Events: An Anthropological Perspective on Contemporary Modern India*. New Delhi: Oxford University Press.

Demleitner, N. 1994. 'Forced Prostitution: Naming an International Offense', *Fordham International Law Journal*, 14: 163–97.

Desai, I. P. 2005. 'The Joint Family in India: An Analysis', in T. Patel (ed.), *The Family in India: Structure and Practice*, pp. 81–94. New Delhi: Sage Publications.

Deshpande, S. and L. Deshpande. 1998. 'Impact of Liberalization on Labour Market in India: What do Facts from NSSO's 50th Round Show?', *Economic and Political Weekly*, 33 (22): L 31–L 39.

Desouza, S. 2004. 'Razing Baina, Goa: In Whose Interest?', *Economic and Political Weekly*, 39 (30): 3341–3343.

Dhruvarajan, V. 1989. *Hindu Women and the Power of Ideology*. Massachusetts: Bergin and Garvey Publishers, Inc.

Ditmore, M. H. 2006. *Encylopedia of Prostitution and Sex Work*. Santa Barbra, CA: Greenwood Publishing Group.

Doezema, J. 1999. 'Loose Women or Lost Women: The Re-emergence of the Myth of White Slavery in Contemporary Discourses of Trafficking in Women', paper presented at the 40th Annual Convention of the International Studies Association, Washington, D. C. 16–20 February. http://www.walnet.org/csis/papers/doezema-loose.html. Accessed 27 July 2009.

———. 2001. 'Ouch! Western Feminists' "Wounded Attachment" to the "Third World Prostitute"', *Feminist Review*, 67: 16–38.

Douzinas, C. 2007. *Human Rights and Empire: The Political Philosophy of Cosmopolitanism*. London: Routledge-Cavendish.

Dreze, J. and R. Khera. 2009. 'The Battle for Employment Guarantee', *Frontline Magazine*, 26 (1): 4–26. 3–16 January.

Dubey, S., P. Donthi, and M. Srivastava. 2007. 'Police Can't Smell the Stink Under its Nose', *Tehelka*. 7 January. http://www.tehelka.com/story_main25.asp?filename=Ne012007Police_cant_CS.asp. Accessed 28 October 2009.

Durbar Mahila Samanwaya Committee (DMSC). 1997. 'Sex Worker's Manifesto', First National Conference of Sex Workers in India, Calcutta. 14–16 November 1997. http://www.nswp.org/rights/dmsc/dmsc-manifesto.html. Accessed 28 October 2009.

———. 2007. *Meeting Community Needs for HIV Prevention and More: Intersectoral Action for Health in the Sonagachi Red-light area of Kolkata*. http://www.who.int/social_determinants/resources/isa_sonagachi_ind.pdf. Accessed 18 November 2009.

Dworkin, A. 1987. *Intercourse*. New York: Free Press.

Ehrenreich, B. and A. R. Hochschild (eds). 2002. *Global Woman: Nannies, Maids and Sex Worker in the New Economy*. New York: Henry Holt and Co.

Eisenstein, Z. 2004. *Against Empire: Feminisms, Racisms and 'The West'*. London: Zed Books.

Elson, D. 1999. 'Labour Markets as Gendered Institutions: Equality, Efficiency and Empowerment Issues', *World Development*, 27 (3): 611–27.

Embree, A. T. 1994. 'The Function of the Rashtriya Swayamsevak Sangh: To Define the Hindu Nation', in M. E. Marty and R. S. Appleby (eds), *Accounting for Fundamentalisms: The Dynamic Character of Movements*, pp. 617–52. Chicago: University of Chicago Press.

Evans, D. 1993. *Sexual Citizenship: The Material Construction of Sexualities*. London: Routledge.

Farely, M. and J. Neuwirth. 2008. 'The New Abolitionists', *Ms. Magazine*. 1 April.

Faulks, K. 2000. *Citizenship*. London and New York: Routledge.

Featherstone, M. 2002. 'Cosmopolis: An Introduction', *Theory Culture and Society*, 19 (1–2): 1–16.

Foucault, M. 1980. *Power/Knowledge: Selected Interviews and Other Writings 1972–1977*. Trans. C. Gordon, L. Marshall, J. Mepham, and K. Soper. New York: Pantheon Books.

Fraser, N. and L. Gordon. 1994. 'Civil Citizenship against Social Citizenship? On the Ideology of Contract-Versus-Charity', in Bart van Steenburgen (ed.), *The Condition of Citizenship*, pp. 90–107. Thousand Oaks, California: Sage Publications.

Freeman, J. 1996. 'The Feminist Debate over Prostitution Reform: Prostitutes' Rights Groups, Radical Feminists, and the (Im)possibility of Consent', in K. Weisburg (ed.), *Applications of Feminist Legal Theory to Women's Lives: Sex, Violence, Work and Reproduction*, pp. 237–49. Philadelphia: Temple University Press.

Gallagher, A. 2002. 'Consideration of the Issue of Trafficking: Background Paper', prepared for the Advisory Council of Jurists at the Asia–Pacific Forum of National Human Rights Institutions. New Delhi. 11–12 November.

Gangoli, Geetanjali. 2006. *Indian Feminisms Law, Patriarchies, and Violence in India*. Hampshire: Ashgate.

Ganguly-Scrase, R. 2003. 'Paradoxes of Globalization, Liberalization and Gender Equality', *Gender and Society*, 17 (4): 544–66.

Gardner, K. and F. Osella. 2004. 'Migration, Modernity and Social Transformation in South Asia: An Introduction', in F. Osella and K. Gardner (eds), *Migration, Modernity and Social Transformation in South Asia*, pp. xi–xlviii. New Delhi, Thousand Oaks, and London: Sage Publications.

Gayen, S. 2005. 'Nightmares on Celluloid', letter, *Daily Telegraph*. 15 March. http://www.cerebration.org/partha.html. Accessed 28 October 2009.

Gavigan, S. 1993. 'Paradise Lost, Paradox Revisited: The Implications of Feminist, Lesbian and Gay Engagement to Law', *Osgoode Hall Law Journal*, 31: 589–624.

———. 1997. 'Feminism, Familial Ideology and Family Law: A Perilous Ménage à Trois', in M. Luxton (ed.), *Feminism and Families: Critical Policies and Changing Practices*, pp. 98–103. Halifax: Fernwood Press.

Gillian, M. 2001. 'Refugees or Infiltrators? The Bharatiya Janata Party and "Illegal" Migration from Bangladesh', *Asian Studies Review*, 26 (1): 73–95.

Gilman, S. L. 1985. 'Black Bodies, White Bodies: Toward an Iconography of Female Sexuality in Late Nineteenth-Century Art, Medicine, and Literature', in H. L. Gates (ed.), *"Race", Writing and Difference*, pp. 223–61. Chicago: Chicago University Press.

Global Alliance Against Trafficking in Women (GAATW). 2001. *Human Rights and Trafficking in Persons: A Handbook*. Bangkok, Thailand: GAATW.

———. 2007. *Collateral Damage: The Impact of Anti-Trafficking Measures on Human Rights around the World*. Bangkok: GAATW.

Global Commission for International Migration (GCIM). 2005. *Migration in an Interconnected World: New Directions for Action*. Geneva: GCIM.

Golwalkar, M. S. 1947. *We or Our Nationhood Defined* (4th edn). Nagpur: Bharat Prakashan.

———. 1966. *Bunch of Thoughts*. Bangalore: Vikrama Prakashan.

Gorringe, H. 2008. 'The Caste of the Nation: Untouchability and Citizenship in South India', *Contributions to Indian Sociology*, 42 (1): 123–49.

Goswami, P. 2009. 'A Critique of the Unorganised Workers' Social Security Act', *Economic and Political Weekly*, 44 (11): 17–19.

Government of India. 1975. 'Towards Equality: Report of the Committee on the Status of Women in India'. New Delhi: Ministry of Education and Social Welfare.

———. 1988. 'The National Perspective Plan for Women, 1988–2000: Report of the Department of Women and Child Development'. New Delhi: Ministry of Human Resource Development.

———. 2002. 'Second National Labour Commission Report'. New Delhi: Ministry of Labour. http://labour.nic.in/lcomm2/nlc_report.html. Accessed 28 October 2008.

Goyal, D. R. 1979. *Rashtriya Swayamsewak Sangh*. New Delhi: Radha Krishna Prakashan.

Gubrium, J. and J. Holstein. 1990. *What is Family?* Mountain View, CA: Mayfield Publications.

———. 1999 *The Self We Live By: Narrative Identity in a Postmodern World*. New York: Oxford University Press.

Guha, R. 1980. 'On Some Aspects of the Historiography of Colonial India', in idem (ed.), *Subaltern Studies I: Writing on South Asian History and Society*, pp. 1–8. Oxford: Oxford University Press.

———. 1996. 'The Small Voice of History', in. S. Amin and D. Chakrabarty (eds), *Subaltern Studies IX: Writings on South Asian History and Society*, pp. 1–12. New Delhi: Oxford University Press.

Gupta, D. 2000. *Mistaken Modernity: India between Worlds*. New Delhi: Harper Collins.

Guru, G. 2005. 'Citizenship in Exile: A Dalit Case', in R. Bharvgava and H. Reifeld (eds), *Civil Society, Public Sphere and Citizenship: Dialogues and Perceptions*, pp. 260–76. New Delhi, Thousand Oaks, and London: Sage Publications.

Hall, S. 1996. 'Cultural Identity and Cinematic Representation', in H. A. Baker Jr, M. Diawara, and R. H. Lindeborg (eds), *Black British Cultural Studies: A Reader*, pp. 210–22. Chicago: University of Chicago Press.

Hameed, S., R. Manorama, M. Ghose, S. George, F. Naqvi, and M. Thekaekara. 2002. *How has the Gujarat Massacre Affected Minority Women: The Survivors Speak*. Ahmedabad: Citizen's Initiative.

Hansen, T. 2004. 'The Ethics of Hindutva and the Spirit of Capitalism', in T. B. Hansen and C. Jaffrelot (eds), *Omnibus: Hindu Nationalism and Indian Politics*, pp. 291–314. New Delhi: Oxford University Press.

Hardt, M. and A. Negri. 2000. *Empire*. Massachusetts: Harvard University Press.

Hazarika, S. 2000. *Rites of Passage: Border Crossings, Imagined Homelands, India's East and Bangladesh*. New Delhi: Penguin Books.

Heisler, M. 1999. 'Contextualizing Global Migration: Sketching the Socio-Political Landscape in Europe', *UCLA Journal of International Law and Foreign Affairs*, 3 (2): 557–93.

Hernandez-Truyol, B. E and M. Hawk. 2005. 'Travelling the Boundaries of Statelessness: Global Passports and Citizenship', *Cleveland State Law Review*, 52: 97–119.

Hertzke, A. 2006. *Freeing God's Children: The Unlikely Alliance for Global Human Rights*. Maryland: Rowland and Littlefields Publishers Inc.

Hindess, B. 2002. 'Neo-Liberal Citizenship', *Citizenship Studies*, 6 (2): 127–43.

Human Rights Watch. 1995. *Rape for Profit: Trafficking of Nepali Girls and Women to India's Brothels*. New York: Human Rights Watch.

———. 2002. *We have No Orders to Save You: State Participation and Complicity in Communal Violence in Gujarat*. New York: Human Rights Watch. http://hrw.org/reports/2002/india/gujarat.pdf. Accessed 5 July 2009.

———. 2004. *Discouraging Dissent: Intimidation and Harassment of Witnesses, Human Rights Activists, and Lawyers Pursuing Accountability for the 2002 Communal Violence in Gujarat*. New York: Human Rights Watch. http://hrw.org/backgrounder/asia/india/gujarat/. Accessed 5 July 2009.

Ignatieff, M. 1987. 'The Myth of Citizenship', *Queen's Quarterly*, 94: 966–85.

Indra, Doreen Marie. 1999. 'Not a "Room of One's Own": Engendering Forced Migration Knowledge and Practice', in idem (ed.), *Engendering Forced Migration: Theory and Practice (Refugee and Forced Migration Studies, Volume 5)*, pp. 1–21. Oxford and New York: Berghahn Books.

International Initiative for Justice (IIJ). 2003. *Threatened Existence: A Feminist Analysis of the Genocide in Gujarat*. Bombay and Delhi: International Initiative for Justice. http://www.onlinevolunteers.org/gujarat/reports/iijg/2003/fullreport.pdf. Accessed 28 October 2009.

International Labour Organization (ILO). 2001. 'Stopping Forced Labour: Global Report under the Follow-up to the ILO Declaration on Fundamental Principles and Rights at Work'. Geneva: ILO.

———. 2004. 'Towards a Fair Deal for Migrant Workers in the Global Economy'. Geneva: ILO.

———. 2005a. 'A Global Alliance against Forced Labour'. Geneva: ILO. http://www.ilo.org/public/english/standards/relm/ilc/ilc93/pdf/rep-i-b.pdf. Accessed 18 November 2009.

———. 2005b. 'ILO Director-General says Global Jobs Crisis Puts Democracy, Freedom at Risk'. 6 June. http://www.ilo.org/global/About_the_ILO/Media_and_public_information/Press_releases/lang—en/WCMS_005166/index.htm. Accessed 28 October 2009.

International Organization for Migration (IOM). 2005. *World Migration Report*. Geneva: IOM.

Jaffrelot, C. 1996. *The Hindu Nationalist Movement and Indian Politics*. New York: Columbia University Press.

———. (ed.). 2005. *The Sangh Parivar: A Reader*. New Delhi: Oxford University Press.

Jain, D. and N. Banerjee (eds). 1985. *Tyranny of the Household: Investigative Essays on Women's Work*. New Delhi: Shakti Books.

Jayanth, K. K. 2004. 'India's Patriot Act: POTA and the Impact on Civil Liberties in the World's Largest Democracy', *Law and Inequality: A Journal of Theory and Practice*, 22 (2): 265–300.

John, M. and J. Nair (eds). 1998. *A Question of Silence? The Sexual Economies of Modern India*. London: Zed Books.

Jolly, S., E. Bell, and L. Narayanaswamy. 2003. *Gender and Migration in Asia: Overview and Annotated Bibliography*. Sussex: Department for International Development.

Joshi, M. M. 1995. 'Women's Liberation: The Indian Way', *The Organiser*. 24 December. http://antibjp.tripod.com/archives/mmj-wlib.html. Accessed 27 July 2009.

Kabeer, N. 2005. 'Introduction: The Search for Inclusive Citizenship — Meanings and Expression in an Interconnected World', in idem (ed.), *Inclusive Citizenship: Meanings and Expressions*, pp.1–27. London: Zed Books.

Kamat Committee Report. 1998. 'Report of the Inquiry Committee Constituted by the National Commission for Women to Study Problems of Women in Prostitution in Baina and the Recommendations for their Rehabilitation' (Justice Kamat Committee Report) New Delhi: Supreme Court.

Kandiyoti, D. 1993. 'Islam and Patriarchy: A Comparative Perspective', in N. Keddie and B. Baron (eds), *Women in Middle Eastern History: Shifting Boundaries in Sex and Gender*, pp. 23–42. New Haven: Yale University Press.

Kannabiran, K. 2006. 'A Cartography of Resistance: The National Federation of Dalit Women', in N. Yuval-Davis, K. Kannabiran, and U. Vieten (eds), *The Situated Politics of Belonging*, pp. 54–75. London, Thousand Oaks, and Delhi: Sage Publications.

Kanungo, P. 2002. *RSS's Tryst with Politics: From Hedgewar to Sarvarkar*. Delhi: Manohar.

Kapadia, K. M. 2005. 'The Family in Transition', in T. Patel (ed.), *The Family in India: Structure and Practice*, pp. 172–203. New Delhi: Sage Publications.

Kaplan, C., N. Alarcón, and M. Moallem (eds). 1999. *Between Woman and Nation: Nationalisms, Transnational Feminisms, and the State*. Durham, N. C.: Duke University Press.

Kapur, R. 2005. *Erotic Justice: Law and the New Politics of Postcolonialism*. London: Glasshouse Press, Cavendish.

———. 2006. 'Human Rights in the 21st Century: Taking a Walk on the Dark Side', *Sydney Law Review*, 28 (4): 665–87.

Kapur, R. and B. Cossman. 1996. *Subversive Sites: Feminist Engagements with Law in India*. New Delhi: Sage Publications.

———. 2001. *Secularism's Last Sigh? Hindutva and the (Mis)Rule of Law* (rpt). New Delhi: Oxford University Press.

Katayama, L. 2005. 'Sex Trafficking: Zero Tolerance', *Mother Jones*. http://www.motherjones.com/politics/2005/05/sex-trafficking-zero-tolerance. Accessed 28 July 2008.

Kaur, R. 2006. 'Migrating for Work: Rewriting Gender Relations', in S. Arya and A. Roy (eds), *Poverty, Gender and Migration (Women and Migration in Asia, Volume 2)*, pp. 192–213. New Delhi, Thousand Oaks, and London: Sage Publications.

Keddie, N. 1999. 'The New Religious Politics and Women Worldwide: A Comparative Study', *Journal of Women's History*, 10 (4): 11–34.

Kelson, G. A. and D. L. DeLaet (eds). 1999. *Gender and Immigration*. New York: New York University Press.

Kempadoo, K. 1998. 'Introduction: Globalizing Sex Workers' Rights', in K. Kempadoo and J. Doezema (eds), *Global Sex Workers: Rights, Resistance and Redefinition*, pp. 1–33. New York: Routledge.

———. 2001. 'Women of Color and the Global Sex Trade: Transnational Feminist Perspectives', *Meridians: Feminism, Race, Transnationalism*, 1 (2): 28–51.

Kennedy, D. 2004. *The Dark Side of Virtue Reassessing International Humanitarianism*. Princeton: Princeton University Press.

Khullar, M. 1999. 'Women's Varing in India: The Intersecting Public and Private Sphere', *Asian Journal of Women's Studies*, 5 (3): 64–79.

Kofman, E. 2005. 'Citizenship, Migration and the Reassertion of National Identity', *Citizenship Studies*, 9 (5): 453–67.

Kosambi, M. 1988. 'Women, Emancipation and Equality: Pandita Ramabai's Contribution to Women's Cause', *Economic and Political Weekly*, 23 (44): WS 38–WS 49.

Koskenniemi, M. 2002. *The Gentle Civilizer of Nations: The Rise and Fall of International Law, 1870–1960*. Cambridge: Cambridge University Press.

Krishna, S. 1996. 'Cartographic Anxiety: Mapping the Body Politic in India', in M. J. Shapiro and R. A. Hayward (eds), *Challenging Boundaries: Global Flows, Territorial Identities*, pp. 193–214. Minneapolis: Minneapolis University Press.

Kristof, N. and S. WuDunn. 2009. *Half the Sky: Turning Oppression into Opportunity for Women Worldwide*. New York: Alfred A. Knopf.

Kristof, N. 2005. 'Sex Slaves? Lock up the Pimps', *New York Times*, A19. 29 January.

———. 2006a. 'Hidden in Brothels: Slavery by Another Name', *New York Times*, A25. 1 June.

———. 2006b. 'Bush Takes on the Brothels', *New York Times*, A27. 9 May.

———. 2006c. 'Hitting Brothel Owners Where it Hurts', *New York Times*, A21. 24 January.

———. 2007. 'Sex Trafficking in India', *New York Times*, A21. 11 May.

Kumar, R. 1993. *The History of Doing: An Illustrated Account of Movements for Women's Rights and Feminism in India, 1800–1990* . New Delhi: Kali for Women.

Kumara B. (ed.). 2006. *Illegal Migration from Bangladesh*. Guwahati: Centre for Northeast Studies and Policy Research.

Kymlicka, W. and N. Wayne. 1994. 'Return of the Citizen: A Survey of Recent Work on Citizenship Theory', *Ethics*, 104 (2): 352–81.

Laczko, F., A. Klekowski von Koppenfels, and J. Barthel. 2002. 'Trafficking in Women from Central and Eastern Europe: A Review of Statistical Data', in F. Laczko, I. Stacher, and A. Klekowski von Koppenfels (eds), *New Challenges for Migration Policy in Central and Eastern Europe*, pp. 153–74. The Hague: Asser Press.

Lajpat Rai, Lala. 1985. *Unhappy India: Being a Reply to Miss Katherine Mayo's "Mother India"* (rpt). Delhi: Anmol Publications.

Lakshmi, R. 2002. 'Mob Attacks Indian Train', *Washington Post*, A13. 28 February.

Liddle, J. and S. Rai. 1998. 'Feminism, Imperialism and Orientalism: The Challenge of the "Indian Woman"', *Women's History Review*, 7 (4): 495–520.

Lingam, L. 1998. 'Locating Women in Migration Studies: An Overview', *The Indian Journal of Social Work*, 59 (3): 715–26.

Linklater, A. 1998. 'Cosmopolitan Citizen', *Citizenship Studies*, 2 (1): 23–41.

Lister, R. 1997. *Citizenship: Feminist Perspectives*. London: Macmillan.

Ludden, D. (ed.). 1996. *Contesting the Nation: Religion, Community and the Politics of Democracy in India*. Philadelphia: University of Pennsylvania Press.

———. (ed.). 2002. *Reading Subaltern Studies: Critical History, Contested Meaning and the Globalization of South Asia*. London: Anthem Press.

MacKinnon, Catherine. 1996. 'Prostitution and Civil Rights', in K. Weisburg (ed.), *Application of Feminist Theory to Women's Lives: Sex, Violence, Work, and Reproduction*, pp. 222–30. Philadelphia: Temple University Press.

Mani, Lata. 1998. *Contentious Traditions: The Debate on Sati in Colonial India*. Berkeley and Los Angeles: University of California Press.

Marcovich, M. 1999. 'Human Rights—A European Challenge?', in D. Hughes and C. Roche (eds), *Making the Harm Visible: Global Sexual Exploitation of Women and Girls, Speaking Out and Providing Services*. The Coalition Agaist Trafficking in Women. http://www.uri.edu/artsci/wms/hughes/mhvtoc.htm. Accessed 2 April 2010.

Marks, S. 2003. 'Empire's Law', *Indiana Journal of Global Legal Studies*, 10 (1): 449–466.

Marshall. T. H. 1950. *Citizenship and Social Class and Other Essays*. Cambridge: Cambridge University Press.

Marshall, T. H. and T. Bottomore (eds). 1992. *Citizenship and Social Class*. London: Pluto Press.

Mayaram, S., M. S. S. Pandian, and A. Skraria. 2007. *Muslims, Dalits and the Fabrications of History*. Visalia, CA: Seagull.

Mayer, T. (ed.). 1999. *Gender Ironies of Nationalism: Sexing the Nation*. London and New York: Routledge.

Mayo, Katherine. 1929. *Slave of the Gods*. London: Jonathan Cape.

McClintock, A. 1995. *Imperial Leather: Race, Gender and Sexuality in the Colonial Contest*. New York and London: Routledge.

McDowell, L. 1996. 'Spatializing Feminism:Geographical Perspectives', in N. Duncan (ed.), *Bodyspace: Destabilizing Geographies of Gender and Sexuality*, pp. 28–44. London: Routledge.

McGill, E. 2002. 'Combating Trafficking of Women and Children in South Asia, Supplemental Study on Legal Frameworks Relevant to Human Trafficking in South Asia', Asian Development Bank Regional Technical Assistance No. 5948. Bangkok: Asian Development Bank.

McGivering, J. 2002. 'Gujarat's Muslims Live in Terror', *BBC News*. 9 May. http://news.bbc.co.uk/2/hi/south_asia/1977246.stm. Accessed 5 April 2010.

Mehta, U. S. 1999. *Liberalism and Empire: A Study in Nineteenth Century British Liberal Thought*. Chicago: University of Chicago Press.

Menon, M. 2001. 'A Test Case in More Ways than One', *The Hindu*. 3 March. http://www.hindu.com/2005/01/03/stories/2005010303341300.htm. Accessed 28 October 2009.

Menon, N. 1998. 'Women and Citizenship', in P. Chatterjee (ed.), *Wages of Freedom: Fifty Years of the Indian Nation State*, pp. 241–66. New Delhi: Oxford University Press.

Menon, R. and K. Bhasin. 1996. 'Abducted Women, the State and Questions of Honour: Three Perspectives on the Recovery Operation in Post-partition India', in K. Jayawardena and M. de Alwis (eds), *Embodied Violence: Communalising Women's Sexuality in South Asia*, pp. 1–31. New Delhi: Kali for Women.

———. 1998. *Borders and Boundaries: Women in India's Partition*. New Delhi: Kali for Women.

Mezzadra, S. 2006. 'Citizen and Subject: A Postcolonial Constitution for the European Union', *Situations*, 1 (2): 31–42.

Mignolo, W. 2002. *Local Histories/Global Designs: Coloniality, Subaltern Knowledges and Border Thinking*. Princeton, New Jersey: Princeton University Press.

Ministry of External Affairs. 2002. 'Report of High Level Committee on the Indian Diaspora'. New Delhi: Ministry of External Affairs.

Ministry of Home Affairs. 2006. 'Annual Report, 2005–2006'. New Delhi: Ministry of Home Affairs.

Ministry of Overseas Indian Affairs. 2007. 'Marriages to Overseas Indians: A Guidance Booklet'. New Delhi: Ministry of Overseas Indian Affairs.

Misra, U. 2007. 'Targeting the Innocent in Assam', *Economic and Political Weekly*, 42 (4): 273–75.

Mohanty, Chandra Talpade. 1991. 'Under Western Eyes: Feminist Scholarship and Colonial Discourses', in C. T. Mohanty, A. Russo, and L. Torres (eds), *Third World Women and the Politics of Feminism*, pp. 51–80. Bloomington: Indiana University Press.

Mohapatra, M. 2004. 'Learning Lessons from India: The Recent History of Anti-terrorist Legislation on the Subcontinent', *The Journal of Criminal Law and Criminology*, 95 (1): 315–44.

Mouffe, C. 1988. 'Hegemony and the New Political Subjects: Towards a New Concept of Democracy', in C. Nelson and L. Grossberg (eds), *Marxism and the Interpretation of Culture*, pp. 89-–101. Trans. S. Grey. Champaign: University of Illinois Press.

Mukherji, D. G. 1928. *A Son of Mother India Answers*. New York: E. P. Dutton.

Munro, V. 2005. 'A Tale of Two Servitudes: Defining and Implementing a Domestic Response to Trafficking of Women for Prostitution in the UK and Australia', *Social and Legal Studies*, 14 (1): 91–114.

Murayama, M. 2006. 'Borders, Migration and Sub-Regional Cooperation in Eastern South Asia', *Economic and Political Weekly*, 41 (14): 1351–1360.

Nair, J. 1996. *Women and Law in Colonial India: A Social History*. New Delhi: Kali for Women.

Nair, P. M. and S. Sen. 2004. 'A Report on Trafficking in Women and Children in India 2002–2003: Volume One'. New Delhi: NHRC, UNIFEM, Institute of Social Sciences.

Nanavati Commission of Inquiry. 2008. 'Part I Sabramati Express Train Incident, Report of the Nanavati–Mehta Commission of Inquiry'. http://www.sacw.net/article101.html. Accessed 28 October 2009.

Nanda, M. 2003. *Prophets Facing Backwards: Postmodern Critiques of Science and the Hindu Nationalism in India*. New Brunswick: Rutgers University Press.

Narain, V. 2007. 'Muslim Women, Family Law, and Equal Citizenship in India', *Journal of Semiotics*, 12 (2): 498–517.

Narayan, U. 2000. 'Essence of Culture and a Sense of History: A Feminist Critique of Cultural Essentialism', in U. Narayan and S. Harding (eds), *Decentering the Center: Philosophy for a Multicultural, Postcolonial, and Feminist World*, pp. 80–100. Bloomington: Indiana University Press.

Narula, S. 2003a. *Compounding Injustice: The Government's Failure to Redress Massacres in Gujarat.* New York: Human Rights Watch. http://www.hrw.org/en/reports/2003/06/30/compounding-injustice. Accessed 28 October 2009.

———. 2003b. 'Overlooked Danger: The Security and Rights Implications of Hindu Nationalism in India', *Harvard Human Rights Journal*, 16: 41–68.

Nathan, D. 2005. 'Oversexed', *The Nation*. 11 August. http://www.thenation.com/doc/20050829/nathan. Accessed 21 April 2009.

National Commission on Enterprises in the Unorganised Sector (NCEUS). 2008. *Report on Conditions of Work and Promotion of Livelihoods in the Unorganised Sector.* New Delhi: Academic Foundation.

National Commission for Women (NCW). 2005a. 'Final Report on Emerging Status of Women Migrants from Bangladesh to West Bengal and Orissa during 1971–2001'. New Delhi: NCW. http://ncw.nic.in/pdfreports/Emerging%20Status%20of%20Women%20Migrants%20from%20Bangladesh%20To%20West%20Bengal%20and%20Orissa.pdf. Accessed 30 July 2009.

———. 2005b. 'Report on Domestic Workers'. New Delhi: NCW.

———. 2005c. General Reports. 'Women in Construction Industry'. http://ncw.nic.in/pdfreports/omen%20Workers%20in%20Construction%20Industry.pdf.

———. n.d. 'Review of the Laws and Legislative Measures Affecting Women, No. 25, The Inter-State Migrant Workmen (Regulation of Employment and Conditions of Service) Act, 1979. New Delhi: NCW. ncw.nic.in/page25.htm#2. Accessed 24 October 2009.

National Perspective Plan for Women, 1988–2002 A. D. 1988. New Delhi: Department of Women and Child Development.

National Policy for the Empowerment of Women. 2001. http://wcd.nic.in/empwomen.htm. Accessed 28 October 2009.

Nessiah, V. and A. Keenan. 2004. 'Human Rights and Sacred Cows: Framing Violence, Disappearing Struggles', in. N. Gordon (ed.), *From the Margins of Globalization: Critical Perspectives on Human Rights*, pp. 261–96. New York: Lexington Books.

Nessiah, V. 2003 'The Ground Beneath Her Feet: "Third World" Feminisms', in A. Anghie (ed.), *The Third World and International Order: Law, Politics and Globalization*, pp. 133–44. Boston: Martinus Nijhoff.

Noorani , A. G. 2002. 'Playing Out a Farce?', *Hindustan Times*. 19 March.

———. 2005. 'Modi and His Visa', *Frontline*. 12–25 March. http://www.hinduonnet.com/fline/fl2208/stories/20050422000704700.htm. Accessed 5 July 2009.

Nussbaum, M. 2002. 'Patriotism and Cosmopolitanism', in M. Nussbaum and J. Cohen (eds), *For Love of Country: Debating the Limits of Patriotism*, pp. 3–20. Boston: Beacon Press.

———. 2003. 'Genocide in Gujarat: The International Community Looks Away', *Dissent Magazine*. Summer. http://www.stopfundinghate.org/resources/news/0803DissentMagazine.htm. Accessed 5 July 2009.

Nussbaum, M. 2004a. 'Body of the Nation: Why Women were Mutilated in Gujarat', *Boston Review*, 29: 33–38.
———. 2004b. *Hiding from Humanity: Disgust, Shame and the Law*. Princeton: Princeton University Press.
Oldenburg, V. 2002. *Dowry Murder: The Imperial Origins of a Cultural Crime*. New York: Oxford University Press.
Oman, J. C. 1973. *The Brahmans, Theists and Muslims of India: Studies of Goddess-Worship in Bengal* (rpt). Delhi: Heritage Publishers.
Orentlicher, D. F. 1991. 'Settling Accounts: The Duty to Prosecute Human Rights Violations of a Prior Regime', *Yale Law Journal*, 100 (8): 2537–2615.
Organization for Economic Co-operation and Development (OECD). 2004. *Migration, Remittances and Development*. Paris: OECD.
———. 2005. *Trends in International Migration and in Migration Policies*. Paris: OECD.
Otto, D. 1999. 'Subalternity and International Law: The Problems of Global Community and the Incommensurability of Difference', in E. Darian-Smith and P. Fitzpatrick (eds), *Laws of the Postcolonial: Law, Meaning and Violence*, pp. 145–80. Ann Arbor: University of Michigan Press.
Oza, R. 2006. *The Making of Neoliberal India: Nationalism, Gender and the Paradoxes of Globalization*. New Delhi: Women Unlimited.
Palriwala, R. and P. Uberoi. 2005. 'Marriage and Migration in Asia: Gender Issues', *Indian Journal of Gender Studies*, 12 (2–3): 5–29.
Pandya, H. 2004. 'Govind Nihalani's Dev in Trouble', *Rediff on the Net*. 16 June. http://in.rediff.com/movies/2004/jun/16dev.htm. Accessed 5 July 2009.
Pandey, G. 1990. *The Construction of Communalism in Colonial North India*. New Delhi, New York, and Oxford: Oxford University Press.
Pardasani, M. 2005. 'HIV Prevention and Sex Workers: An International Lesson in Empowerment', *International Journal of Social Welfare*, 14: 116–26.
Parker, A., M. Russo, D. Sommer, and P.Yaeger (eds). 1992. *Nationalisms and Sexualities*. New York and London: Routledge.
Parrenas, R. S. 2001. *Servants of Globalization: Women, Migration and Domestic Work*. Stanford: Stanford University Press.
Patel, T. (ed.). 2005. *The Family in India: Structure and Practice*. New Delhi: Sage Publications.
Patnaik, U. 1999. 'The Costs of Free Trade: The WTO Regime and the Indian Economy', *Social Scientist*, 27 (11–12): 3–26.
Pederson, J. D. 2000. 'Explaining Economic Liberalization in India: State and Society Perspectives', *World Development*, 28 (2): 265–82.
Percot, Marie. 2006. 'Indian Nurses in the Gulf: From Job Opportunity to Life Strategy', in A. Agrawal (ed.), *Migrant Women and Work (Women and Migration in Asia, vol. 4)*, pp. 155–76. New Delhi, London, and Thousand Oaks: Sage Publications.
People's Union for Civil Liberties (PUCL). 2002. 'An Interim Report to the National Human Rights Commission'. New Delhi: PUCL. http://www.pucl.org/Topics/Religion-communalism/2002/gujarat-nhrc-submission.htm. Accessed 28 October 2009.
People's Union for Democratic Rights (PUDR). 2004. 'Obsessive Pursuit'. Delhi: PUDR. http://www.pudr.org/index.php?option=com_docman&task=cat_view&gid=56&Itemid=63. Accessed 5 July 2009.

Porras, Ileana M. 1995. 'On Terrorism: Reflections on Violence and the Outlaw', in D. Danielsen and K. Engle (eds), *After Identity: A Reader in Law and Culture*, pp. 294–313. New York: Routledge.

Portes, A., M. Castells, and L. Benton (eds). 1989. *The Informal Economy: Studies in Advanced and Less Developed Countries*. Baltimore: The Johns Hopkins University Press.

Prabhakara, M. S. 2007. 'Assam: Updating the Past', *Economic and Political Weekly*, 42 (4): 271–72.

Prakash, G. 2000. 'Writing Post-Orientalist Histories of the Third World: Perspectives from Indian Historiography', in V. Chaturvedi (ed.), *Mapping Subaltern Studies and the Postcolonial*, pp. 163–90. New York: Verso.

Prayas. 2005. 'A Study of the Socio Economic Situation and Rehabilitation Needs of Women in Dance Bars'. Bombay: Prayas.

PTI. 2002. 'Every Citizen of India is a Hindu: Sudarshan', *Rediff on the Net*. 6 April. http://www.rediff.com/news/2002/apr/06rss.htm. Accessed 5 July 2009.

———. 2005. 'Zaheera Sheikh a "Self Condemned Liar": SC Panel', *Express India*. 30 August. http://www.expressindia.com/fullstory.php?newsid=53608 Accessed 5 July 2009.

Puri, J. 1999. *Women, Body, Desire in Post-Colonial India: Narratives of Gender and Sexuality*. New York: Routledge.

Puri, S. and T. Ritzema. 1999. 'Migrant Worker Remittances, Micro-Finance, and the Informal Economy: Prospects and Issues', Working Paper No. 21, Enterprise and Co-operative Development Department, Social Finance Unit. Geneva: ILO.

Rajan, N. 1990. *Within the Fragments: A Non-holistic Approach to Indian Culture*. New Delhi: Affiliated East West Press.

Raju, S. and S. K. Sasikumar. 2006. 'Into the Persian Gulf to Return: Remittance, Consumption and Development', in M. John, P. K. Jha, and S. Jodhka (eds), *Contested Transformations: Changing Economies and Identities in Contemporary India*, pp. 200–11. New Delhi: Tulika.

Ramakrishnan, V. 2002. 'Hindutva Institutions in Education: The Spreading Network of RSS', *South Asia Documents*. http://indowindow.net/sad/article.php?child=30&article=32. Accessed 5 July 2009.

Ramachandran, S. 1999. 'Of Boundaries and Border Crossings: Undocumented Bangladeshi "Infiltrators" and the Hegemony of Hindu Nationalism in India', *Interventions*, 1 (2): 235.

Ramachandran, S. 2003. '"Operation Pushback": Sangh Parivar, State, Slums and the Surreptitious Bangladeshis in New Delhi', *Economic and Political Weekly*, 38 (7): 637–47.

Ranga Iyer, C. S. 1928. *Father India: A Reply to Mother India*. New York: Lewis Carrier & Co.

Rao, U. 1992. 'Gaps in Definition and Analysis: A Sociological Perspective', in K. Saradomoni (ed.), *Finding the Household: Conceptual and Methodological Issues*, pp.49–74. New Delhi: Sage Publications.

Raymond, J. 2005. 'Sex Trafficking is not "Sex Work"', *Conscience*, 26 (1). Accessed 28 October 2009. www.rediff.com. 2004a. 'Zaheera is under Vadodara Police Protection: Commissioner'. 4 November. http://in.rediff.com/news/2004/nov/04best.htm .Accessed 5 July 2009.

———. 2004b. 'Majlis-e-Shura Declares Zaheera an Outcast'. 24 December. http://in.rediff.com/news/2004/dec/24best.htm. Accessed 5 July 2009.

Raymond, J. 2005. 'Supreme Court Panel Calls Zahira a Liar'. 29 August. http://www.rediff.com/news/2005/aug/29best.htm. Accessed 5 July 2009.

———. 2006. 'Best Bakery Case: 9 Accused Convicted'. 24 February. http://in.rediff.com/news/2006/feb/24gujarat.htm. Accessed 5 July 2009.

Richardson, D. 2000. *Rethinking Sexuality*. London: Sage Publications.

Roberts, N. 1992. *Whores in History: Prostitution in Western Society*. London: Harper Collins.

Rodrigues, V. 2005. 'Citizenship and the Indian Constitution', in R. Bharghava and H. Reifeld (eds), *Civil Society, Public Sphere and Citizenship*, pp. 209–35. New Delhi: Sage Publications.

Roy, A. 2005. *Gendered Citizenship: Historical and Conceptual Explorations*. New Delhi: Orient Longman.

———. 2006. 'Overseas Indian Citizen: A New "Setubandhan?"', *Economic and Political Weekly*, 41 (15): 1421–1424.

———. 2008. 'Between Encompassment and Enclosure: The "Migrant" and the Citizen in India', *Contributions to Indian Sociology*, 42 (2): 219–48.

Rubin, G. 1992. 'Thinking Sex: Notes for a Radical Theory of the Politics of Sexuality', in C. Vance (ed.), *Pleasure and Danger: Exploring Female Sexuality*, pp. 267–319. London: Pandora Press.

Rushdie, Salman. 1983. *Shame*. London and New York: Knopf.

———. 1991. *Imaginary Homelands*. London: Granta.

SAARC. 2002. 'SAARC Convention on Preventing and Combating Trafficking in Women and Children for Prostitution'. 5 January. http://www.december18.net/traffickingconventionsSAARC2002.pdf. Accessed 21 April 2009.

Said, E. 1978. *Orientalism*. New York: Vintage Books.

———. 1993. *Culture and Imperialism*. New York: Vintage Books.

Salgaonkar, S. 2007. 'Violence, Employment and Citizenship: A Case of Self-Employed Women in the Unorganised Sector in Goa', *Indian Journal of Gender Studies*, 14 (1): 117–35.

Samaddar, R. 1999. *The Marginal Nation: Transborder Migration from Bangladesh to India*. New Delhi: Sage Publications.

Sangari, K. K. and S. Vaid. 1989. 'Introduction', in K. K.Sangari and S. Vaid (eds), *Recasting Women: Essays in Colonial History*, pp.1–26. New Delhi: Kali for Women.

Sarkar S. 1997. *Writing Social History*. New Delhi: Oxford University Press.

Sarkar, Tanika. 1993. 'The Women of the Hindutva Brigade', *Bulletin of Concerned Asian Scholars*, 25 (4): 16–25.

———. 1996. 'Colonial Lawmaking and Lives/Deaths of Indian Women: Different Readings of Law and Community', in Ratna Kapur (ed.), *Feminist Terrains in Legal Domains: Interdisciplinary Essays on Women and Law in India*, pp. 210–42. New Delhi: Kali for Women.

———. 2001. *Hindu Wife and Hindu Nation*. New Delhi: Permanent Black.

———. 2002. 'Semiotics of Terror: Muslim Children and Women in Hindu Rashtra', *Economic and Political Weekly*, 37 (28): 2872–2876.

Sassen, S. 1996. *Losing Control?: Sovereignty in an Age of Globalization*. New York: Columbia University Press.

———. 1998. *Globalization and its Discontents*. New York: The New Press.

Savarkar, V. D. (1923) 1989. *Hindutva: Who is A Hindu?* Bombay: S. S. Savarkar.

———. (1929) 1971. *The Six Glorious Epochs of Indian History*. Trans. S. T. Godbole. Bombay: Bal Savarkar Prakashan.

Sen, Amartya. 2006. *The Argumentative Indian: Writings on Indian History, Culture and Identity*. London: Penguin Books.

Sen, I. 2002. *Woman and Empire: Representations in the Writings of British India, 1858–1900*. New Delhi: Orient Longman.

Sethi, A. 2007. 'House of Death', *Frontline*, 24 (1): 27–29. 13–26 January.

Shah, A. M. 2005. 'Lineage, Structure and Change in a Gujarat Village', in P. Uberoi (ed.), *Family, Kinship and Marriage in India* (rpt), pp.119–45. New Delhi: Oxford University Press.

Shah, Svati. 2006. 'Solicitation, Migration and Day Wage Labour', in S. Arya and A. Roy (eds), *Poverty, Gender and Migration* (*Women and Migration in Asia, vol. 2*), pp. 236–50. New Delhi: Sage Publications.

Shapiro, N. 2004. 'The New Abolitionists', *Seattle Weekly*. 30 August. http://www.bayswan.org/swed/newabolish.html. Accessed 28 July 2009.

Sharma, A. and A. Piush. 2001. *Women Workers in the Unorganised Sector: The More the Merrier?* New Delhi: Institute for Human Development.

Siddiqui, T. 2003. 'An Anatomy of Forced and Voluntary Migration from Bangladesh: A Gendered Perspective', in M. Morokvasic-Muller, E. Umut, and S. Kyoko (eds), *Crossing Borders and Shifting Boundaries*, pp. 155–76. Opladen: Leske and Budrich.

Singh, J. 2002. 'Gujarat Muslim Women "Rape Victims"', *BBC News*. 16 April. http://news.bbc.co.uk/2/hi/south_asia/1933521.stm. Accessed 5 July 2009.

Singha, R. 1998. *A Despotism of Law: Crime and Justice in Early Colonial India*. New Delhi and London: Oxford University Press.

———. 2009.'Passport, Ticket, and India — Rubber Stamp: "The Problem of the Pauper Pilgrim" in Colonial India ca. 1882–1925', in H. Fischer-Tine and A. Tambe (eds), *The Limits of British Colonial Control in South Asia : Spaces of Disorder in the Indian Ocean Region* (Routledge Studies in the Modern History of Asia, 50), pp. 49–83. London: Routledge.

Sinha, A., N. Sangeeta, and K. A. Siddiqui. 2000. 'Study of the Impact of Alternate Policies on the Economy with Special Reference to the Informal Sectors: A Multisectoral Study' (mimeo). New Delhi: NCAER.

Sinha, Mrinalini. 1995. *Colonial Masculinity: The 'Manly' Englishman' and the 'Effeminate Bengali' in the Late Nineteenth Century*. Manchester and New York: Manchester University Press.

———. (ed.). 2000. *Katherine Mayo: Mother India: Selections from the Controversial 1927 Text*. Ann Arbor: University of Michigan Press.

———. 2006. *Spectres of Mother India: The Global Restructuring of an Empire*. Durham: Duke University Press.

Skeldon R. 2004. 'More than Remittances: Other Aspects of the Relationship between Migration and Development', UN/POP/MIG/2004. 9 November.

Smith, J. 2000. 'Sex Trade Enslaving East Europeans: A Survivor's Brutal Tale', *International Herald Tribune*. 26 July.

Smith, Zadie. 2000. *White Teeth: A Novel*. London: Penguin Books.

SNDT Women's University and Forum Against Oppression of Women. 2005. 'Working Women in Mumbai Bars, Truth Behind The Controversy'. Mumbai: SNDT.

Som, R. 1992. 'Jawaharlal Nehru and the Hindu Code: A Victory of Symbol Substance?' *Occasional Papers on Perspectives in Indian Development*. New Delhi: Centre for Contemporary Studies, Nehru Memorial Museum and Library.

Sparke, M. 2004, 'Passports into Credit Cards: On the Borders and Spaces of Neoliberal Citizenship' in Joe S. Migdal (ed.), *Boundaries and Belonging: States and Societies in the Struggle to Shape Identities and Local Practices*, pp. 251–83. Cambridge: Cambridge University Press.

Spivak, G. 1985. 'Three Women's Texts and a Critique of Imperialism', *Critical Inquiry*, 12: 242–61.

———. 1988. 'Can the Subaltern Speak?' in C. Nelson and L. Grossberg (eds), *Marxism and the Interpretation of Culture*, pp. 271–313. Urbana and Chicago: University of Illinois.

———. 1993. *Outside in the Teaching Machine*. London: Routledge.

Srinivasan, T. N. and J. Bhagwati. 1999. 'Outward-orientation and Development: Are Revisionists Right?', Discussion Paper No. 806. New Haven, California: Economic Growth Centre, Yale University.

Standing, H. 1991. *Dependence and Autonomy: Women's Employment and the Family in Calcutta*. London: Routledge.

Stoler, A. 1995. *Race and the Education of Desire: Foucault's History of Sexuality and the Colonial Order of Things*. Durham and London: Duke University Press.

———. 2002. *Carnal Knowledge and Imperial Power: Race and the Intimate in Colonial Rule*. Berkeley: University of California Press.

Strobel, M. 1992. 'Gender, Sex and Empire', pamphlet for American Historical Association series, *Essays on Global and Comparative History*. Washington, D.C.: American History Association.

Sunder Rajan, R. 1993. *Real and Imagined Women: Gender, Culture and Postcolonialism*. London and New York: Routledge.

———. 2003. *The Scandal of the State: Women, Law and Citizenship in Postcolonial India*. New Delhi: Permanent Black.

Sung, G. 2001. 'Europe to Deal a Blow to Human Trafficking', *The Straits Times*. Singapore. 6 December.

Swaminathan, H., N. Bhutla, and S. Chakraborty. 2007. *Women's Property Rights as an AIDS Response: Emerging Efforts in South Asia*. Washington, D.C.: International Centre for Research on Women.

Tafadar, S. and A. Khadijah. 2002. *Gujarat: Ongoing Genocide*. London: Islamic Human Rights Commission.

Terre des hommes and Partnership Nepal. 2004. 'Interim Report: A Study of the "Destination Side" of the Trafficking of Nepalese Girls to India'. Kathmandu: Terre des Hommes. 20 August.

Thapan, M. 2005a. '"Making Incomplete": Identity, Women and the State', in idem (ed.), *Transnational Migration and the Politics of Identity* (*Women and Migration in Asia*, vol. 1), pp. 23–62. New Delhi: Sage Publications.

———. (ed.). 2005b. *Transnational Migration and the Politics of Identity* (*Women and Migration in Asia*, vol. 1). New Delhi: Sage Publications.

Thapar, R. 1975. *The Past and Prejudice*. New Delhi: National Book Trust.

———. 1989. 'Imagined Religious Communities?: Ancient History and the Modern Search for a Hindu Identity', *Modern Asian Studies*, 23 (2): 209–31.

———. 2002. *History and Beyond*. New Delhi: Oxford University Press.

Thapar, R. 2007. 'Secularism, History and Contemporary Politics in India', in A. D. Needham and R. Sunder Rajan (eds), *The Crisis of Secularism in India*, pp. 191–207. Durham and London: Duke University Press.

The Hindu. 2002. 'Shabana flays RSS leaders'. 3 May. http://www.hinduonnet.com/2002/05/03/stories/2002050307121100.htm. Accessed 5 July 2009.

———. 2003. 'On the Ground in Gujarat'. 26 October. http://www.hindu.com/2003/10/26/stories/2003102600081400.htm. Accessed 5 July 2009.

———. 2004. 'BJP Criticizes Decision to Retain IMDT Act'. 30 October. http://www.hinduonnet.com/thehindu/2004/10/30/stories/2004103015971300.htm. Accessed 21 July 2009.

———. 2005. 'Nanavati Commisson Report of 1984 Anti-Sikh Riots Submitted'. 10 February. http://www.hinduonnet.com/2005/02/10/stories/2005021005880900.htm. Accessed 5 July 2009.

The Telegraph. 2005. 'Calcutta Sex Workers Respond to Born into Brothels', letter. 15 March. http://www.16beavergroup.org/monday/archives/001535.php. Accessed 25 November 2009.

The Times of India. 2005. 'Dance Bar Bill Passage Major Boost for Patil'. 22 July. http://timesofindia.indiatimes.com/articleshow/1180390.cms. Accessed 21 July 2009.

———. 2006. 'Age, Sex Bar for Maids in Gulf'. 10 January. http://timesofindia.indiatimes.com/articleshow/1365204.cms. Accessed 2 April 2009.

Thompson, E. 2000. *Colonial Citizens: Republican Rights, Paternal Privilege and Gender in French Syria and Lebanon*. New York: Columbia University Press.

Thomas, D. and S. Jones (eds). 1993. *A Modern Form of Slavery: Trafficking of Burmese Women and Girls into Brothels in Thailand*. Washington: Women's Rights Project, Asia Watch, Division of Human Rights Watch.

Todd, E. 1985. *The Explanation of Ideology: Family Structures and Social Systems*. Trans. D. Garrioch. Oxford: Basil Blackwell.

Uberoi, P. (ed.). 2005. *Family, Kinship and Marriage in India* (rpt). New Delhi: Oxford University Press.

Ujjwala. 2007. 'A Comprehensive Scheme for Prevention of Trafficking and Rescue, Rehabilitation, Reintegration, and Repatriation of Victims of Trafficking for Commercial Sexual Exploitation'. New Delhi: Ministry of Women and Child Development, Government of India.

United Nations. 2006. 'World Population Monitoring, Focusing on International Migration and Development: Report of the Secretary-General', E/CN.9/2006/3. New York: United Nations.

United Nations AIDS (UNAIDS). 2008. 'Report on the Global AIDS Epidemic'. New York: United Nations.

United Nations Commission on Human Rights (UNCHR). 1988. 'Guiding Principles on International Displacement', UN Doc. E/CN.4/998/Add.2. 11 February.

United Nations Department of Economic and Social Affairs (UNESA).1998. 'Recommendations on Statistics of International Migration–Revision 1', 12-15 ST/ESA/STAT/SER.M/58/Rev 1. New York: Statistics Divison, United Nations.

———. 2002. 'International Migration Report'. New York: United Nations.

———. 2005. 'World Survey on the Role of Women in Development: Women and International Migration', A/59/287/Add.1, ST/ESA/294. New York: Division for the Advancement of Women, United Nations.

United Nations Department of Economic and Social Affairs (UNESA). 2006. 'Trends in Total Migrant Stock: 2005 Revision', POP/DB/MIG/Rev.2005. Spreadsheet. New York: Population Division, United Nations.

United Nations Family Planning Association (UNFPA). 2006. 'State of World Population: A Passage to Hope — Women and International Migration. http://www.unfpa.org/swp/2006/english/introduction.html. Accessed 1 April 2009.

United States Department of State. 2005. 'Victims of Trafficking and Violence Protection Act of 2000: Trafficking in Persons Report'. http://www.state.gov/documents/organization/47255.pdf. Accessed 21 July 2009.

———. 2009. 'Victims of Trafficking and Violence Protection Act of 2000: Trafficking in Persons Report, 2009 Report'. Washington, D.C.: U.S. State Department. http://www.state.gov/g/tip/rls/tiprpt/2009/index.htm. Accessed 27 July 2009.

Vamp News. 2002. 'Rehabilitation: Against their Will?', vol. 1 (2). June. www.sangram.org/vampnews/vol01no02/against.html. Accessed 13 April 2009.

Vajpayee, A. B. 2002. 'Who are These People Accusing Us, India was Secular Even Before Muslims and Christians', *Indian Express*. 24 April. http://www.indianexpress.com/full_story.php?content_id=1402. Accessed 5 July 2009.

Varia, N. 2007. 'Globalization Comes Home: Migrant Domestic Workers' Rights', 'World Report, 2007', pp. 51–62. Washington, D. C.: Human Rights Watch. http://www.hrw.org/en/reports/2007/01/10/world-report-2007. Accessed 28 October 2009.

Vasan, S. 2007. 'Gendering Resource Rights and Democratic Citizenship', *Indian Journal of Gender Studies*, 14 (1): 17–32.

Voet, R. 1998. *Feminism and Citizenship*. London: Sage Publications.

Walkowitz, J. 1982. *Prostitution and Victorian Society: Women, Class, and the State*. Cambridge and New York: Cambridge University Press.

Walzer, M. 1970. *Obligations: Essays on Disobedience, War and Citizenship*. Cambridge, Mass: Harvard University Press.

Weeks, J. 1999. 'The Sexual Citizen', *Theory, Culture and Society*, 15 (3–4): 35–52.

Wilks, R., R. Netting, and E. Arnould (eds). 1984. *Households: Comparative and Historical Studies of the Domestic Group*. Berkeley: University of California Press.

World Bank. 2006. 'Global Economic Prospects 2006 — Economic Implications of Remittances and Migration'. New York: World Bank.

World Trade Organization (WTO). 2004. 'World Trade Report: Exploring the Linkage between Domestic Policy Environment and International Trade'. Geneva: WTO. http://www.wto.org/english/res_e/booksp_e/anrep_e/world_trade_report04_e.pdf. Accessed 28 October 2009.

Young, I. M. 1995. 'Polity and Group Difference: A Critique of the Ideal of Universal Citizenship', in R. Beiner (ed.), *Theorizing Citizenship*, pp. 175–208. Albany: State University of New York Press.

Yuval-Davis, N. and P. Werbner. 1999. 'Introduction: Women and the New Discourse of Citizenship', in idem (eds), *Women, Citizenship and Difference*, pp. 1–38. London: Zed Press.

CASES

Air India Cabin Crew Association v Yeshawinee Merchant All India Reports 2004 Supreme Court 187.

Bandhua Mukhti Morcha v. Union of India All India Reports 1984 Supreme Court 802.

Bangladesh Society for the Enforcement of Human Rights vs. Government of Bangladesh Volume LIII, 2001, Dhaka Law Reports.

Chetan Dutt v. Municipal Corporation of Delhi, Civil Writ Petition No. 3170 of 2001.

Dr. Ved Vyas Mahajan, Secretary Bharatiya Janata Party, Delhi v. The Election Commission of India, Civil Writ Petition of 2003.

Dhanurjaya Putel and Another v. State of Orissa 2002 (II) Orissa Law Reports 412.

Gaurav Jain vs. Union of India, 1997, 8 Supreme Court Cases 114.

Dharwad District Public Works Department Literate Daily Wages Employees Association vs. the State of Karnataka, All India Reports 1990 Supreme Court 883.

Gaurav Jain vs. Union of India, All India Reports 1990 Supreme Court 292.

Gaurav Jain vs. Union of India All India Reports 1997 Supreme Court 302.

Indian Hotel and Restaurants Association (AHAR) v. State of Maharashtra (MANU/MH/0088/2006).

Kulathil Mammu v. State of Kerala, All.India.Reports 1966, Supreme Court 1614.

Mubarak Ali v. State of Bombay, All India Reports 1957, Supreme Court 857.

Lucy D'Souza v. State of Goa MANU/MH/0048/1990.

Mackinnon, Mackenzie & Co v. Audrey D'Costa, All India Reports 1987 Supreme Court 1281.

Mahabubnagar District Palamoori Contract Labour Union v. M/S Nagarjuna Construction Company, 1998, (1), *Karnataka Law Journal* 639.

Municipal Corporation of Delhi vs. Female Workers (Muster Roll) and Another All India Reports 2000 Supreme Court 1274.

National Domestic Workers Welfare Trust and Others vs. Union of India and Another Supreme Court Writ Petition (Civil) 160/2003.

National Human Rights Commission v. State of Gujarat, Special Leave Petition (Criminal) of 2003 (India 2003). http://www.ielrc.org/content/c0302.pdf. Accessed 28 October 2009.

People's Union for Democratic Rights v. Union of India, All India Reports 1982 Supreme Court 1473.

Phul Singh v. State of Haryana (1979) 4 Supreme Court Cases 413.

Prosecutor v. Akayesu, Case No. ICTR-96-4-T (Sept. 2 1998). http://69.94.11.53/default.htm (follow "Status of Cases" hyperlink; then follow 'AKAYESU, Jean Paul (ICTR-96-4) hyperlink under 'Completed Cases') *Prosecutor v. Delalic,* Case No. IT-96-21-A 20 (Feb. 20 2001).

Public at Large vs. The State of Maharashtra (1997) (4) Bombay Criminal Law Reports 171.

Salal Hydroelectric Project v. State of Jammu and Kashmir, (1984) 3 Supreme Court Cases 538.

Sahyog Mahila Mandal and Another vs. State of Gujarat and Others (2004) 2 Gujarat Law Reports 1764.

Sarbananda Sonowal v. Union of India and Another (2005) 5 Supreme Court Cases, 665.

Savera vs. the State of Goa (MANU/MH/0888/2003).

State of Gujarat v. Baria et. al (*Best Bakery Case*) No. 248/2002 (Gujarat Fast Track Ct. June 27 2003). http://www.sabrang.com/cjp/best/vadjudgement.pdf. Accessed 29 October 2009.

State of Andhra Pradesh v. Abdul Khader, All India Reports 1961 Supreme Court 1467.

State of Madhya Pradesh v. Peer Mohammed, All India Reports, 1963 Supreme Court 645.

Sudhansu Sekhar Sahoo vs. State of Orissa (2002) 10 Supreme Court Cases 743.

The Cooperative Store Ltd. (Super Bazar) vs. Bimla Devi and Ors. (MANU/DE/0731/2005).

Union of India v. Dharam Pal and Others All India Reports, 1996, Supreme Court 3234.

About the Author

Ratna Kapur is a leading scholar on human rights law, feminist legal theory, and postcolonial theory. Her extensive repertoire of publications spans these and other issues of contemporary relevance and debate. She is Director of the Centre for Feminist Legal Research in New Delhi and is on the faculty of the Geneva School of International Relations. She has been a legal practitioner in India and continues to work as a legal consultant, associated with the United Nations and various other organisations. As an international scholar, Kapur has been invited as visiting faculty to a number of law schools including New York University School of Law, Yale Law School, Georgetown University Law Centre, the United Nations Peace University (Costa Rica), and the National Law School of India University. Some of her important publications include *Erotic Justice: Law and the New Politics of Postcolonialism* (2005), *Secularism's Last Sigh?* (co-authored, 2001), and *Subversive Sites: Feminist Engagements with Law in India* (co-authored, 1996).

Index

abuse 33, 66, 80, 98–100, 122, 125, 129, 132
Adi Brahmo Samaj 51–52
age of consent 41, 112, *see also* child marriage; marriage
Age of Consent Act, 1891 110
Alberuni 53
and non-government initiatives 178; and prosecution recommendation 179–80; responses to victims of 190; riots force 184; and violence on women 180
anti-trafficking 196; campaign 10; domestic law 102–108; initiatives 107; international law 99–100; intervention 123, 128–29; law 105, 198, 131; legal regime 98; South Asian regional initiative 100–102
anti-immigration policies 10
anti-prostitution movement 99, *see also* anti-trafficking
anti-trafficking, laws 34, 59, 97, 105, 123; provisions, 104, 106
Arya Samaj (Society of Aryans) 52
Assam 140, 150, 151, 152, 153, 154, 164; to 'oust Bangladeshis' 9, *see also* Bangladesh migrant

Baina beach habitation, eviction and demolition of 61–63; and High Court 62; and sex workers 61–62
Bajrang Dal (BD — Hanuman Squad) 173
balance of payment problems 35
Bangladesh migrants 9, 12, 28, 30, 149–52, 154, 156, 157, 165; Muslims as 167, *see also* migrants
bar dancing in Bombay 198; ban on 7–8
Basu, Amrita 194
belonging' 29, 33, 39, 41, 59,
Best Bakery Case, The 177, 186–87; and Zaheera Sheikh 186–89, 194
between Burma and Thailand 124, 137*n*19
Bharatiya Janata Party (BJP) 136–37*n*16, 151; led coalition at Centre 183; as political wing of Hindu Right 173, 188
bhumipuja (grand prayer) 168
bodies, women's 86, 92, 121, 122
Bombay 121, 130, 165
Bombay High Court, on brothels and sexual services 60–63; and anti-trafficking 61
borders 11; migration across 12, *see also* cross-border movement
Born into Brothels by Ross Kaufman and Zana Briski 97, 117–18, 130, 133; Gender Lens Award to 118
Building and Other Construction Workers (Regulation of Employment and Conditions of Services) Act, 1996 77, 78–79
Bumiller, Elizabeth 135*n*6
Butler, J. 197

Calcutta 97, 117, 118, 121, 122, 133, 136, *see also* sex workers in Calcutta, union of; sex workers in Sonagachi
campaigns on violence against women 122
casual workers, regularisation of 73
CATW (Coalition Against Trafficking in Women) 114, 115, 119, 125, 126
Chae Chan Ping, US Supreme Court decision in 153
chastity 40, 42-43, 58, 146
child marriage 41, 108, 110, 112, 113; and Hindu tradition 113; Mrinalini Sinha on 41
Child Marriage Restraint Act, 1929 41
child trafficking 27, 134

Christian Evangelicals, USA 113–14, 135*n*8
Christian Right 121, 135*n*8
Cisik, Richard 114
citizenship 15–19, 29, 139, 140–48, 149–50, 151–63, 164, 165; alternative conception of 198; cultural and religious identity for 155–56; definition of 33; in India 200; law and migrant 149–51; laws 19, 198; liberal argument on 16, 139; as mechanisms of power 139; and migrant 18, 139–40; in modern nation-state 138; in postcolonial India 142–49; rights and practices of 18, 51; role of 140; social security of 84; T. H. Marshall on 15–16; technologies of 5
Citizenship Act, 149, 165
Citizenship Amendment Act (CAA 2005) 149
Citizenship Rules of 1956 149
civilising mission/civilisational maturity 15, 141, 163
colonial 40, 41, 42, 43, 51, 110, 111, 112, 113, 123, 126, 141, 157; power 40, 41, 43, 52, 110, 111, 112, 123, 163
colonial citizenry 140–42
colonial encounter 29, 40–43, 47, 51–52, 97, 123, 157; culture and sex 40; and Indian tradition 47; and women 29; and women's sexual purity 41
communalism 189
concubine system 110
crimes 66
cross-border movement 33, 55, 56, 107; traffic 56
cultural, identity 142; norms 50–55; purity 51; values of India 51
culture 42, 51–52, 54, 87, 90–91, 108, 155; Indian 53, 55; Partha Chatterjee on 40, 41

daughters 45, 47, 48, 56, 57, 146, *see also* wives
Day My God Died, The by Andrew Levine 121–25, 97, 134
Delhi High Court ruling, on women workers 72; for same wage as male 72
Denning, Lord 153
Derozians 51
Dev by Govind Nihalani 168–70, 190–91
discrimination 69, 70, 71, 72, 74, 85, 103, 141, 166
domestic workers and NCW 81–82; and sexual misconduct or exploitation 80
dual nationality 200, *see also* citizenship
Durban Mahila Samanwaya Committee, 130, 96

economic, liberalisation 34–99; regulation of migrant women 69–71
Ehrenreich, B. 95*n*10
emancipation of women 108
emigrant women workers 80
Empire 42, 108, 126, 140, 141
Equal pay for equal work 73–74, *see also* Delhi High Court ruling, for same wage as male
Equal Remuneration Act, The 1976 (ERA 1976) 71–73
equality 47, 51, 64, 70–71, 89, 107, 113–14, 119–20, 145–46; discourse of 111, 144–45, 148; rights 147, 148; women's 96, 111, 113
Equality Now 114
essentialism gender and cultural 185
evictions 59, 61, 62, 64, 65, 68
exclusion 29, 57, 139, 141, 157, 163; and citizenship 139, 141; and colonialism 157; and migrants, 155; of Other 157
exploitation 33, 66, 80, 100, 102, 103, 109, 116, 160

familial norms 43–50; cross-cultural 46–47
familial roles, women's 71, 89, 158
family 43–44, 45–46, 48–49; diversity in formations 57*n*6; ideology of 44–45, 49–50; law 145; and sexual division of labour 46

fear 28, 39, 55, 62, 94, 112, 124, 143, 146, 155
female 128–31; infanticide 110; morality 113–21; 'Other' 108–13, 127, sexuality 43; workers in organised sector 71–76
female migrants 6–8, 22, 38, 96–97, 195, 196–97, 202–203, 206; in informal sector 38; and international migration 6; and legal regulation of 9–10, 42, 55, 67; from Nepal 51; as Other 93; re-regulation of 86; Svati Shah for 68; in vulnerable position of 9; workers 71, 74, 75, 101
feminine, characteristics of 10; virtues of 50
feminism 19–20, 128
feminist responses to 125–28; Kathleen Barry work on 126; in Nepal–India border 124; in Persons Report (TIP Report), USA 116; and rescue 59; rescue and rehabilitation 126–27; woman 131; of young girls into prostitution 102
First World countries 197
foreigners 149, 152, 155, 165, 166

Gangoli, Geetanjali 67
gender 39, 69, 73, 206; difference, 29, 71, 141, 144, 147; identity, 41; dimensions of migration 6; and nationalism 87; relations, 36, 44, 45; roles, 69, 71, 94, 161
General Agreement on Trade and Services (GATS) 31, 32; and migration 31–32
girls 41, 56, 59, 60, 61, 89, 98, 103, 105, 118, 121, 124, 132, 133, 134, 137, *see also* daughters
global 28, 30–33, 39, 86; anti-trafficking initiatives 122; anti-trafficking interventions 116; capital 85; economic process 94; economic recession 31, 32; economy 30, 82, 86, 91, 120; encounter with national identity 39; job crisis 30; labour flow 33; migration 30; movement of cross border 28
globalisation, 28, 32, 34–39, 54–55, 85–87, 89–90, 93, 107
Godhra carnage, 58 168; as murder of Hindu martyrs 175; and Narendra Singh Modi 175–76; projection of 176; refugees of 177, *see also* Gujarat riots
Golwalkar, Madhav Sadashiv 13, 188
government, social spending of 37
governmentality 17
Gujarat riots 167–68, 174–76, 188; *Hindutva* and anti-Muslim ideology 190; Human Rights Watch report on 191; Muslim in 171

Hindu Adoption and Maintenance Act 147
Hindu Code Bill 147
Hindu Marriage Act, The 147
Hindu Minority and Guardianship Act 147
Hindu nation 29, 52, 119, 144,
Hindu nationalism 52, 94, 119, 157
Hindu nationalists 57*n*2, 113; and Pakistan 143; and 'regeneration' of Hinduism 52
Hindu rights 5, 12–14, 53, 167, 173; and citizenship 150; and mosque 168; and Other 93; political agenda of 185; in politics 94; precepts of ideology of 173; religious right-wing 135*n*8; strategy 172; and women, 87–93, 185
Hindu Succession Act 147
Hindu, culture 12; family 120; identity as Hindu nation 52, 53; majoritarianism 172–74; masculinity 184; for resisting colonialism 174; revivalism 149; woman and identity 91
Hindus 26*n*; as Aryans 14
Hindus–Muslims, struggle between 13
Hindutva 53, 167, 173–74; and call of unity 174; concept of 14; in constructing 'alien' 182; as

genocidal project 178; militant 188; politics 182; politics of 174–75
HIV/AIDS prevention 59–60, 102, 136*n*15; and sex workers 130
home workers/home-based workers 83
homosexuality 50–51
Hoschschild, A. R. 95*n*10
household as economic unit 57*n*4
Hughes, Donna 119
human rights 62, 64, 79, 101, 106, 114–15, 117; violations 171
Human Rights Law Network 81
Human Rights Watch 123–24, 137*n*18, 19
human trafficking 7

identity, cultural 41, 123, 142, 156, 162; gendered 39, 49; Hindu nationalist 119, 158; nation's 39, 56; women's 41, 86, 88, 89, 90, 92, 120
Illegal Migrants (Determination by Tribunal) Act (IMDT Act) of 1983 152–53, 154, 155
illegal, immigrants 154, 155, 161; migrants, 149, 150, 152, 153, 154, 155, 165; deportation of 152, 154
ILO (International Labour Organization) 73
Immoral Traffic (Prevention) Act (ITPA) Amendment Bill, 2006 117
Immoral Traffic Prevention Act, 1956 (ITPA) 64, 102–105
inclusion 29, 57, 141, 157, 163
India, borders of 29; division of history 93; identity of, 29, 39; lineage of 201; Muslims of 167, 171; as transit country 30
Indian nation 30
Indian woman 60, 66, 111, 120–21, 145, 163; citizenship 158; identity of 158; sexuality of 42
Indian womanhood 128, 144–46, 149
Indian-ness/Hindu-ness 201
Indirect taxation 35
influx 64, 151–54
International Initiative for Justice (IIJ) 178–79, 192
interracial sex 110
Interstate Migrant Workmen (Regulation of Employment and Conditions of Services Act 1979 (ISMWA), 77–78; Arya and Roy on 77

joint family 47, 48, *see also* familial norms
Joshi, Murli Manohar 175
judicial 55, 58, 106, 107; activism 106
judicial decisions, and migrant women 58; and sexual promiscuity 58
juridical entitlements 140, 151, 158
justice, in Gujarat 185; for Muslim women 179; proliferation of 177–85
Juvenile Justice (Care and Protection of Children) Act, The 2000 134*n*5

Kamat Committee, The 62
Kannabiran, K. G. 193
Koli, Surender 27, *see also* Nithari
Krishna Iyer, V. R. 193

labour abuses, US Act, 2000 on 115–16
labour force, casualisation of 37; exploitation in 30
labour market 35; and neoliberal policies 38; women in 45
labour, casual 37; forced 65, 99, 102; market 35, 37, 38, 45, 46, 48, 49, 69, 70, 73, 76, 82, 85, 89; power 76; migration to Gulf 31; sexual division of, 29–30, 34, 36, 38, 44–46, 48, 50, 69, 71, 73, 79, 82; women's 37, 38, 85, 90
law 205–206; and rights, role of 167–68
Lederer, Laura 115, Laura 136*n*12

legal regulation, of domestic work 79–83; of female migrants 51, 69, 98; of migrant 202–203
Levine, Andrew 132
liberalism 52, 54
'licensing raj' 34

MacKinnon, Catharine 126
Mackinnon, Mackenzie & Co v. Audrey D'Costa 72
majoritarianism 150, 169–70, 172, 189; HINDU 173–74; ideologies of 190; politics of 187
marriage 41–43, 48, 66, 67, 106, 112, 114, 132, 145
massacres 151
Maternity Benefits Act (MBA), 1961 74–76; and construction industry 74–75; Arya and A. Roy on 75–76; nursing provisions of 74; in unorganised sector 74; to women employed on daily wages 75
Mayo, Katherine 135*n*6; in *Mother India* 108–109; on sexuality 123
middle-class nationalism 40
Migrant Rights Convention 204
Migrant Workers Convention 204
migrants 4–5, 26; claims legitimacy 196; and families 204; and Hindu nation 11–15; settlement and legal responses 61; sexuality 55; subaltern position of 20–21
migration 3, 22–23, 28, 30, 31, 32, 107; benefits of 31–32; clandestine 33–34; contextualising 30–39; and foreign remittances 120–21; M. Thapan, on 75; of marginalised groups 33; from Nepal and Bangladesh 30; and poor countries 30–31
Ministry of Women and Child Development (MWCD) 117
modernity 52, 88, 90, 140, 142, 158
Modi, Narendra Singh 175–78, 192*n*4; as Chief Minister, Sarkar's analysis on 183, *see also* Gujarat riot
moral regulation of migrant women 58–59
Mother India 150
Municipal Corporation of Delhi vs. Female Workers 75
Muslim 5; as alien 189; of Bangladesh 22; depiction of 171, 172; Hindu Right's portrayal of 14–15; mechanisms for justice for 177; migrants into Assam 151; militant organisations 153; minorities in India 190; as 'Other' or 'outsider' 22, 175, 188,195
Muslim women 142, 143, 166; constituted genocide 178; Urvashi Butalia on 142–43

Nanavati Commission 177, 189, 192
National Commission for Enterprises in Unorganised Sector (NCEUS) 37
National Commission of Women 67–68
National Domestic Workers Welfare Trust 81
National Human Rights Commission, The (NHRC) 62, 177–78
national identity 28–29
National Policy for Empowerment of Women 70
National Rural Employment Guarantee, The (NREG) scheme 39, 205
nationalism 34, 35, 36, 40, 42, 51, 85–94, 144
native woman, representation of 113; sexual liaisons 201; as victim 97
neoliberal, citizen 200, 202; economic reforms 36
neoliberalism, Wendy Brown on 199–200
Nepal 30, 51, 60, 64, 123, 124; women of 121, 122
Neuwirth, Jessica 115
new economic policies and female migrants 85–94
new Indian woman 89, 119
NGOs, interventions on violence on Muslim women 182–83; and 'justice' in Gujarat 186
Nightingale, Florence 49
Nithari 27, 28, 56

non-governmental mechanism and Concerned Citizen's Tribunal 179
non-Hindus 13–14
non-resident Indian 200
normative, boundaries 4; sexuality 197
norms 4, 59
Nussbaum, Martha 180–82

oppression, women's 122
Others 4, 19–20, 107

Pandher, Moninder Singh 27
partition 4, 11
polis 198–99
postcolonial 127, 130, 133, 136, 140, 141, 142, 157
postcolonial India 28, 29, 30, 43, 54, 97, 109, 119, 138, 157, 162; citizenship in 141, 142; and citizenship law 138; and female sexuality 97 and women's rights agenda 119; culture in 54; liberal feminists in 109; migration and law in 29; normative sexuality in 43; religious minorities in 30
postcolonialism *viii*, 20
poverty 30, 31
Prevention of Genocide and Crimes Against Humanity Act 193
Prevention of Terrorism Act (POTA) 192
Prevention of Terrorism Ordinance 176
property rights, equal 147
proselytising campaigns 93
prostitution 66; and sex 66; Sigma Huda on criminalisation of 126
purity 41, 42, 43, 128, 146

Rai, Lala Lajpat 52
Ram Mandir (Ram Temple) movement 168
rape 194, *see also* violence against women
Rashtriya Swayamsevak Sangh (RSS) 173
Raymond, J. 115
rehabilitation of rescued sex workers 69
religion 15, 143–44
religious, identity 150; minorities 29, 150; right 113–21
rights 203–204; and justice for migrants 205; of female migrants 168; of migrant women's 76
right-wing forces 201
Roy, Aruna 193
Roy, Raja Ram Mohan 61
RSS, militaristic nationalism by 188

Said, Edward, work of 109
Sarkar, Tanika 41; and Concerned Citizen's Tribunal 182–83
sati, Lata Mani on 88
Savarkar, V. D. 13–14; *Hindutva* of 12–13
Savera, NGO 61, 62; and rights of sex workers 66–67
Sawant, P. B. 193
self-employed workers 84, *see also* women's employment
Sen, Amartya 53; on subaltern 54
sex trade *see* sex industry
sex trafficking 97, 98, 100, 102, 113–21, 136; George Bush on 114, 116, 135*n*9, *see also* trafficking
sex work 42, 51, 60, 62, 65, 68, 79, 101, 104, 107, 115, 129, 160; and anti-trafficking interventions 59–68; commercial 59, 61, 62, 63, 64, 65, 66, 67, 83, 102, 103, 104, 117, 118, 128, 130; forced 100; as occupation 96
sex workers 64, 66, 198, 203; in Calcutta, union of 117; migrant as 67, 129–30, *see also* migrants; migrated from Nepal 64; and police abuse 64; schools for children of 106–107; in Sonagachi 118, 130, 136*n*14, in Surat 64; as victims of trafficking 59, 68
sex, industry 51, 61, 62, 64, 80, 104, 105, 115, 117, 121, 122, 125, 130; and Bangladesh Supreme Court 64–65; in Chakla Bazaar 64

sexual division of labour 43–50, 69, 73; and familial ideology 85; Chandra Talpade Mohanty on 45–46
sexual, exploitation of domestic workers and Middle East 82; normativity 39–43; stereotypes 197; symbols 110; violence 178; violence against Muslim community 179
sexuality, normative 42, 43, 97, 162; women's, 113, 127
Sheikh, Zaheera *see Best Bakery* case
Shetty, Shilpa, Richard Gere kissing 50
Shiv Sena (SS — 'foot-soldiers of Lord Shiva') 173
Singh, Dev Pratap 169
Skeldon, R. 32
social, reformers 111–12; spending, and India 35, 37; welfare 31
Sonowal case 201
South Asian Association for Regional Cooperation Convention on Preventing and Combating Trafficking in Women and Children for Prostitution, 2002 (SAARC Convention) 98, 100–101
special export zones (SEZs) 34
Sri Lanka 30
state-sponsored crimes 179
Steinem, Gloria 126
subaltern 40, 54, 139, 149
subaltern studies 20, 54, 55
Subramaniam, K. S. 193
Sudarshan, K. C. 191
Supreme Court of India, on air hostesses retirement 78; on recognition of prostitution 65; on regularisation of workers 73; in *Sonowal* case 151; on women in sex work 65

Tales of Night Fairies of Shohini Ghosh 97, 130–31
Teesta, Setalvad, of Citizens for Peace and Justice 186
Teresa, Mother 49
terror, global war on 167
Third World 136*n*11
Third World women 197; Kempadoo on 126–27; victimisation of 122, 131
Traffic Signal 1–3, 25, 195
trafficking 10–11, 100–101, 124, 127, *see also* anti-trafficking

UC Bannerjee panel 178; exonerating Narendra Modi 178
UN Protocols on Smuggling and Trafficking 98, 99, 100
unemployment 35, 39, 82, 84; domestic 31
UNESCO Trafficking Statistics project 134*n*4
Uniform Civil Code 146
United Nations Office of Commissioner for Human Rights (UNOCHR) 115
United Progressive Alliance (UPA) coalition 192
universalism 197
universality 141
Unlawful Activities (Prevention) Amendment Act, 2004 192
unorganised sector 76–77, 83–84
Unorganised Workers Social Security Act, 2008, 77, 83–85
Valentine's Day 50, *see also* culture, Indian

Vedic Golden Era 52
veiling or purdah, practice of 110
violence 92, 100, 104, 115, 122, 124, 125, 129, 172; on Muslim, Sarkar as 183–84; against women 184; against Muslim community 185
Vishwa Hindu Parishad (VHP—World Hindu Council) 14, 168, 173

wage labour 45, 48, 49
wages 31, 45, 73, 76, 77, 81, 84; lower 35, 37, 71, 77; women's 73, 76
widows, oppression of 110
wives 38–39, 45–46, 48, 50, 87, 89, 91–92, 119, 148, 158

womanhood and nationalism 144, *see also* Indian womanhaood
women 95*n*7, 196; abroad as domestic workers 80; cross-border movements of 7, 131; as dependants 6–7; discrimination 9; economic dependency of 36, 45, 69; and education 89; equality of 111, 112–13; G. Spivak on 111; gendered identities of 39–50; in Hindu tradition 111; identity of 41, 49, 86; infantilising 126; labour and reproduction 36; as lower races 109–10; mobility of 86; as 'modern but not western' 81–92, 119–20; oppression of 197; Oza on 39; protection for 94, 124; in public sphere 41; Rajeswari Sunder Rajan on 89–90; of religious minority and discrimination 9; responsibilities of 36–37, 38–39; roles of 38, 48–49, 89, 145–46; status of 149, 187; suffrage 144, 146; as symbols of nation 9; as symbols of nation 8–12; Tanika Sarkar on 92; upholders of national identity 41; upholders of family integrity 5, 89, 147, 195; upholders of purity of nation 9, 43, 128; as victims of culture 22, 197; as wives, construction of 8
women workers, and Factories Act, 1948 95*n*8; and labour market 37; police harassment of 68; protection of 69; sexual exploitation of 67; in unorganised sector 70, 76; wage discrimination and 71, 76
women's movement 144–45; campaigns for political representation of 144, 146; upliftment of 145
women's employment 70–71; and economic liberalisation 82–83; and identity 90–91; within labour market 90; violence against 91–92
women's gendered identities 39
women's rights, Hindu nationalists 119–21; to work and education 113–14
women's sexuality 197; and sexual purity 41–42, 58, 96
women-headed households 48
workers, casual 73; regular 73
work-force in informal sectors 36
world citizen 198–99
World Trade Organization (WTO) 31; and migration 31–32; negotiations 32

For Product Safety Concerns and Information please contact our EU
representative GPSR@taylorandfrancis.com
Taylor & Francis Verlag GmbH, Kaufingerstraße 24, 80331 München, Germany

www.ingramcontent.com/pod-product-compliance
Ingram Content Group UK Ltd.
Pitfield, Milton Keynes, MK11 3LW, UK
UKHW022156190926
475702UK00003B/52

* 9 7 8 0 4 1 5 5 9 6 2 9 9 *